39

Yale Language Series

EDITED BY SANDRA J. SAVIGNON

Interpreting Communicative Language Teaching

CONTEXTS AND

CONCERNS IN

TEACHER

EDUCATION

Yale University Press

New Haven &

London

Publisher: Mary Jane Peluso
Editorial Assistant: Emily Saglimbeni
Manuscript Editor: Noreen O'Conner-Abel
Marketing Manager: Mary Coleman
Marketing Assistant: Michelle Schrag
Production Coordinator: Maureen Noonan

Set in Minion type by Keystone Typesetting. Printed in the United States of America.

Library of Congress Cataloging-in-Publication Data
Interpreting communicative language teaching : contexts and concerns in teacher education/edited by Sandra J. Savignon.
        p.   cm.—(Yale language series)
Includes bibliographical references and index.
ISBN 0-300-09156-7 (pbk.: alk. paper)
1. Languages, Modern—Study and teaching. 2. Language teachers—Training of. 3. Communicative competence in children. I. Savignon, Sandra J. II. Series.
LB1578 .I56 2002
418'.0071—dc21   2001056761

A catalogue record for this book is available from the British Library.

10   9   8   7   6   5   4   3   2   1

Lovingly dedicated to Joseph, Caitlin, Madeleine, Julien, Charlotte, Patrick, Nicolas, and Jasper, great-grandchildren of Joy and Harold. May they live to know a world that celebrates languages and language learning for peace and understanding.

Contents

Prologue

SANDRA J. SAVIGNON

In the literature on communicative language teaching, or CLT, teacher education has not received adequate attention. My purpose in conceiving and editing this volume was to bring together a horizon-broadening variety of initiatives, projects, and activities related to teacher education that can make language teaching communicative in the broadest, most meaningful sense. The collection showcases some of the best work being done internationally to make CLT an attainable goal.

Ordering the chapters was a challenge. Themes appear and reappear, voices heard in one text are echoed in another. These links and recurrences contribute significantly to the cohesion and strength of the collection. As editor I have taken a hands-off approach to shaping individual chapters, striving, rather, to preserve the unique, contextualized perspective of each contributing author. Together, the contributors offer thought-provoking insights into the construct of CLT, as it has come to be known worldwide, and provide practical examples for meeting the challenges of educating language teachers in the new millennium.

For the most part, the chapter authors look at CLT from the perspective of practicing teachers. The impression throughout is one of hearing voices from the classroom. In some chapters, we hear from teacher educators, researchers, and national policy makers, in addition to teachers. The result is a vivid representation of language teaching as the collaborative and context-specific human activity that it is.

I would like to thank Susan Welch, dean of the College of Liberal Arts, Jim Lantolf, director of the Language Acquisition Center, and the graduate students in the Linguistics and Applied Language Studies program at Penn State for their contributions to our applied linguistics community that encourages inquiry and innovation. Also, I would like to acknowledge the reviewers of this text, Mary McGroarty of Northern Arizona University, Elizabeth Bernhardt of Stanford University, Margie Berns of Purdue University, Bill Johnston of Indiana University, and Fred Davidson of the University of Illinois at Urbana-Champaign. Finally, I would like to thank Mary Jane Peluso for including me in the new Yale University Press language collection, and Noreen O'Connor and Philip King for their excellent suggestions and attention to detail. Foremost, however, I thank the contributors from around the globe without whom this collection would not have been possible.

Communicative Language Teaching: Linguistic Theory and Classroom Practice

SANDRA J. SAVIGNON

Communicative language teaching (CLT) refers to both processes and goals in classroom learning. The central theoretical concept in communicative language teaching is "communicative competence," a term introduced into discussions of language use and second or foreign language learning in the early 1970s (Habermas 1970; Hymes 1971; Jakobovits 1970; Savignon 1971). Competence is defined in terms of the *expression, interpretation,* and *negotiation* of meaning and looks to both psycholinguistic and sociocultural perspectives in second language acquisition (SLA) research to account for its development (Savignon 1972, 1997). Identification of learners' communicative needs provides a basis for curriculum design (Van Ek 1975).

Understanding of CLT can be traced to concurrent developments in Europe and North America. In Europe, the language needs of a rapidly increasing group of immigrants and guest workers, and a rich British linguistic tradition that included social as well as linguistic context in description of language behavior, led the Council of Europe to develop a syllabus for learners based on notional-functional concepts of language use. The syllabus was derived from neo-Firthian systemic or functional linguistics, in which language is viewed as "meaning potential," and the "context of situation" (Firth 1937; Halliday 1978) is viewed as central to understanding language systems and how they work. The syllabus described a threshold level of language ability for each of the major languages of Europe in view of what learners should be able to *do* with the language (Van Ek 1975). Language functions based on an assessment of the communicative needs of learners specified the end result, or *goal,* of an instructional program. The term *communicative* attached itself to programs that used a notional-functional syllabus based on needs assessment, and the language for specific purposes (LSP) movement was launched.

Concurrent development in Europe focused on the *process* of communicative classroom language learning. In Germany, for example, against a backdrop of Social Democratic concerns for individual empowerment, articulated in the writings of the philosopher Jürgen Habermas (1970), language teaching methodologists took the lead in developing classroom materials that encouraged learner choice (Candlin 1978). Their systematic collection of exercise types for communicatively oriented English language teaching was used in teacher in-service courses and workshops to guide curriculum change. Exercises were designed to exploit the variety of social meanings contained within particular grammatical structures. A system of "chains" encouraged teachers and learners to define their own learning path through principled selection of relevant exercises (Piepho 1974; Piepho and Bredella 1976). Similar exploratory projects were initiated in the 1970s by Candlin at the University of Lancaster, England, and by Holec (1979) and his colleagues at the University of Nancy, France. Supplementary teacher resources promoting classroom CLT became increasingly popular in the 1970s (for example, Maley and Duff 1978), and there was renewed interest in building learners' vocabulary.

Meanwhile, in the United States, Hymes (1971) had reacted to Chomsky's characterization of the linguistic competence of the ideal native speaker and, retaining Chomsky's distinction between competence and performance, proposed the term "communicative competence" to represent the ability to use language in a social context, to observe sociolinguistic norms of appropriateness. Hymes's concern with speech communities and the integration of language, communication, and culture was not unlike that of Firth and Halliday in the British linguistic tradition (see Halliday 1978). Hymes's "communicative competence" can be seen as the equivalent of Halliday's "meaning potential." Similarly, Hymes's focus was not language learning but *language as social behavior*. In subsequent interpretations of the significance of Hymes's views for learners, methodologists working in the United States tended to focus on the cultural norms of native speakers and the difficulty, if not impossibility, of duplicating them in a classroom of non-natives. In light of this difficulty, the appropriateness of communicative competence as an instructional goal was called into question (Paulston 1974).

At the same time, in an empirical research project at the University of Illinois, Savignon (1971) used the term "communicative competence" to characterize the ability of classroom language learners to interact with other speakers, to make meaning, as distinct from their ability to recite dialogues or perform on discrete-point tests of grammatical knowledge. At a time when pattern practice and error avoidance were the rule in language teaching, this study of adult classroom acquisition of French looked at the effect of practice in the use of coping strategies as part of an instructional program. By encouraging learners to ask for information, to seek clarification, to use circumlocution and whatever other linguistic and nonlinguistic resources they could muster to negotiate meaning, to stick to the communicative task at hand, teachers were invariably leading learners to take risks, to venture beyond memorized patterns. The communication strategies identified in this study became the basis for subsequent identification by Canale and Swain (1980) of *strategic competence* as one of the components in their well-known framework for communicative competence, along with grammatical competence and sociolinguistic competence. (The classroom model of communicative competence proposed by Savignon [1983] includes the three components identified by Canale and Swain plus a fourth component, discourse competence, added by Canale [1983]. We shall look more closely at this framework below.) In the Savignon research, test results at the end of the eighteen-week instructional period provided convincing evidence that learners who had practiced communication in lieu of pattern drills in a laboratory performed with no less accuracy on discrete-point tests of grammatical structure. Nevertheless, their communicative competence, as measured in terms of fluency, comprehensibility, effort, and amount of communication in unrehearsed communicative tasks, significantly surpassed that of learners who had had no such practice. Learners' reactions to the test formats lent further support to the view that even beginners respond well to activities that let them focus on meaning as opposed to formal features.

A collection of role-playing exercises, games, and other communicative classroom activities was developed subsequently for inclusion in the adaptation of the French CREDIF materials, *Voix et Visages de la France* (CREDIF, or the Centre de Recherche et d'Etude pour la Diffusion du Français, is a university-based institution that contributed to the dissemination of French outside France). The accompanying guide (Savignon 1974) described their purpose as that of involving learners in the experience of communication. Teachers were encouraged to provide learners with the French equivalent of expressions like "What's the word for . . . ?" "Please repeat," and "I don't understand," expressions that would help them participate in the negotiation of meaning. Not unlike the efforts of Candlin and his colleagues working in a European English as a foreign language (EFL) context, the focus was on classroom process and learner autonomy. The use of games, role playing, and activities in pairs and other small groups has gained acceptance and is now widely recommended for inclusion in language-teaching programs (see Chapter 5).

Communicative language teaching derives from a multidisciplinary perspective that includes, at the least, linguistics, psychology, philosophy, sociology, and educational research. The focus has been the elaboration and implementation of programs and methodologies that promote the development of functional language ability through learners' participation in communicative events. Central to CLT is the understanding of language learning as both an educational and a political issue. Language teaching is inextricably linked with language policy. Viewed from a multicultural intranational as well as international perspective, diverse sociopolitical contexts mandate not only a diverse set of language-learning goals but a diverse set of teaching strategies. Program design and implementation depend on negotiation between policy makers, linguists, researchers, and teachers (see Chapter 6). Evaluation of program success requires a similar collaborative effort. The selection of methods and materials appropriate to both the goals and the context of teaching begins with an analysis of learners' needs and styles of learning, socially defined.

Focus on the Learner

By definition, CLT puts the focus on the learner. Learners' communicative needs provide a framework for elaborating program goals with regard to functional competence. Functional goals imply global, qualitative evaluation of learner achievement as opposed to quantitative assessment of discrete linguistic features. Controversy over appropriate language testing persists, and many a curricular innovation has been undone by failure to make corresponding changes in evaluation. Current efforts at educational reform favor essay writing, in-class presentations, and other more holistic assessments of learner competence. Some programs have initiated portfolio assessment, the collection and evaluation of learners' poems, reports, stories, videotapes, and similar projects in an effort to represent and encourage learner achievement. Assessment initiatives of this kind do not go unopposed. They face demands for accountability from school boards, parents, and governmental funding agencies. Measurement of learning outcomes remains a central focus in meeting educational challenges worldwide. (See Chapters 3, 5, and 7.)

Depending upon their own preparation and experience, teachers differ in their reactions to CLT. Some feel understandable frustration at the seeming ambiguity in discussions of communicative ability. Negotiation of meaning may be a lofty goal, but this view of language behavior lacks precision and does not provide a universal scale for assessment of individual learners. Ability is viewed, rather, as variable and highly dependent on context and purpose as well as on the roles and attitudes of all involved. Other teachers welcome the opportunity to select or develop their own materials, providing learners with a range of communicative tasks. They are comfortable relying on more global, integrative judgments of learning progress.

An additional source of frustration for some teachers is research findings on the acquisition of a second language that show the route, if not the rate, of language acquisition to be largely unaffected by classroom instruction. (See, for example, Ellis 1985, 1997.) First language (L1) cross-linguistic studies of developmental universals initiated in the 1970s were soon followed by second language (L2) studies. Acquisition, assessed on the basis of unrehearsed oral communication, seemed to follow a similar morphosyntactical sequence regardless of learners' age or the learning context. Although the findings supported teachers' informal observations, namely that textbook presentation and drill do not ensure learners' use of the same structures in their own spontaneous expression, the findings were nonetheless disconcerting. They contradicted both the grammar-translation method and audiolingual precepts that placed the burden of acquisition on the teacher's explanation of grammar and the learner's controlled practice of syntactical and phonological patterns with a goal of near native "accuracy." The findings were further at odds with textbooks that promise "mastery" of "basic" French, English, Spanish, and so forth. Teachers' rejection of research findings, renewed insistence on tests of discrete grammatical structures, and even exclusive reliance in the classroom on the learners' native or first language, where possible, to be sure students "get the grammar," have in some cases been reactions to the frustration of teaching for communication.

Moreover, with its emphasis on sentence-level grammatical features, the dominant second language acquisition (SLA) research paradigm itself has obscured pragmatic and sociolinguistic issues in language acquisition. (See, for example, Firth and Wagner 1998.) Renewed interest in sociocultural theories of second language acquisition offer promise for expanding the research paradigm and bringing much needed balance (Lantolf 2000). In her discussion of the contexts of competence, Berns (1990) stresses that the definition of appropriate communicative competence for learners requires an understanding of the sociocultural contexts of language use (see Chapter 7). In addition, the selection of a methodology suited to the attainment of communicative competence requires an understanding of sociocultural differences in styles of learning. Curricular innovation is best advanced by the development of local materials, which, in turn, rests on the involvement of classroom teachers. (See Chapters 3 and 6 and Markee 1997.) Berns (1990, 104) provides a useful summary of eight principles of CLT:

1. Language teaching is based on a view of language as communication. That is, language is seen as a social tool that speakers use to make meaning; speakers communicate about something to someone for some purpose, either orally or in writing.
2. Diversity is recognized and accepted as part of language development and use in second language learners and users, as it is with first language users.
3. A learner's competence is considered in relative, not in absolute, terms.
4. More than one variety of a language is recognized as a viable model for learning and teaching.
5. Culture is recognized as instrumental in shaping speakers' communicative competence, in both their first and subsequent languages.
6. No single methodology or fixed set of techniques is prescribed.
7. Language use is recognized as serving ideational, interpersonal, and textual functions and is related to the development of learners' competence in each.
8. It is essential that learners be engaged in doing things with language—that is, that they use language for a variety of purposes in all phases of learning.

It has increasingly been recognized that learners' expectations and attitudes play a role in advancing or impeding curricular change. Among the available scales measuring learners' attitudes, the BALLI (Beliefs About Language Learning Inventory) scale developed by Horwitz (1988) is designed to survey learners' views on issues affecting language learning and teaching. The scale includes five parts: (1) difficulty of language learning, (2) foreign language aptitude, (3) the nature of language learning, (4) learning and communication strategies, and (5) motivations and expectations. As Horwitz (1988) suggests, classroom realities that contradict learners' expectations about learning may lead to disappointment and ultimately interfere with learning. At the same time, classroom practices have the potential to change learners' beliefs (see Chapter 4 and Kern 1995).

What About Grammar?

Discussions of CLT not infrequently lead to questions of grammatical or formal accuracy. The perceived displacement of attention toward morphosyntactical features in learners' expression in favor of a focus on meaning has led in some cases to the impression that grammar is not important, or that proponents of CLT favor learners' ability to express themselves, without regard to form.

While involvement in communicative events is seen as central to language development, this involvement necessarily requires attention to form. Communication cannot take place in the absence of structure, or grammar, a set of shared assumptions about how language works, along with a willingness of participants to cooperate in the negotiation of meaning. In their carefully researched and widely cited paper proposing components of communicative competence, Canale and Swain (1980) did not suggest that grammar was unimportant. They sought rather to situate grammatical competence within a more broadly defined communicative competence. Similarly, the findings of the Savignon (1971) study did not suggest that teachers forsake grammar instruction. Rather, the replacement of structure drills in a language laboratory with self-expression focused on meaning was found to be a more effective way to develop communicative ability with no loss of morphosyntactical accuracy. Learners' performance on tests of discrete morphosyntactical features was not a good predictor of their performance on a series of integrative communicative tasks.

The nature of the contribution to language development of both form-focused and meaning-focused classroom activity remains a question in ongoing research. The optimal combination of these activities in any given instructional setting depends no doubt on learners' age, the nature and length of instructional sequence, the opportunities for language contact outside the classroom, teacher preparation, and other factors. For the development of communicative competence, however, research findings overwhelming support the integration of form-focused exercises and meaning-focused experience. Grammar is important; and learners seem to focus best on grammar when it relates to their communicative needs and experiences (Lightbown and Spada 1993; Ellis 1997). Nor should explicit attention to form be perceived as limited to sentence-level morphosyntactical features. Broader features of discourse, sociolinguistic rules of appropriateness, and communication strategies themselves may be included.

How Has CLT Been Interpreted?

The classroom model we shall present shows the hypothetical integration of four components of communicative competence (Savignon 1972, 1983, 1987, 2000; Canale and Swain 1980; Canale 1983; Byram 1997). Adapted

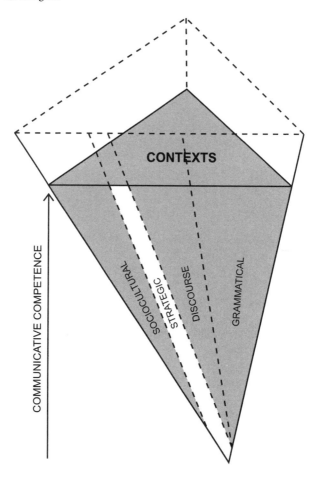

Figure 1.1. Components of communicative competence.

from the familiar "inverted pyramid" classroom model proposed in Savignon (1983), the current model shows how, through practice and experience in an increasingly wide range of communicative contexts and events, learners gradually expand their communicative competence, which comprises grammatical competence, discourse competence, sociocultural competence, and strategic competence (Figure 1.1). Although the relative importance of the various components depends on the overall level of communicative competence, each is essential. Moreover, all the components are interrelated. They cannot be developed or measured in isolation, and one cannot go from one component to the other as when stringing beads on a necklace. Rather, when an increase occurs in one area, that component interacts with other components to produce a corresponding increase in overall communicative competence.

Grammatical competence refers to sentence-level grammatical forms, the ability to recognize the lexical, morphological, syntactical and phonological features of a language and to make use of those features to interpret and form words and sentences. Grammatical competence is not linked to any single theory of grammar and does not include the ability to state rules of usage. One demonstrates grammatical competence not by stating a rule but by using a rule in the interpretation, expression, or negotiation of meaning.

Discourse competence is concerned not with isolated words or phrases but with the interconnectedness of a series of utterances or written words or phrases to form a text, a meaningful whole. The text might be a poem, an e-mail message, a sportscast, a telephone conversation, or a novel. Identification of isolated sounds or words contributes to interpretation of the overall meaning of the text. This is known as bottom-up processing. In contrast, top-down processing involves understanding of the theme or purpose of the text, which in turn helps in the interpretation of isolated sounds or words. Both kinds of processing are essential for communicative competence. (See Chapter 10 for additional perspective on discourse.)

Two other familiar concepts that arise in discussions of discourse competence are text coherence and cohesion. Text coherence is the relation of all sentences or utterances in a text to a single global proposition. The establishment of a global meaning, or topic, for a whole poem, e-mail message, sportscast, telephone conversation, or novel is an integral part of both expression and interpretation and makes possible the interpretation of the individual sentences that make up the text. Local connections or structural links between individual sentences provide cohesion. Halliday and Hasan (1976) are widely recognized for their identification of various cohesive devices used in English, and their work has influenced materials for teaching English as a second or foreign language (ESL/EFL). (For an illustration, see Celce-Murcia and Larsen Freeman 1999.)

Sociocultural competence, a broader view of what Canale and Swain (1980) identified as sociolinguistic competence, extends well beyond linguistic forms and is an interdisciplinary field of inquiry having to do with the social rules of language use. Sociocultural competence requires an understanding of the social context in which language is used: the roles of the participants, the information they share, and the function of the interaction. Although we have yet to provide a satisfactory description of grammar, we are even further from an adequate description of sociocultural rules of appropriateness. Yet we use them to communicate successfully in many different situational contexts.

Learners cannot be expected to anticipate the sociocultural dimension of every situation. The likelihood of encountering the unexpected is easily seen for a language like English, which serves not only as a first language in many countries, and within different cultural groups in those countries, but also as a language of wider communication across national and cultural boundaries. Subtler, perhaps, but no less real variations in style and use in different settings can be observed for all languages. Participants in multicultural communication are sensitive not only to the cultural meanings attached to the language itself but to social conventions concerning language use, such things as taking turns, appropriateness of content, nonverbal language, and tone. These conventions influence how messages are interpreted. In addition to cultural knowledge, cultural sensitivity is essential. Just knowing something about the culture of an English-speaking country will not suffice. What must be learned is a general empathy and openness toward other cultures. Sociocultural competence includes a willingness to engage in the active negotiation of meaning along with a willingness to suspend judgment and take into consideration the possibility of cultural differences in conventions of use. Together these features might be subsumed under the term "cultural flexibility," or "cultural awareness." The "ideal native speaker," someone who knows a language perfectly and uses it appropriately in all social interactions, exists in theory only. None of us knows all there is to know of a language in its many manifestations, both around the world and in our own backyards. Communicative competence is always relative. The coping strategies that we use in unfamiliar contexts, with constraints arising from imperfect knowledge of rules, or such impediments to their application as fatigue or distraction, are represented as strategic competence. With practice and experience, we gain competence in grammar, discourse, and sociocultural adaptability. The relative importance of strategic competence thus decreases; however, the effective use of coping strategies is important for communicative competence in all contexts and distinguishes highly effective communicators from those who are less so.

Shaping a Communicative Curriculum

Today, many proposed innovations in curriculum planning offer both novice and veteran teachers an array of alternatives. Games, tasks, juggling, and jazz have been proposed as aids to language learning. Rapidly increasing opportunities for computer-mediated communication, both synchronous—via on-line chat rooms—and asynchronous—through the full spectrum of information and interactions available on the Internet as well as specialized bulletin boards and e-mail—hold promise for increased communicative opportunities for learners worldwide.

In attempting to convey the meaning of CLT to both preservice and in-service teachers of English as a second or foreign language in a wide range of contexts, I have found it helpful to think of a communicative curriculum as potentially having five components (Savignon 1983, 1997). These components can be regarded as thematic clusters of activities or experiences related to language use. They provide a way to categorize teaching strategies that promote communicative competence. Use of the word "component" to categorize these activities seems particularly appropriate in that it avoids any suggestion of sequence or level. Experience with communicative teaching methods has shown that the five components can be profitably blended at all stages of instruction. Organization of learning activities into the following components serves not to sequence an instructional program, but rather to highlight the range of options available in curriculum planning and to suggest ways in which their very interrelatedness can benefit the learner.

Language Arts
Language for a Purpose
My Language Is Me: Personal Second Language Use
You Be . . . , I'll Be . . . : Theater Arts
Beyond the Classroom

Language arts, or language analysis, is the first component on the list. Language arts includes the skills at which language teachers often excel. In fact, it may be all they have been taught to do. Language arts includes many of the exercises used in school programs throughout the world to help learners focus on formal accuracy in their mother tongue. Language arts in a second or foreign language program focuses on forms of the language, including syntax, morphology and phonology. Spelling tests, for example, are important if writing is a goal. Familiar activities such as translation, dictation, and rote memorization can be helpful in bringing attention to form. Vocabulary can be expanded through definition, synonyms and antonyms, and study of cognates and false cognates. Pronunciation exercises and patterned repetition of verb paradigms and other structural features can be used to lead students to focus on form, to illustrate regular syntactic features, or rules of grammar. Learners of all ages can also enjoy numerous language arts games or activities for the variety and group interaction they provide. So long as they are not overused and are not promoted as the solution to all manner of language learning problems, games and other activities that focus on language arts in a wide range of formats are a welcome addition to a teacher's repertoire.

Language for a purpose, or language experience, is the second component on the list. In contrast with language analysis, language experience is the use of language for real and immediate communicative goals. Not all learners are taking a new language for the same reasons. It is important for teachers to pay attention, when selecting and sequencing materials, to the specific communicative needs of the learners. Regardless of how distant or unspecific the communicative needs of the learners, every program with a goal of communicative competence should pay heed to opportunities for meaningful language use, opportunities to focus on meaning as well as form.

In a classroom where the language of instruction is of necessity the second language, learners have an immediate and natural need to use it. Where this happens, language for a purpose is a built-in feature of the learning environment. In those settings where the teacher shares with learners a language other than the second language, special attention needs to be given to providing learners with opportunities for experience in their new language. Exclusive use of the second language in the classroom is an option. In so-called content-based instruction, the focus is something other than the language. The content, history, music, or literature, for example, is taught in the second language. Immersion programs at the elementary, secondary, or even university level, where the entire curriculum is taught in the second language, offer greatest possible exposure to language for a purpose. In addition, task-based curricula are designed to provide learners with the most opportunity to use language for a purpose.

Learners who are accustomed to being taught exclusively in their first language may at first be uncomfortable if the teacher speaks to them in the second, expecting them not only to understand but, perhaps, to respond. When this happens, teachers need to take special care to help learners understand that they are not expected to understand every word, any more than they are expected to express themselves in the second language as if they had been using it since childhood. Making an effort to get the gist and using strategies to enhance comprehension are important to the development of communicative competence. With encouragement and help from their teacher in developing the strategic competence they need to interpret, express, and negotiate meaning, learners often express satisfaction and even surprise (see Chapter 4).

My language is me: personal second language use, the third component in a communicative curriculum, relates to the learner's emerging identity in the new language. Attitude is without a doubt the single most important factor in a learner's success. Whether the learner's motivations are integrative or instrumental, the development of communicative competence fully engages the learner. The most successful teaching programs are those which take into account the affective as well as the cognitive aspects of language learning and seek to involve learners psychologically as well as intellectually.

In planning for CLT, teachers should remember that not everyone is comfortable in the same role. Within classroom communities, as within society at large, some people are leaders and some prefer to be followers. Both are essential to the success of group activities. In group discussions, a few always seem to do most of the talking. Those who often remain silent in larger groups may participate more easily in pair work. Or they may prefer to work on an individual project. The wider the variety of communicative, or meaning-based, activities, the greater the chance for involving all learners.

"My language is me" implies, above all, respect for learners as they use their new language for self-expression. Although language arts activities provide an appropriate context for focus on form, personal second language use does not. Most teachers know this and intuitively focus on meaning rather than form, as learners assume a new identity and express their personal feelings or experiences. Repeated emphasis on structural features in textbooks or on tests, however, may cause teachers to feel uncomfortable about their exclusive focus on meaning on these occasions. An understanding of the importance of opportunities for the interpretation, expression, and negotiation of meaning and of the distinction between language arts and "my language is me" can help to reassure teachers that what they are doing is in the best interests of the learners for continued second language development.

Respect for learners as they use their new language for self-expression requires more than simply paying less attention to formal "errors" (see Chapter 10) that do not interfere with meaning. It includes recognition that so-called near-native performance, in fact, may not even be a goal for learners. Language teaching has come a long way from audiolingual days when "native" pronunciation and use was held up as an ideal for learners. Reference to the terms "native" or "near native" in the evaluation of communicative competence is inappropriate in today's postcolonial, multicultural world. We now recognize that native speakers are never "ideal" and, in fact, vary widely in range and style of communicative abilities. Moreover, the decision about what is or is not one's "native" language is arbitrary and is perhaps best left to the individual concerned. Such is the view of Chenny Lai, a MATESL candidate studying in the United States:

> As to the definition of "native" or "first" language we discussed in today's class, I came up with the idea that we have no say about whether a person's native language is this one or that one. It is the speaker who has the right to feel which language is his native one. The native language should be the one in which the speaker feels most comfortable or natural when engaged in daily communication or, more abstractly, the one in which the speaker does all his thinking. There are two major languages spoken in Taiwan: Mandarin and

Taiwanese. I don't have the slightest problem using either of them since I use both every day in equal proportion. But when I do my thinking, considering things, or even kind of talking to myself, my "mental" language is Mandarin. Because of this, I would say that my native language is Mandarin. We probably can say that a person's native language can actually "switch" from one to another during stages of his life.

Since personality inevitably takes on a new dimension through expression in another language, learners need to discover that dimension on their own terms. Learners should not only be given the opportunity to say what they want to say in the second language; they should be encouraged to develop a personality in the second language with which they are comfortable. They may feel more comfortable maintaining a degree of formality not found in the interpersonal transactions of native speakers. The diary entry of a Japanese learner of English offers important insight into the matter of identity:

I just don't know what to do right now. I might have been wrong since I began to learn English; I always tried to be better and wanted to be a good speaker. It was wrong, absolutely wrong! When I got to California, I started imitating Americans and picked up the words that I heard. So my English became just like Americans'. I couldn't help it. I must have been funny to them, because I am a Japanese and have my own culture and background. I think I almost lost the most important thing I should not have. I got California English, including intonation, pronunciation, the way they act, which are not mine. I have to have my own English, be myself when I speak English. (Preston 1981, 113)

At the same time, learners may discover a new freedom of self-expression in another language. When asked what it is like to write in English, a language that is not her native tongue, the Korean writer Mia Yun (1998), author of *House of the Winds,* replied that it was "like putting on a new dress." Writing in English made her feel fresh, see herself in a new way, offered her freedom to experiment. When expressing themselves in a new language, writers are not the only ones to experience the feeling of "putting on a new dress." The component "my language is me" calls for recognition and respect for the individual personality of the learner. (We shall return to the "native–nonnative" distinction with respect to users of English later in this chapter.)

Theater arts is the fourth component of a communicative curriculum. In the familiar words of Shakespeare, "all the world's a stage" (*As You Like It,* II, 7). And on this stage we play many roles, roles for which we improvise scripts from the models we observe around us. Child, parent, foreigner, newcomer, employer, employee, doctor, or teacher, all are roles that embrace certain expected ways of behaving and using language. Sociocultural rules of appropriateness have to do with these expected ways. Familiar roles may be played with little conscious attention to style. New and unfamiliar roles require practice, and an awareness of the way the meanings we intend are being interpreted by others. Sometimes there are no models. In the second half of the twentieth century, women who suddenly found themselves in what had been a "man's world," whether as firefighters, professors, or heads of state, had to adapt existing male models to develop a role in which they could be comfortable. The transition is far from complete. Although women comprise more than 50 percent of the world population, their participation in many professional and political arenas remains limited. Men, for their part, often feel constrained in choosing roles more often assumed by women, for example, homemaker, secretary, or nurse. If current social trends continue, however, by the end of the twenty-first century both women and men may find they have many more established models from which to choose.

If the world can be thought of as a stage, with actors and actresses who play their parts to the best of their ability, theater may be seen as an opportunity to experiment with roles, to try things out. Fantasy and play-acting are a natural and important part of childhood. Make-believe and the "you be . . . , I'll be . . ." improvisations familiar to children the world over are important to self-discovery and growth. They allow young learners to experiment, to try things out, like hats and wigs, moods and postures, gestures and words. As occasions for language use, role playing and the many related activities that constitute theater arts are likewise a natural component of language learning. They allow learners to experiment with the roles they play or may be called upon to play in real life. Theater arts can provide learners with the tools they need to act—that is, to interpret, express and negotiate meaning in a new language. Activities can include both scripted and unscripted role playing, simulations, and even pantomime. Ensemble-building activities familiar in theater training have been used very successfully in language programs to create a climate of trust so necessary for the incorporation of theater arts activities (see Savignon 1997). The role of the teacher in theater arts is that of a coach: to provide support, strategies, and encouragement for learners as they explore new ways of being.

Language use beyond the classroom is the fifth and final component of a communicative curriculum. Regardless of the variety of communicative activities in the classroom, their purpose remains preparing learners to use the second language in the world beyond. This is the world on which learners will depend for the maintenance and development of their communicative competence once classes are over. The classroom is but a rehearsal. Language use beyond the classroom in a communicative curriculum begins with discovery of learners' interests and needs and opportunities not only to respond to but, more important, to explore those interests and needs through second language use beyond the classroom itself.

In a second language environment, opportunities to use the second language outside the classroom abound. Systematic "field experiences" may successfully become the core of the course, which then becomes a workshop where learners can compare notes, seek clarification, and expand the range of domains in which they learn to function in the second language. Classroom visits to a courtroom trial, a public auction, or a church bazaar provide introductions to aspects of the local culture that learners might not experience on their own. Conversation partners, apprenticeships, and host families can be arranged. Residents of nearby retirement communities can be recruited as valuable resources for a range of research projects. Senior citizens often welcome the opportunity to interact with international visitors or new arrivals and can offer a wealth of knowledge and experience. They might be interviewed about noteworthy historical events, child rearing in earlier decades, or their views on politics, health care, or grandparenting.

In other than a second language setting, the challenge for incorporating language use beyond the classroom may be greater, but it is certainly not insurmountable. Such incorporation remains essential for both learners and teacher. Radio and television programs, videos, and feature-length films may be available along with newspapers and magazines. Residents who use the second language, or visitors from the surrounding community, may be able to visit the classroom. The Internet now provides opportunities to interact on a variety of topics with other language users around the world. These opportunities for computer-mediated communication (CMC) will increase dramatically in the years ahead. In addition to prearranged exchanges, learners can make use of World Wide Web sites to obtain a range of information, schedules, rates, locations, descriptions, and sources.

Putting It All Together

How do we put it all together? Is there an optimum combination of language arts, personal language use, language for a purpose, theater arts, and language use beyond the classroom? These questions must be answered by individual language teachers for their learners in the context in which they teach. Cultural expectations, goals, and styles of learning are but some of the ways in which learners may differ one from another. To the complexity of the learner must be added the complexities of teachers and of the settings in which they teach. Established routines, or institutional beliefs about what is important, weigh heavily in a teacher's decisions about what and how to teach and often make innovation difficult (see Chapters 3 and 7). Finally, the need for variety must be taken into account. Learners who are bored with recitation of rules or with sentence translation may just as easily lose interest in games or role-play if either is allowed to become routine. Difficult as it is, the teacher's task is to understand the many factors involved and respond to them creatively.

Teachers cannot do this alone, of course. They need the support of administrators, the community, and learners themselves. Methodologists and teacher-education programs have a responsibility as well. They should provide classroom teachers with the perspective and experiences they need if they are to respond to the realities of their world, a changing world in which the old ways of language teaching may not be the best ways. The optimal combination for a given context of the analytical and the experiential is a focus of ongoing inquiry. A now well-established research tradition in second and foreign language learning and teaching, however, has clearly shown the importance of attention to language use, or experience, in addition to language usage, or analysis. The overwhelming emphasis in most school programs remains on the latter, though, often to the complete exclusion of experience in language use (for examples, see Chapters 3, 4, and 7).

Sociolinguistic Issues

Numerous sociolinguistic issues await attention. Variation in the speech community and its relationship to language change are central to sociolinguistic inquiry. Sociolinguistic perspectives on variability and change highlight the folly of describing the competence of a native speaker, let alone that of a non-native speaker, in terms of "mastery" or "command" of a system. All language systems show instability and variation. The language systems of learners show even greater instability and variability in both the amount and rate of change. Moreover, sociolinguistic concerns with identity and accommodation help explain the construction by bilingual speakers of a "variation space" which is different from that of a native speaker. This may include retention of any number of features of a previously acquired code or system of phonology and syntax as well as features of discourse and pragmatics, including communication strategies. The phenomenon may be individual or, within a community of learners, general. Differences not only in the code itself but in the semantic meanings attributed to different encodings contribute to identification with a speech community or culture, the way a speech community views itself and the world. This often includes code mixing and code switching, the use by bilingual speakers of resources from more than one speech community.

Sociolinguistic perspectives have been important in understanding the implications of norm, appropriateness, and variability for CLT and continue to suggest avenues of inquiry for further research and development of teaching materials. Use of authentic language data has underscored the importance of context—setting, roles, genre, and so on—in interpreting the meaning of a text. A range of both oral and written texts in context provides learners with a variety of language experiences, experiences they need to construct their own "variation space," to make determinations of appropriateness in their own expression of meaning. "Competent" in this instance is not necessarily synonymous with "near native." Negotiation in CLT highlights the need for interlinguistic—that is, intercultural—awareness on the part of all involved (Byram 1997). Better understanding of the strategies used in the negotiation of meaning offers the potential for improving classroom practice of the needed skills.

NATIVES AND FOREIGNERS

As a starting point, we might begin by asking ourselves whose language we teach and for what purpose. What is our own relationship with the language? Do we consider it to be foreign, second, native, or target?

Webster's New International Dictionary, second edition, was published in 1950, a time when language teaching in the United States was on the threshold of a period of unprecedented scrutiny, experimentation, and growth. The dictionary provides the following definitions of these terms we use so often with respect to language. "Foreign" derives from Middle English *foraine, forene,* Old French *forain,* and Latin *foris,* meaning "out-of-doors." Modern definitions include

> situated outside one's own country; born in, belonging to, derived from, or characteristic of some place other than the one under consideration . . . alien in character; not connected; not pertinent; not appropriate. Related to, or dealing with, other countries; not organically connected or naturally related; as a foreign body (biology, medicine), a substance occurring in any part of the body or organism where it is not normally found.

Those who are identified as teaching a foreign language, perhaps in a department of foreign languages, should ponder the meaning of the term. What does the label "foreign" signal to colleagues, learners, and the community at large? Today we are concerned with global ecology and the global economy. The "foreign" students who used to walk university campuses and whose numbers have become increasingly important for balancing budgets in higher education have been replaced by international students. To excite national pride and assail their opponents, politicians are fond of evoking the dreaded "F" word, in phrases such as "foreign influence," "foreign money," and "foreign oil."

Nonetheless, one might object, "foreign" is still a useful term to use in distinguishing between teaching English in Osaka, Japan, and teaching English in, say, Youngstown, Ohio. In Youngstown, English is taught to non-native speakers as a second language, whereas in Osaka it is a foreign language. The contexts of learning are not the same, to be sure. Neither are the learners—or the teachers. Do these facts change the nature of the language, though? What about the teaching of Spanish in Chicago, in Barcelona, in Buenos Aires, in Guatemala City, in Miami, or in Madrid? In what sense can Spanish in each of these contexts be described as "foreign" or "second," and what are the implications for the learners of the label selected or for the teacher?

On the one hand, having taught French in Urbana, Illinois, for many years, I can easily identify with the problems of teachers of English in Osaka. More so, perhaps, than can those who teach ESL in Urbana with easy access to English-speaking communities outside the classroom. On the other hand, however, teaching French in Urbana or English in Osaka is no excuse for ignoring or avoiding opportunities for communication, either written or oral. In this age of satellite television and the World Wide Web, a multitude of language communities is for some as close as the computer keyboard. In the decades ahead, the potential for language learning and language change that is inherent in computer-mediated negotiation of meaning will be increasingly recognized, both inside and outside language classrooms.

What may be a problem is the teacher's communicative competence. Is she a fluent speaker of the language she teaches? If not, does she consider herself to be bilingual? If not, why not? Is it a lack of communicative competence, or rather a lack of communicative confidence? Is she intimidated by "native" speakers?

The example of English as an international or global language is instructive. Such wide adoption of one language in both international and intra-national contexts is unprecedented. English users today include (1) those who live in countries where English is a primary language, the United States, the United Kingdom, Canada, Australia, and New Zealand; (2) those who live in countries where English is an auxiliary, intranational language of communication—for example, Bangladesh, India, Nigeria, the Philippines, Tanzania;

and (3) those who use primarily English in international contexts, in countries like China, Indonesia, Japan, Saudi Arabia, and Russia. By conservative estimates the number of non-native speakers of English in the world today outnumbers native speakers by more than two to one, and the ratio is increasing. Models of appropriateness vary from context to context. The use of the English language has become so widespread that some scholars speak not only of varieties of English but of world Englishes, the title of a professional journal devoted to discussion of issues in the use, description, and teaching of these many varieties. Depending on the context, "native" speakers may or may not be appropriate models (Kachru 1992).

For an interpretation of the term "native speaker," *Webster's International Dictionary,* second edition, is not very helpful. A "native" is defined as "one that is born in a place or country referred to; a denizen by birth; an animal, a fruit or vegetable produced in a certain region; as, a native of France." The dictionary cites, among expressions containing "native" as a modifier, "native bear," "native bread," "native cabbage," "native dog," and "native sparrow." There is no mention of native speaker.

To understand the meaning of "native speaker" in language teaching today, we must look to American structural linguistics and its use of "native speaker informants" to provide data for previously undescribed, unwritten languages, as well as to Chomsky's representation of the "ideal native speaker" in his elaboration of transformational-generative grammar. In both cases the native speaker, real or imagined, was the authority on language use. In audiolingual language teaching, the native speaker became not only the model for but the judge of acceptable use. See, for example, the *ACTFL Oral Proficiency Guidelines* level descriptor that tolerates errors in grammar that "do not disturb the native speaker" (American Council on the Teaching of Foreign Languages 1986). That phrase has always conjured up for me images of people sitting around with big signs that say, "native speaker. do not disturb." Having lived most of my adult life with a native speaker of French, I suppose I am no longer intimidated, or even impressed. Nor, I should add, is he intimidated or impressed by my American English. Native speakers of French, American English, or whatever language are fine, but they do not own the language they use; nor are they by definition competent to teach and evaluate learners. (A more recent version of the ACTFL level descriptor refers to errors that do not "distract" the native speaker. For discussion, see Chapter 10.)

There remains the term "target language," used frequently by methodologists and language-acquisition researchers alike. "Target language" is laden with both behavioristic and militaristic associations. A target is not unlike the "terminal behavior" or end result identified in behaviorist learning theory. "Target language" evokes the Army Specialized Training Program (ASTP) that provided an experimental setting for the audiolingual methods and materials developed in the 1960s. Evoking as it does a monolithic, fixed goal for all, reference to language as a target misrepresents both process and progress in language learning.

THE CLASSROOM AS SOCIAL CONTEXT

Along with other sociolinguistic issues in language acquisition, the classroom itself as a social context has been neglected. Classroom language learning was the focus of research studies in the 1960s and early 1970s. Language classrooms were not a major concern, however, in the SLA research that gathered momentum in the years to follow. The full range of variables present in educational settings—for example, teacher preparation and experience, class size, learner needs and attitudes—was an obvious deterrent. Other difficulties included the lack of well-defined classroom processes and lack of agreement on what constituted successful learning. Confusion between form-focused drill and meaning-focused communication persisted in many of the textbook exercises and language test prototypes that influenced curricula. Not surprisingly, researchers eager to establish SLA as a worthy field of inquiry turned their attention to narrower, more quantitative studies of the acquisition of selected morphosyntactic features.

Increasingly, however, researchers' attention is now being directed to the social dynamics and discourse of the classroom. What does teacher-learner interaction look like? What happens during pair or group work? How much is the second language being used and for what purposes? If language use is essential for the development of communicative competence, then the nature and amount of second language use in the classroom setting needs to be examined closely. Is the aim truly communication, that is, is the focus on the negotiation of meaning, rather than on practice of grammatical forms? What are the opportunities for interaction in the second language? Who participates? Who initiates discourse in the second language? What are the purposes of this discourse (Savignon 1997)?

Questions related to patterns of communication and opportunities for learners to negotiate meaning become all the more compelling as technological advances increase dramatically and alter the nature of such opportunities. E-mail, chat rooms, on-line teaching materials, and video-conferencing are, in effect, redefining the concept of "classroom" and, with it, the roles of teachers and learners. (For an example, see Chapter 8.)

What CLT Is Not

Disappointment with both grammar-translation and audiolingual methods for their inability to prepare learners for the interpretation, expression, and negotiation of meaning, along with enthusiasm for an array of activities increasingly labeled communicative (see Chapters 2, 5, 6, 7, and 10) has resulted in no little uncertainty over what constitutes the essential features of CLT. Thus, a summary description would be incomplete without mention of what CLT is not.

The concern of CLT is not exclusively with face-to-face oral communication. The principles apply equally to reading and writing activities that involve readers and writers in the interpretation, expression, and negotiation of meaning. (For an illustration of the interactive, interpretive nature of the reading process, see Fish 1980.) Communicative language teaching does not require work in small groups or pairs; group tasks have been found helpful in many contexts as a way of increasing the opportunity and motivation for communication. Classroom work in groups or pairs should not, however, be considered an essential feature and may well be inappropriate in some contexts.

Communicative language teaching need not entail complete rejection of familiar materials. Materials designed to promote communicative competence can be used as aids to memorization, repetition, and translation, or for grammar exercises. Similarly, a teacher who has only a grammar-translation manual can certainly teach for communicative competence. What matters is the teacher's understanding of what language learning is and how it happens. The basic principle is that learners should engage with texts and meaning through the process of use and discovery.

Finally, CLT does not exclude a focus on metalinguistic awareness or knowledge of rules of syntax, discourse, and social appropriateness. Focus on form can be a familiar and welcome component in a learning environment that provides rich opportunity for focus on meaning; but focus on form cannot replace practice in communication.

The essence of CLT is the engagement of learners in communication to allow them to develop their communicative competence. Terms sometimes used to refer to features of CLT are "task-based" (see Chapter 5), "content-based," "process-oriented," "interactive," "inductive," and "discovery-oriented." CLT cannot be found in any one textbook or set of curricular materials. Strict adherence to a given text is not likely to be true to the processes and goals of CLT. In keeping with the notion of context of situation, CLT is properly seen as an approach, grounded in a theory of intercultural communicative competence, that can be used to develop materials and methods appropriate to a given context of learning. No less than the means and norms of communication they are designed to reflect, communicative language teaching methods will continue to be explored and adapted.

Teacher Education and CLT

Considerable resources, both human and monetary, are being used around the world to respond to the need for language teaching that is appropriate for the communicative needs of learners. The key to success in this endeavor is the education of classroom teachers. The remaining chapters directly address issues of CLT and teacher education. The contributors present accounts of teacher response to communicative English language teaching (CELT) in situations outside native-English-speaking countries (Japan, Taiwan, Hong Kong, and the Netherlands), a report on an innovative technology-intensive program for elementary Spanish language instruction at a major U.S. research university, and a report on the promotion of learner autonomy in a multilingual European setting. The collection also includes a first-person narrative account of English language teaching by a Japanese teacher with many years' experience, an account of the first U.S. attempt to promote national standards for language learning, and a philosophical final chapter that offers a modern critical perspective on applied linguistics and teacher education.

The research reports included provide a global perspective on language teaching for communicative competence in the twenty-first century. I have made a deliberate effort to blur the distinction between the contexts for foreign language teaching and for second language teaching, a distinction that, while useful in delineating features of access to the second language and of teacher preparation, obscures the common goals of multilingualism: the empowerment of learners and world understanding. In accordance with these goals, contexts for learning a range of different languages are included. Too often, accounts of second language acquisition (SLA) and CLT leave readers with the impression that English is the only language worth studying and that English language teachers, methodologists, and researchers are the only "experts" worth reading.

Moreover, I have sought to highlight the diverse nature of contributions to understanding CLT and educating language teachers. In writing about CLT, British scholars, on the one hand, have focused on the concepts and contributions of writers who are monolingual, predominantly male, and British. Their names appear in the publications of British university presses that include a broad range of materials intended for use by classroom teachers. These same names are also well known to employees of the government-funded British Council that conducts a variety of English language teaching programs worldwide. For U.S. foreign language teachers, methodologists, and researchers, on the other hand, the "proficiency-oriented" language teaching promoted by the American Council for Teaching of Foreign Languages often remains the default descriptor. For U.S. scholars concerned with the teaching of Spanish, French, German, and other modern languages to speakers of English, CLT has tended until recently to be seen as a predominantly European and, perhaps, ESL concern. Although they share a concern for language learning, foreign language and ESL teachers in U.S. schools often function as two quite distinct professional groups.

The collection represents at least three different streams of scholarship. Some chapters are based on survey results, one is a somewhat reflective, personal account, two are conceptually more philosophical and historical than empirical. The difference in research paradigms, or ways of knowing, serves to strengthen the collection. Each chapter provides an example of sound research design or an original interpretation and approach to problems of coordination between language teachers and teacher educators over language policy and curricular and methodological change and innovation. Together, the chapters serve as models for inspiration, adoption, and adaptation in other contexts where CLT is a goal.

It is important to see what happens when teachers try to make changes in their teaching in accordance with various types of advice, whether directives from Ministries of Education, advice from so-called experts in teacher education and research, or other sources. The information provided on language policy, methods, and materials specific to CLT in multiple contexts highlights the international interest in promoting CLT and provides important insights for researchers, program administrators, and prospective or practicing teachers.

Chapters 2, 3, and 4 look at English language education in Japan from the perspective of the Japanese Ministry of Education, a teacher educator, and a classroom teacher, respectively. In Chapter 2, Minoru Wada, a former member of Mombusho (the Japanese Ministry of Education, Science, and Culture) takes justifiable pride in the recent redirection of English language education by the Japanese government, including the introduction of a communicative syllabus, the Japan Exchange and Teaching (JET) Program, and overseas in-service training for teachers. Although Mombusho had previously encouraged attempts to make classrooms more "communicative" through the addition of "communicative activities," it was apparent that teachers felt constrained by a structural syllabus that rigidly controlled the introduction and sequence of grammatical features. The perception that learners could not talk about their past experiences until their second year of study, when past tenses had been introduced, severely constricted communication. With the introduction of a new national syllabus, structural controls were relaxed and teachers were allowed more freedom in determining the sequence for introducing syntactical features. The theoretical rationale underlying the curriculum change in Japan includes both the well-known Canale and Swain (1980) model of communicative competence and the hypothetical classroom model of communicative competence, or "inverted pyramid," proposed by Savignon (1983). In the conclusion to Chapter 2, Wada offers sobering evidence of the failure of previous attempts to introduce ELT reform in Japan. Nonetheless, he remains optimistic about the current efforts. The stakes are indeed higher, and the major difference between this and previous efforts may well be the involvement of Japanese educators themselves.

Chapter 3 is illustrative of current research on teacher development that focuses on teachers' beliefs in relation to their practices, rather than on teaching skills mandated by educators or policy makers. Kazuyoshi Sato follows the educational research model for classroom language teaching adapted by Kleinsasser (1993) in considering language teachers' beliefs and practices in the Japanese context. His yearlong study focuses on the department of English in a private senior high school. Multiple sources, including interviews, observations, surveys, and documents, yield valuable insight into how EFL teachers learn to teach in this particular school environment.

A third compelling voice in the case study of Japan is that of a classroom teacher, Kiyoko Kusano Hubbell, a fluent speaker of English with twenty years of classroom experience. In Chapter 4, in a welcome departure from mainstream academic prose, Kusano Hubbell offers a poignant narrative of her own struggles and triumphs as a teacher of English, from the perspective of her native Japanese language and culture. The insights she provides into learners' and teachers' attitudes and experiences and the context in which they are shaped richly complement the findings presented in Chapters 2 and 3.

Chapter 5, by Liying Cheng, uses both qualitative and quantitative methods to examine the influence of a new, more communicative English language test on the classroom teaching of English. The context for this particular study is Hong Kong, where ELT is moving toward a task-based model. In keeping with curricular redesign, alternative public examinations have been developed to measure learners' ability to make use of what they have learned, to solve problems and complete tasks. At the time curricular changes were introduced, ELT was characterized as "test-centered, teacher-centered, and textbook-centered" (Morris et al. 1996). The ambitious multiyear award-winning study (TOEFL Award for the Outstanding Doctoral Dissertation Research in Second/Foreign Language Testing for 1998) that is the basis for this report reveals data on the extent to which the change in public examinations has influenced change in classroom teaching.

National standards are the focus of Chapter 6 by Ana Schwartz. Schwartz reports on efforts to establish and diffuse National Standards for Foreign Language Learning for U.S. schools. The standards were adopted in 1995 after extensive lobbying efforts by the American Council on the Teaching of Foreign Languages and the National Committee on Languages to include foreign languages in the national Goals 2000 Educate America Act that endorsed curricular standards in the subject areas of math, English, history, and science. Goals 2000 marked an important turning point in the educational history of the United States, where issues of curriculum and assessment have remained the concern of individual states and local school districts. The new U.S. federal curricular standards remain voluntary, however. A decentralized system of education, along with distorted representation of the concept of communicative competence for purposes of language evaluation, represents an obstacle to true and meaningful implementation of communicative goals.

Chapter 7 offers the perspective of prominent language teacher educators involved in a national initiative to promote CLT in schools. Adopting a sociocultural perspective on language use and language learning as prerequisite to pedagogical innovation, Chaochang Wang considers attitude, function, pedagogy (Berns 1990), and learner beliefs with respect to the use and teaching of English in the Taiwanese context. This report of teacher educators' views is part of a larger study of CLT in Taiwan. Data for the study were both quantitative and qualitative and included teachers', learners', and parents' responses to questionnaires, in addition to the analysis of data from interviews with teacher educators reported here (Wang 2000).

Cutting-edge advances in computer-mediated instruction are the focus of Chapter 8, by Diane Musumeci. Taking advantage of the technological resources available at a major research university, Musumeci designed and implemented an introductory multisection Spanish language program that has attracted considerable administrative attention for its cost-saving potential. This report looks at the new program from the perspective of a second language researcher and teacher educator. It discusses teachers' persistent concern with grammar teaching, for which there is seemingly never enough class time, and considers the potential of technology as a tool for in-service teacher education.

Chapter 9, by Eus Schalkwijk, Kees van Esch, Adri Elsen, and Wim Setz, a team of teacher educators at the University of Nijmegen, in the Netherlands, looks at important and challenging implications of CLT not only for what is learned in a foreign language but for how it is learned. Autonomous learning influences teaching methodology and dramatically changes the roles of the language teacher and the language learner. To cope with these changes, future teachers have to be prepared both practically and academically. The historical overview of culture orientations in the first part of the chapter provides an important perspective on the influence of social views and values on the education of language teachers in generations past. (For a provocative and relevant discussion of their education as far back as the Middle Ages, when Latin was the lingua franca of the Western world, see Musumeci 1997a.) The multilingual nature of the European context in which these teacher educators work underscores the importance of innovation in language teaching in the effort to meet rapidly increasing demands for communicative competence in two or more languages.

In conclusion, Chapter 10, by Celeste Kinginger, provides a useful discussion of both theoretical and practical issues in language teacher education from the perspective of postmodern critical theory. Adapting the categories of primary discourse, or ways of understanding, proposed by Kramsch (1995a, 1995b), Kinginger cites the notion of "error" in language learning and teaching to illustrate how teachers can develop interpretive skills to evaluate competing forms of discourse and cull from them in making decisions about their own teaching practice. The development of interpretive and reflective skills offers a practical alternative for educating language teachers, who currently seem compelled to choose a single methodological stance from a bewildering smorgasbord of options: audiolingual, grammar-translation, CLT, content-based, or total physical response, for example. This overview of the competing forms of discourse in language teacher education provides a useful perspective on the previous chapters in the collection, each responding to a particular context for language teaching.

PART I

Case Study: Japan

2

Teacher Education for Curricular Innovation in Japan

MINORU WADA

Since the decision in the mid-1980s of the national Ministry of Education, Science, and Culture of Japan (hereafter referred to as Mombusho) to emphasize the development of communicative competence in English language education in the Japanese school system, the central issue has remained the gap between the national government's initiatives to promote innovation and the response of the Japanese teachers of English. In this chapter, I shall examine some key features of the implementation process.

The design of the innovations that were introduced has become increasingly visible to outsiders who take an interest in English education in Japan. At the same time, though, this process is very difficult for them to understand because it is affected by "complex cultural, ideological, historical, political, economic, administrative, institutional, technological, sociolinguistic, and language planning factors" (Markee 1997, 12). Without an understanding of the process of syllabus *implementation,* as opposed to syllabus design, however, it is impossible to appreciate fully the degree to which communicative language teaching (CLT) has spread in the English as a foreign language (EFL) context in Japan.

The issues involved include (1) the national government's role in educational reform, (2) the administrative measures taken to achieve the reform, and (3) practicing teachers' response to the government reform. Discussion of the first issue requires an explanation of the 1989 Mombusho Guidelines, or national guidelines for school curricula, in which the communicative syllabus was introduced. The administrative measures included the Mombusho Japan Exchange and Teaching (JET) program, an unprecedented project sponsored by the national government to accelerate its initiatives to reform English education and teacher-training programs. Examination of the third issue, reactions by Japanese classroom teachers of English to governmental reform initiatives, is based on the findings of an exploratory survey of teachers in both general and vocational high schools in Chiba prefecture in Tokyo.

The 1989 Mombusho Guidelines

The Mombusho Guidelines or course of study is one of the most important sets of legal precepts in the Japanese educational system. It establishes national standards for elementary and secondary schools. It also regulates content, the standard number of annual teaching hours at lower-level secondary (junior high) schools, subject areas, subjects, and the standard number of required credits at upper-level secondary (senior high) schools.

The course of study for the teaching of English as a foreign language announced by Mombusho in 1989 stands as a landmark in the history of English education in Japan. For the first time it introduced into English education at both secondary school levels the concept of *communicative competence*. In 1989, Mombusho revised the course of study for primary as well as secondary schools on the basis of proposals made in a 1987 report by the Council on the School Curriculum, an advisory group to the minister of education, science, and culture (Kyoikukateishingikai 1987). The basic goal of the revision was to prepare students to cope with the rapid pace of change toward a more global society. The report urged Japanese teachers to place much more emphasis on the development of communicative competence in English. Some specific changes were made in accordance with this main principle of the revision. In order to illustrate those changes, let me offer examples for both junior and senior high schools.

Before the 1989 reform, the Mombusho Guidelines stated that English teachers were expected to make their classes "communicative" by implementing "communicative activities" in their classrooms. Close examination of the *content* of the Mombusho Guidelines, however, revealed them to be quite structurally based. For example, they prescribed that the simple present and present progressive tenses be taught in the first year of junior high school, and the simple past tense in the second year. Consequently, Japanese teachers could not have their students tell their past experiences in English until their second year. This was a great obstacle to the construction of "real" and "communicative" English language classes. Therefore, in the 1989 guidelines the rigid restrictions on the sequencing of grammatical and syntactical structures were revised to provide more flexibility and allow teachers more freedom in their use of the language. This change is a prime example of the move that has occurred on the junior high school level from a structurally oriented to a communicatively oriented program.

At the upper secondary school level the main objective of the 1989 guidelines has been the creation of three new courses: Oral Communication A, Oral Communication B, and Oral Communication C. Oral Communication A comprises mainly daily conversations. Oral Communication B focuses on the development of listening-comprehension skills by giving learners practice in identifying the main points in a speech or lecture and requiring them to take notes while listening. Oral Communication C emphasizes the development of public speaking skills.

With the purpose of providing a rationale for these new moves to reform the teaching of English in secondary schools, the developers of the reform have often referred to the framework for communicative competence proposed by Canale and Swain (1980) and Canale (1983). In addition, the hypothetical classroom model of communicative competence proposed by Savignon (1983), also referred to as the "inverted pyramid," has attracted the attention of many Japanese teachers of English. (For further discussion of this classroom model, see Chapter 1.)

The Mombusho Initiatives

In accordance with the revised 1989 Mombusho Guidelines (Mombusho 1989a, 1989b), Mombusho has supported initiatives seen as key to the improvement of English language teaching in Japanese schools. One of these measures is the recruitment of native speakers of English as assistants to Japanese teachers of English. The other is the in-service training of Japanese teachers of English.

THE RECRUITMENT OF NATIVE SPEAKERS OF ENGLISH

Before the 1989 revision of the guidelines, Mombusho had been employing native speakers of English to assist both Japanese teachers of English and English education teaching consultants for prefectural and municipal boards of education. Two such projects were the Mombusho English Fellows (MEF) and the British English Teachers Scheme (BETS) programs. In order to meet the increasing demand for native speakers of English at secondary schools throughout Japan, the Japanese government decided to expand and reorganize the MEF and the BETS programs as a single national project, jointly sponsored by Mombusho, the Ministry of Internal Affairs, and the Ministry of Foreign Affairs. A new project, the Japan Exchange and Teaching program (JET), thus emerged as the synthesis of the two previously existing programs. From August 1987 to July 1988, approximately eight hundred native speakers of English participated in the new program.

The rationale behind the JET project has been "to bring the L2 community into the classroom" (Savignon 1983, 220). It has been difficult for Japanese teachers to provide their students with opportunities to use English outside the classroom. Therefore, it is necessary to bring "representatives of the L2 community into the classroom so that [second language teachers'] students can try out their English in a communicative situation and develop the strategies needed to interact with and learn from a native speaker" (220).

The JET program has encouraged an increasing number of prefectures and municipalities to employ native English speakers on their own. It is estimated that in 1999 there were approximately ten thousand native speakers of English teaching the language throughout Japan. Half of these assistants were employed directly by local governments and the other half entered through the JET program. There appears to be general agreement that native speakers of English have contributed to English education in Japanese schools in three ways: they increase learners' positive attitude toward communicating with native speakers of English; they enhance the ability of Japanese teachers to speak English, and their confidence in that ability; and they bring with them into Japanese classrooms innovative language teaching techniques.

IN-SERVICE TRAINING OF JAPANESE TEACHERS OF ENGLISH

The effectiveness of any educational program depends ultimately on the quality of teachers. To improve teaching, therefore, a high priority must be given to the in-service training of teachers. Current in-service training of Japanese teachers of English includes one-month domestic training programs sponsored by Mombusho and six-month and one-year study programs overseas that are coordinated with the domestic programs and aimed at improving both teaching skills and English language proficiency.

The official name of the domestic training program is the Institute for Educational Leadership on the Teaching of English. The participants are English teaching consultants for the prefectural and municipal boards of education and senior high school teachers who play a leading role in the field of English education within a prefecture or municipality. In 1998, domestic in-service training programs were held at six different locations in Japan; a total of three hundred junior high and three hundred senior high school teachers participated. The main objectives of the program seminars are (1) to enhance participants' communicative ability with regard especially to their listening and speaking skills, (2) to familiarize participants with innovative methodologies for the teaching of English, and (3) to improve participants' teaching skills to facilitate the implementation of these innovative methods in English language classrooms.

Mombusho has also been trying to expand overseas study programs in conjunction with domestic programs. Teachers who successfully complete domestic seminars qualify for programs abroad to further improve their teaching and language skills. In 1998, 136 teachers who participated in these overseas programs studied in the United States, the United Kingdom, Australia, or New Zealand.

Teachers' Reactions to the Mombusho Initiatives

My discussion of English language teaching reform for the development of communicative competence in the Japanese school system has focused thus far on the initiatives of Mombusho. But as Markee (1997) observes, "End users are unlikely to adopt innovations unless there is a realistic match between change agents' expectations, the resources that are available to support the introduction of the innovation, and end users' levels of knowledge, commitment, and skills" (61). The wide discrepancy between what the government hopes to achieve and what Japanese teachers of English are actually doing in their classrooms has been noted frequently. To develop baseline quantitative data about Japanese high school teachers of English, Charles Browne of Aoyama University and I conducted a survey of teachers' perceptions about several important issues related to the Mombusho initiatives already described.

A twenty-six-item survey was sent to approximately twelve hundred high school English teachers working in college preparatory (*Ippan*) and vocational (*Jitsugyo*) high schools throughout the Chiba prefecture (Browne and Wada 1998). Chiba prefecture in Tokyo is one of forty-seven prefectures in Japan. Ippan schools in Chiba prefecture number 131, with 1,151 teachers of English; Jitsugyo schools number 17, with 71 teachers of English. The response rate was 18.7 percent (or 216 questionnaires returned) for Ippan teachers and 16.9 percent (or 12 surveys returned) for Jitsugyo schools, for an overall rate of return of 18.6 percent.

The results of the survey identified the problems these teachers face in their

Table 2.1 Reported In-Service Seminar Attendance Rate

	Jitsugyo (Vocational)	Ippan (College Preparatory)
Teachers attending seminars	75%	67%
Average number of private seminars attended	3.66	3.12
Average number of public seminars attended	2.75	2.29

Table 2.2 Most Popular Topics for In-Service Seminar

Topic	Number of Teachers Reporting
Communicative methods/techniques	123
Reading	18
Speech/pronunciation	13
Team teaching	11
Writing	8

classrooms as well as the extent to which the 1989 Mombusho Guidelines have influenced their teaching practice. As can be seen in Table 2.1, vocational (Jitsugyo) high school teachers reported attending in-service training seminars more often than did general, or college preparatory (Ippan), high school teachers. Several possible explanations present themselves for this higher rate of attendance by vocational high school teachers. One explanation might have to do with the grammar-translation method of teaching English. Since the focus of the grammar-translation method closely corresponds to the content of college entrance examinations, it continues to be favored by Ippan teachers. In addition, both because classroom instruction in the grammar-translation method is familiar and teacher-centered and because it requires no communicative ability in the second language on the part of the teacher, it is more easily adopted by teachers with no previous teacher training. Thus, Ippan teachers may feel less need for in-service training than do Jitsugyo teachers, who are more likely to experiment with communicative teaching methods and techniques. Indirect support for this claim may be found in the fact that the overwhelming majority of seminar topics reported by the participants in this study are related to communicative language teaching, as illustrated in Table 2.2. In addition, it seems reasonable to suspect that, given the relatively low overall rate of response to the survey for both Ippan and Jitsugyo teachers (18.6 percent), the attendance rate reported by those teachers who did respond was higher than for the groups as a whole. Teachers who did attend the seminars and express interest in communicative methods of language teaching were more likely to respond to the survey than were those who lacked interest or did not attend.

COMMUNICATIVE COMPETENCE IN THE CLASSROOM

As explained earlier, the 1989 Mombusho Guidelines for Japanese high school English classes emphasized for the first time the development of learners' communicative competence in English as the primary goal of instruction. In the survey of teachers conducted by Browne and Wada (1998), 67 percent of Jitsugyo high school teachers and 68 percent of Ippan high school teachers reported having read the revised guidelines. When asked to identify their most important classroom goal, 100 percent of the Jitsugyo teachers and 64 percent of the Ippan teachers gave as their first choice the development of learners' communicative ability.

Although their responses may appear promising, it is possible that these participating teachers answered the questions as they thought they were expected to answer. In fact, numerous other studies indicate that more traditional translation-oriented methods still prevail in Japanese classrooms. (For further discussion of what goes on in Japanese ELT classrooms, see Chapters 3 and 4.) Moreover, when asked what goal most influenced their teaching style, both Jitsugyo and Ippan teachers said their top-ranked goal was "to teach the contents of the textbook." These rankings are shown in Table 2.3.

Inasmuch as the operationalization of the Mombusho Guidelines includes the use of Mombusho-approved textbooks and teachers feel compelled to teach the contents of these textbooks, communicative language teaching should be flourishing. Appropriate textbooks are most certainly a key factor in successful innovation. It is, however, debatable whether the approved textbooks are in fact a clear reflection of the Mombusho Guidelines. Research is needed in this area. The comprehensive set of guidelines for the analysis of textbooks and materials as described by Savignon (1997) could provide a framework for this much-needed research.

TEAM TEACHING

With the JET program now in its twelfth year, not surprisingly 90 percent of the Ippan teachers and 100 percent of the Jitsugyo teachers in our survey reported having had some experience team teaching with native speakers of English. Table 2.4 shows the distribution of these reported experiences. In

Table 2.3 Three Most Important Influences on Classroom Teaching

Jitsugyo	Ippan
To teach the contents of the textbook	To teach the contents of the textbook
To make parents happy	To prepare students for the entrance examination
To prepare students for the entrance examination	To follow the Mombusho Guidelines

Table 2.4 Teachers' Team-Teaching Experiences

Number of Lessons	Jitsugyo	Ippan
Never	0%	6%
1–5	25%	10%
6–10	8%	10%
11–15	0%	9%
16–24	25%	11%
25 or more	42%	54%
TOTAL	100%	100%

the early years of the program, most Japanese teachers of English showed hesitation about teaching together with English-speaking assistant teachers. In fact, at that time the most common obstacle to team teaching cited by Japanese teachers of English was their lack of confidence in their ability to communicate in English with a native speaker. Although it may be debated whether the JET program has upgraded the quality of communicative language teaching in Japanese schools, the program has clearly had an impact on the English language ability of Japanese English teachers and on their level of self-confidence at the prospect of working with a native speaker of English.

ORAL COMMUNICATION CLASSES

As can be seen in Table 2.5, only 9 percent of the general high school teachers and none of the vocational high school teachers reported teaching Oral C (public speaking) courses. One possible reason for the avoidance of this class is teachers' lack of confidence in their ability to teach public speak-

Table 2.5 Types of Oral English Classes Taught in Chiba Prefecture

	Oral A (Conversation)	Oral B (Listening Comprehension)	Oral C (Public Speaking)
Jitsugyo	75%	25%	0%
Ippan	38%	67%	9%

ing and debate skills, owing to a lack of formal training in these areas. Another interesting finding was the almost opposite rates of implementation of Oral A (conversation) and Oral B (listening comprehension) classes at both types of high school. A likely explanation for this result is that Japanese teachers in Ippan schools feel better prepared to teach listening comprehension than to teach speaking skills.

Although it might be expected that oral English classes A, B, and C would be conducted in English, the Jitsugyo teachers in this study reported that in a typical fifty-minute English class they used English only 33 percent of class time, on average. Ippan teachers reported a slightly greater (41 percent) use of English in their classes. (For further insight into this phenomenon, see Chapter 4.)

With reference to the diffusion of innovation in educational contexts, Markee (1997) has observed that "center-periphery relationships exist in the educational system in Japan. The power to promote educational changes rests with a small number of senior ministry educational officials who are at the center of the decision-making process, and teachers, who are on the periphery of this decision-making process, merely implement the decisions that are handed down to them" (14). He cites Adams and Chen (1981), who estimate that approximately 75 percent of all innovations do not survive in the long run. With further specific reference to Japan, Markee observes that "Harold Palmer attempted to introduce his Oral Method into Japanese secondary schools. Similarly, Charles Fries attempted to introduce the Audiolingual Method in Japan in the 1950s and 1960s. Both attempts ultimately failed" (9). Given the past history of innovation in language teaching in Japan, it seems reasonable to wonder whether current moves initiated by Mombusho to promote communicative language teaching are similarly doomed to fail. It seems too early to give a definitive answer to this question.

As an "insider" who has held an appointment in Mombusho and remains actively involved in current moves by the central government to implement communicative language teaching, I can say with confidence that within the past decade there has been a clear improvement in English education in our schools. At the same time, many obstacles clearly remain. In light of the growing importance of English language skills for international communication in the twenty-first century, the stakes are high. Successful innovation this time around will come only through more research, collaborative efforts, and fuller understanding of the many and sometimes conflicting perspectives of those involved.

3

Practical Understandings of Communicative Language Teaching and Teacher Development

KAZUYOSHI SATO

Despite the theoretical development of communicative language teaching (CLT), understanding among practitioners remains limited (Sato and Kleinsasser 1999a). Moreover, a growing number of studies indicate that classrooms in which CLT is effectively used are rare. Nevertheless, little is known about why it is so difficult to implement CLT and how teachers learn to teach in various school contexts. With the exception of research on technical cultures by Kleinsasser (1989, 1993; also Kleinsasser and Savignon 1991), the question of how school contexts influence what teachers think and do and how teachers learn to teach remains unanswered (Freeman 1996). This chapter reports how EFL teachers in Japan understand English language teaching and learning under the new Mombusho (Ministry of Education, Science, and Culture) guidelines for CLT (see Chapter 2), how they actually teach in their classrooms, and how they learn to teach in a given context.

Theoretical Overview

The focus of teacher development is teachers' learning in school. In essence, teacher development requires teachers to develop their beliefs and practices (Foss and Kleinsasser 1996; Johnson 1994; Pajares 1992; Richardson 1994, 1996; Sato and Kleinsasser 1999a). Today, the question of how teachers learn to teach, whether in general or in second language disciplines, concerns more what teachers actually *know* and how they develop their practices than what teachers *need to know* and how they can be trained (Carter 1990; Golombek 1998; Lange 1990; Richardson 1994, 1996; Sato and Kleinsasser 1999a). In other words, current research on teacher development focuses on teachers' beliefs with relation to their practices rather than on the teaching skills mandated by educators or policy makers (Carter 1990; Richardson 1994). Studies on teacher beliefs have been few, however (Clark and Peterson 1986; Pajares 1992), and have only recently gained prominence (Richardson 1996). Pajares (1992) reviewed research on beliefs and argued that "teachers' beliefs can and should become an important focus of educational inquiry" (307). No comprehensive investigation has been undertaken, though, of the relation between teaching context and teachers' beliefs and practices (Lee and Yarger 1996).

Only a few researchers have examined and clarified particular features. Kleinsasser (1989, 1993) applied the work of Rosenholtz (1989) with high school foreign language teachers. Data were collected from thirty-seven teachers in eleven schools through interviews, observations, and surveys. The results indicated two distinctive technical cultures. One was a routine/uncertain culture, where teachers were uncertain about their instructional practice but were engaged in day-to-day routine. These teachers reported lack of communication about teaching issues. The other was a nonroutine/certain culture, where teachers were confident about their instruction, and their daily practices were not predictable. In addition, Kleinsasser found that teachers in nonroutine/certain cultures incorporated more communicative activities, whereas those in routine/uncertain cultures relied on established approaches. In conclusion, Kleinsasser (1989, 1993) revealed the strong relation between school context and teaching performance.

Other general educational studies have clarified the relation between practices and organizational contexts. Smylie (1988) examined the association between school contexts, classroom teachers' efficacy and certainty, and teachers' practices. He concluded that among the variables of organizational contexts, the most influential are interactions with colleagues through which "teachers may develop a body of technical knowledge about what teaching practices are likely to be effective" (24).

Although research on socialization has focused on student teachers (Richardson 1996), only a few studies have followed beginning teachers to learn how they adapt to school cultures (Briscoe 1996; Lee 1993; Powell 1997). Lee (1993) did a case study of one first-year elementary school teacher over a seven-month period, examining how the new teacher was socialized in the environment. He found four organizational rules, which the beginning teacher deduced from roles and relationships within the technical culture. They were: (1) teachers manage students to maintain a quiet, orderly environment, (2) teachers manage time and schedules to work as efficiently as possible, (3) teachers view students' performance as important because it reflects teachers' competence, and (4) teachers uniformly pace their instruction to correspond to other teachers' (vi).

Powell (1997) completed a cross-case study on two science teachers: a first-career teacher who majored in zoology and marine biology and had limited knowledge of science, and a second-career teacher who had well-developed beliefs and knowledge about science after six years as a field hydrogeologist. He found that by the end of the school year teachers with different levels of content expertise came to teach the same way according to the textbooks. He inferred that these beginning teachers adapted their beliefs and practices to the classroom environment. Both Lee's and Powell's studies showed that beginning teachers have difficulty developing their beliefs and practices in their school contexts.

Briscoe (1996) conducted a one-year case study of a science teacher who, in keeping with his ideal goal, wished to modify his teaching practices to make them more cooperative. He focused on how the teacher learned to teach in the context and developed practices consistent with his goal. Briscoe reported that the teacher tried to implement his ideal practices, only to find it difficult to change. His beliefs, based on his own experiences as a learner as well as the school context, which emphasized control of the teaching and learning process, impeded change. Briscoe concluded that "the construction of intelligible and plausible alternative images and schemes for practices consistent with them may be unlikely if long-held meaning systems constructed within educational settings conflict with information from new experiences" (327) and called for creating collaborative "learning environments which foster conceptual change among teachers" (315).

COMMUNICATIVE LANGUAGE TEACHING AND TEACHER DEVELOPMENT

Change in Beliefs and Practices. Pajares (1992) claims that beliefs are inflexible and basically unchanging. He refers to Rokeach (1968) in saying, "Beliefs differ in intensity and power; beliefs vary along a central-peripheral dimension; and the more central a belief, the more it will resist change" (Pajares 1992, 318). In fact, empirical studies represent the difficulty of changing beliefs and practices. Foss and Kleinsasser (1996), for example, studied preservice mathematics elementary teachers' beliefs and practices during a mathematics methods course. The authors concluded that while preservice teachers were supposedly developing pedagogical and content knowledge, the teachers' beliefs and practices were little altered. Richardson and others (1991) conducted a three-year research project on thirty-nine elementary teachers' beliefs and practices about reading instruction. They found that a majority of teachers lacked reading theories to implement in the classroom. Only one teacher changed her beliefs and practices. Five others showed slight changes in beliefs but did not change their practices.

In the area of foreign language teaching, Lamb (1995) did research on twelve ESL teachers after they had completed a one-year in-service course. He found that their practices did not change, a result he attributed to their interpretation of information from the course to fit their own beliefs. He pointed out that ideas from in-service programs were mediated by teachers' existing beliefs. Johnson (1994) conducted a study on four preservice language teachers. She concluded that prior beliefs based on formal language learning experiences were so powerful that preservice teachers could not alter their beliefs without sufficient alternative instructional practices "to test out their emerging beliefs" (451). Masumi-So (1981) observed six Japanese classes in Australia. Among the six teachers, one was a native Japanese speaker and three of the five Australian teachers had done university coursework in education. She found that most lessons were drill-based and mechanical and that only the two teachers who had *not* been enrolled in preservice programs used open-ended role-play after practicing a model dialogue. She implied that teaching practices might be influenced not by teacher-development courses or proficiency but rather by teachers' beliefs about foreign language teaching and learning.

Beliefs About CLT and Practices. Although communicative language teaching (CLT) is widely promoted through preservice and in-service programs, workshops, and university courses, little is actually known about what teachers understand by "CLT" and how they implement it in the classroom. Despite the rich theoretical base for CLT, different interpretations and variations exist at the level of design and procedure (Richards and Rodgers 1986); even foreign language professionals vary in their presentations (see Sato 1997). As a result, many teachers appear confused. For instance, Thompson (1996) summarized different views from his colleagues and outlined four misconceptions of CLT, as follows: (1) CLT means not teaching grammar, (2) CLT means teaching only speaking, (3) CLT means pair work, which means role-play, and (4) CLT means expecting too much from the teacher. He noted that "A surprisingly large number of teachers that I have spoken to criticize or reject CLT for what seem to me to be wrong reasons" (10). He concluded that for its future development, misconceptions must be cleared away. Fox (1993) conducted a survey of 147 first-year graduate teaching assistants in French at twenty universities in the United States. He reported that teaching assistants did not conceptualize language according to the model of communicative competence (Canale and Swain 1980). Instead, they showed a strong emphasis on grammar at the expense of communicative activities. He concluded that their beliefs about language teaching and learning should be elicited so that they could develop their beliefs and knowledge about CLT.

Furthermore, a growing number of studies indicate that CLT classrooms are rare (Burns 1990; Nunan 1987; Walz 1989; Kumaravadivelu 1993; Lamb 1995; Karavas-Doukas 1996; Sato 1997; Sato and Kleinsasser 1999a). Nunan (1987), for example, investigated CLT as manifested in the classroom. He contended that although teachers were highly qualified, with graduate diplomas in TESOL, and had goals for communicative classes, there were few opportunities for genuine communicative language use. Karavas-Doukas (1996), using attitude surveys, did research on 101 Greek EFL teachers' attitudes about the communicative approach, observed fourteen teachers' classes and followed up with interviews. She found that although teachers expressed favorable attitudes toward the communicative approach, under observation they taught very few communicative classes. Noting the discrepancy in results between the surveys and the observations, she recommended the addition of interviews to clarify teachers' beliefs about CLT.

Using interviews, observations, and surveys, Sato (1997; see also Sato and Kleinsasser 1999a) conducted research on ten teachers of Japanese in Australia concerning their beliefs and practices with respect to CLT. He found that even though the teachers had participated in preservice or in-service programs about CLT, they did not understand it well. He identified four tendencies in these teachers' beliefs about CLT: (1) CLT is learning to communicate in the second language, (2) CLT relies mainly on speaking and listening, (3) CLT involves little grammar instruction, and (4) CLT relies on (time-consuming) activities. In short, teachers had fragmented knowledge of CLT, and their beliefs about language teaching and learning were based on their own second language learning and teaching experiences, as opposed to formal knowledge. Furthermore, observations revealed that few classes were actually communicative. Most were teacher-centered, with few interactions among learners. Grammatical points were explained deductively in the absence of contextual clues and followed by mechanical drills. In other words, teachers relied on established practices. Interview data revealed the challenges these teachers faced in their efforts to implement CLT. These challenges were divided into two main types: CLT challenges and organizational challenges. The CLT challenges included the teacher's role as a facilitator promoting interactions among learners, teaching grammar in context, integrating language skills, and evaluating them. The organizational challenges included lack of school support, preparation time, materials, or in-service programs, as well as difficulty with classroom management and different student learning styles. These organizational challenges were seen to influence teachers' practices.

Context, Problem Statement, and Research Questions

With respect to the teaching of English in Japan, an orientation toward CLT has been emphasized since a new syllabus was introduced in both junior and senior high schools in the 1990s (see Chapter 2). The syllabus stresses the significance of communication-oriented English in classes that have traditionally been taught through the *yakudoku* (grammar-translation) method. According to "The Course of Study for Senior High School," guidelines published by Mombusho (Wada 1994), the overall objectives of foreign language study are "To develop learners' ability to understand and express themselves in a foreign language; to foster a positive attitude towards communicating in a foreign language, and to heighten learner interest in language and culture, thus deepening international understanding" (1). With regard to content, "To respond appropriately to learner aptitude and achievement, use of individualized and small-group instruction, and audio-visual aids should be encouraged. The assistance and cooperation of native speakers should be sought in order to develop learner communicative competence and deepen international understanding" (10).

In addition, a new subject, oral English communication, became mandatory for two hours a week in either the first or second year of senior high school (see Chapter 2), and various oral communication textbooks were published to reflect the new syllabus. It seems, however, that many teachers who rely on established practices are at a loss when it comes to teaching oral communication. A survey conducted by ALC Press (1996) revealed that 59 percent of 129 senior high school teachers responded that their oral communication classes were ineffective. The main reasons given were (1) ineffective instruction (33 percent), (2) low motivation of students (22 percent), (3) low motivation of teachers (16 percent), (4) lack of support from the school (10 percent), and (5) poor textbooks (6 percent). In addition, the survey showed that owing to the pressure of university entrance examinations, 16 percent of the teachers changed oral communication classes into other lessons, such as grammar. As a result, oral communication classes are sidelined, and Japanese teachers rely heavily, if not completely, on native English-speaking teachers for this new subject. Japanese teachers continue to emphasize grammar and translation and pay little attention to the use of

English in classrooms (Chapter 4). It seems that the yakudoku method is still effective in preparing students for university entrance examinations that emphasize grammar and translation.

In their university preparation, "teachers of English receive no formal training with respect to team teaching and little information on how to implement communicative teaching on a regular basis in all of the various skill areas" (Scholefield 1997, 20). To obtain a teaching license, students are required to complete only a two-week teaching practicum. As a result, "many Japanese teachers of English are not well-informed about recent developments in the various subfields of linguistics" (20; see also Ogasawara 1983). Although Mombusho initiated in-service programs to improve teachers' English language proficiency and teaching skills, "annual participation is restricted to approximately 100 teachers" (37) and "many English teachers are unable to find time to be released from their daily school commitments to attend in-service programs or undertake further study" (37). Pacek (1996) conducted a survey of forty-three high school English teachers in Japan after they had attended a one-year in-service program at the University of Birmingham, England. Thirty-six teachers reportedly attempted to introduce changes in their classes, such as pair and group work, more English in the classroom, less teacher talk, use of task-based methodology, use of authentic materials, and avoidance of translation. Pacek found their responses to be imprecise, however, and the actual number of communicative activities used in their lessons was unconfirmed. The remaining seven teachers reported finding it impossible to introduce innovation, for reasons such as peer resistance, parental resistance, and poor textbooks. Pacek concluded that the "top-down innovation currently being attempted by Mombusho might not bring about the expected results" (336).

Mindful of the fact that the Japanese government mandates certain instruction, this study aims to discover the relationships among EFL teachers' context, beliefs, and practices. The questions that will be addressed include: (1) What are the context, beliefs, and practices of EFL teachers who work together in a high school? (2) What is the interrelation of the teaching context and individual EFL teachers' beliefs and practices? (3) How is teacher learning manifested for EFL teachers in their school, department, and classrooms?

Overview: Participants, Data Collection, and Data Analysis

This yearlong study employed multiple data sources (see Sato and Kleinsasser 1999b) including interviews, observations, a survey, and documents, to reveal how EFL teachers learn to teach in the school context. Data

Table 3.1 *Participants in the Study*

Name	Sex	Age	Teach. Exper.	Degree	Major, Minor	Section Assignment	Completed Survey	Number of Interviews	Classes Observed
Japanese teachers									
Full-time									
Yasuda	M	32	3	BA	Psychology, English	Student affairs	X	3	2
Kondo	M	44	19	BA	Education, English	Student management (chair)	X	3	2
Sudo	M	53	27	BA	E-literature	Career guidance (chair)	X	3	2
Higuchi	F	24	1	BA	Psychology, English	Student affairs	X	3	2
Goto	M	49	22	BA	Religion, English	School affairs	X	3	2
Terada	M	40	17	BA	Psychology, English	Teaching affairs	X	3	2
Hatano	M	48	25	BA	E-literature	School affairs	X	3	2
Inoue	M	53	25	BA	English	Career guidance	X	3	2
Toda	M	26	2	BA	English	Student management	X	3	2
Yoneda	M	55	32	BA	English	Vice-principal	X	3	0
Sakamoto	F	33	11	BA	Education, English	School affairs	X	3	0
Kobayashi	M	50	26	BA	Education, English	Teaching affairs	X	3	0
Hori	M	26	1	BA	E-literature	Student management	X	2	2
Part-time									
Koide	F	28	4	BA	Sociology, English		X	1	1
Noguchi	F	23	0	BA	Japanese, LTEnglish		X	1	1
Native English-speaking teachers									
Full-time									
Brad	M	29	6	BA, MA	Engineering		X	2	2
Tim	M	27	3	BA	Asian Studies		X	1	1
Part-time									
Tony	M	33	4	BA	History, E-literature		X	2	2
Mick	M	25	2	HS			X	1	1

Note: All teacher names are pseudonyms. Teaching experience indicates years as of April 1998.

collection began in September 1997 after a letter was sent to the principal to obtain permission from the school. Japanese schools begin classes in April and usually have three terms. After forty days' summer vacation, the second term begins in September. Following the school culture survey, interviews and classroom observations were repeated in each term until the end of the first term in 1998.

PARTICIPANTS

The context for this study is a department of English in a private senior high school in a metropolitan area in Japan. The school was founded in 1958 as a coeducational high school. In addition to general and commercial courses, in 1967 the school opened music and nursing courses for women only. In the school year of 1997 the three-story building accommodated thirty-seven homeroom classes with 1,384 students in all. There are three grade levels in Japanese high schools. Teachers from various subjects belong to each grade-level cohort and discuss educational policies in cohort meetings. Each grade level had eight or nine general classes, two commercial classes, one music class, and one nursing class. The approximate number of students per class was 38 for general studies, 40 for commercial, 33 for music, and 40 for nursing. There were seventy-one full-time teachers (fifty-seven males and fourteen females) including a principal, a vice-principal, two head teachers, and a school nurse, sixty-two part-time teachers (twenty-five males and thirty-seven females), and two assistants (females). Seven full-time staff members (three males and four females) worked in the school office. All full-time teachers belong to sections concerned with such things as school affairs, teaching affairs, student management, career guidance, student affairs, and recruiting. They are also responsible for club activities including baseball, judo, track and field, soccer, basketball, volleyball, rugby, broadcasting, art, calligraphy, drama, English, orchestra, journalism, and photography.

INTERVIEWS

As shown in Table 3.1, all nineteen EFL teachers participated in interviews. Twelve teachers were interviewed three times, in accordance with Foss's recommendation (1993) that repeated measures be incorporated. Foss noted that "in sequential interviewing, the researcher can make it progressively more difficult for respondents to submit contrived answers" (32). The first interviews were conducted at the beginning of the second term in 1997, followed by second interviews at the end of the third term and third interviews at the end of the first term in 1998.

Following the ethnographic model of Spradley (1979), and adapting interview questions from Sato (1997), the researcher developed descriptive questions to reveal teachers' beliefs and practices along with the school culture. In addition, questions about the school context were adapted from Lee (1993). Ethnographic interviews have many features in common with friendly conversations (Spradley 1979). Open-ended interview questions encourage participant response. Moreover, a structured protocol enables the interview to focus on certain issues (Spradley 1979). This interview protocol was piloted with two EFL teachers from different schools and modified before the interviews began. Each interview lasted approximately thirty minutes. With the exception of those with the four native speakers of English, interviews were conducted in Japanese. With the permission of the participants, interviews were tape-recorded and transcribed for analysis. Interviews with Japanese teachers were then translated into English by the researcher.

OBSERVATIONS

English classes employing both regular and oral communication were observed. As shown in Table 3.1, twelve teachers participated in the first and the second classroom observations, thirteen teachers in the third observation. Each observation period lasted for about one month during the term. A total of eighty-eight classes were observed. At least two different classes per teacher were observed in each term so that different classroom contexts could be taken into consideration.

As a participant observer, the researcher documented the setting, participants, events, acts, and gestures (Glesne and Peshkin 1992). In other words, the focus was on what was directly observable, as opposed to things not observable—for example, motivations or attitudes (Silverman 1993)—and an effort was made to avoid early generalizations. Lest the researcher become involved in class activities, care was taken to maintain a balance of intimacy and marginality (Glesne and Peshkin 1992). The researcher usually sat at the back of the class, occasionally moving around the room and documenting in field notes what was happening. With teachers' permission, audiotapes were made of all classroom lessons and used to supplement field notes. This method freed the researcher to use his eyes and ears during observations (Silverman 1993). In addition, daily interactions among teachers in the staff room, halls, departmental meetings, and workshops were noted, as well as informal conversations between teachers and the researcher.

SURVEY

A school culture survey adapted for this study from Kleinsasser (1989) following Rosenholtz (1989) was administered to all EFL teachers at the beginning of the second term, September 1997. The adapted survey consisted of 104 questions about nine organizational variables with a Likert-type scale ranging from "strongly disagree" to "strongly agree" or from "almost never" to "almost always." In order to understand the complexities of the context, the survey data were integrated with other data from interviews, observations, and documents.

DOCUMENTS

Documents were useful in this study to better understand the school context. Guba and Lincoln (1981) suggested that using documents "lends contextual richness and helps to ground an inquiry in the milieu of the writer. This grounding in real-world issues and day-to-day concerns is ultimately what the naturalistic inquiry is working toward" (234). Therefore, documentation of teaching materials, examination papers, curricula, department goals, and school handbooks were examined and integrated with interviews, observations, and surveys. Such documents offered historical, demographic, and personal evidence of the school culture and corroborated other data sources (Glesne and Peshkin 1992).

DATA ANALYSIS

Mathison (1988) proposed that analysis of multiple data sources, or triangulation, requires researchers to avoid a singular proposition and to construct "plausible explanations about the phenomena being studied" (17). When multiple data are systematically analyzed and interpreted, more trustworthy conclusions result (Eisner 1991; Glesne and Peshkin 1992). Inductive approaches were used to analyze the qualitative data from interviews, observations, and documents. Following the constant comparative method of Glaser and Strauss (1967), data were categorized and incidents were compared so that theory would emerge (see also Lincoln and Guba 1985; Silverman 1993).

With respect to the timing of data analysis, the researcher started simultaneously with data collection so that he could "focus and shape the study as it proceeds" (Glesne and Peshkin 1992, 127). By writing memos, making analytic files, developing coding schemes, and writing monthly reports as you go, you find yourself "reflecting on both the research process and the data collected, you develop new questions, new hunches, and, sometimes, new ways of approaching the research" (131).

Findings

Repeated measures based on multiple data sources revealed four themes: school norms and values, tension between individual ideas and a hidden goal, a pattern of teaching, and lack of learning opportunities. In this summary of research findings I shall consider each of these themes in turn, with illustrations from the supporting data.

SCHOOL NORMS AND VALUES

Comprehensive data analysis identified two persistent norms: (1) managing students and various task assignments took precedence over teaching and (2) communication and collaboration centered on keeping pace with others and getting through the day. These school norms and values remained consistent throughout the yearlong study. Sakamoto, a department head, explained that good teachers at the school were considered to be those who emphasized homeroom management. Even in the English department, "the most important thing is order and classroom management." Throughout the extracts that follow, pseudonyms are used, to maintain the participants' anonymity.

> Sakamoto: Those who make efforts to manage their homerooms, for example, collecting signatures for a petition, selling tickets for a festival to parents, writing many homeroom newsletters, and so forth, are highly valued. The union newsletter also treats these activities as major news. In particular, at big school events such as a school festival, those who put more effort into managing homerooms so that their projects will be successful are considered good teachers. I think we have such a school atmosphere. In the English department, as far as the class is concerned, the most important thing is order and classroom management. Then, if learners understand the subject matter and their classroom average is good, the teacher in charge is considered to be a good instructor. Therefore, for example, how diligently learners prepare for lessons appears to be an important criterion. I think teachers are evaluated in these ways. (1)[1]

In addition, Brad, with three years' teaching experience in this school, noticed that those who were involved in extracurricular activities and attended lots of meetings were considered good teachers.

> Brad: There are a lot of extracurricular activities, and I think teachers taking part in those are considered better teachers. And to an extent, I think people just have to turn up for class and keep the students under control. And I think teachers who spend a lot of time in meetings are more likely to be considered good teachers. (1)

Those who were busy working hard for homerooms, school events, extracurricular activities, and union affairs appeared to be the more highly regarded as teachers. Evaluations centered on teachers' ability to manage students, keep order, and get things done, as opposed to actually teach. As

Sakamoto observed, "This is the school atmosphere," to which everyone was expected to conform.

The busy EFL teachers in this school had a tacit agreement that they would keep pace with others and get things done. With other EFL teachers, in particular, they did discuss the progression of teaching according to the textbook and share handouts, but they did not seem to have enough time to talk about instructional issues. Goto's remarks are representative of teachers' view that a weekly department meeting was insufficient.

> Goto: We have a departmental meeting once a week. We report what we did and talk about the problems, if any. We try to share these things with one another. But we actually lack time and don't have enough time to discuss big issues. Nonetheless, I think this department encourages sharing and collaboration. (1)

Toda wished he could talk more about teaching issues.

> Toda: With other teachers of English, I want to talk a little bit more about goals and objectives. But we mainly talk about what to do next, which lesson we will cover before the exam, who will make a supplementary handout, or which section we have finished so far. I wish I could talk more about other important things. (1)

Consequently, collaboration seemed to be limited to talking about the progression of classes and some sharing of materials. In other words, they did not or could not collaborate to solve teaching problems or develop the curriculum. Two novice teachers, Hori and Higuchi, had many teaching problems, for example, but they kept them to themselves.

> Hori: Since I am a new teacher, I have so many things to talk about. But other teachers are so busy that I cannot afford to joke or talk about topics other than classes. Though I want to ask other teachers many questions, I dare not. I try to solve problems by myself, because I don't want to bother other teachers. To be honest, I myself am busy and still have many problems that I have not yet solved. (1)

> Higuchi: I have many things to discuss about English classes but have few opportunities. We share materials, but rarely talk about them. In the first term, one of my students came to me after the term exam and said, "I don't think this point was covered for the exam." So we should discuss which points will be covered before starting a new lesson. But everyone is busy and I cannot go to other teachers to consult on the matter. (1)

In summary, keeping pace with others as a group seemed to be a priority in this school context. EFL teachers collaborated to talk about the progression, make supplementary handouts, and keep things moving. Owing to lack of time, however, they rarely discussed classes or collaborated to address their teaching concerns.

TENSION BETWEEN INDIVIDUAL IDEAS AND A HIDDEN GOAL

These teachers reiterated in their interviews that they had experienced a dilemma between their individual ideas of communication-oriented English and a hidden goal of examination-oriented English.

Individual Ideas. Teachers of English as a foreign language were asked to describe or define their understanding of English language teaching and the way students learned English. Although a majority did express their individual ideas or knowledge of communication-oriented English, their responses also reflected the dichotomy between their wishes and the reality they faced: in their workplace they could not ignore the influence of examination-oriented English. Most teachers were puzzled by the questions and considered them difficult. They could not delineate or further describe their views, and their remarks showed that they were uncertain and confused about how to teach. Terada confessed, for example, that he had not yet discovered how to teach English.

> Terada: A difficult question, isn't it? I think we need techniques to teach English as a means of communication. One example is to teach by speaking English for a whole class hour. Although we have to teach in completely different ways from native English-speaking teachers, we have not learned how to teach English as a second language. I have no clear answers for this question. I am still looking for the answer. (1)

In addition, none of the participants in this study used the term "communicative language teaching." They expressed their views of communication-oriented English in broad terms: use of English (activities/authentic materials); and focus on listening/integrating language skills.

Using the English language (activities/authentic materials): Most teachers expressed their understanding of using English as a means of communication in general terms. Two gave explicit examples.

> Sakamoto: I think students learn English by actually communicating with native English speaking teachers in oral communication classes rather than by learning from our reading and grammar classes based on the textbook. So, I think they learn English by actually using it. When it comes to examination-oriented English, students learn it if they want to get into universities. Other than that, students need to get involved in learning by themselves. They should be responsible for their own learning. Otherwise, I don't think they can learn English. (1)

Noting the importance of learner motivation, Inoue recommended home-stay programs.

> Inoue: One thing for sure is learner interest. Despite their limited skills, in the bottom of their hearts, I think they have the desire to communicate in English, express their thoughts, and understand English. For example, home-stay programs might foster learner motivation. Other things such as interesting reading materials and famous speeches are also good. It is true that we have to compromise with examination-oriented English. But I suppose the ideal way of teaching should be based on learner interest. (1)

Focus on listening/integrating skills: Other teachers expressed their concern about listening skills, in particular, and integrating listening, speaking, reading, and writing skills. Two teachers explicitly stressed the importance of listening. For example, Tony seemed to have been influenced from his experiences learning French and Japanese. He believed that a second language is learned naturally, as one learns a first language.

> Tony: Again, I think any language teaching has to come from the teachers getting the students to open up and not to fear mistakes. It's very embarrassing to make mistakes, especially when there are students of different abilities, you know. So I know that from my experience of studying different languages, now studying Japanese, but French before. I was very self-conscious about speaking. The sound and pronunciation, and just making simple mistakes—it's something that many many students fear. And it's been my experience in Japan that students are extremely self-conscious about that. So I think once you make the students comfortable and reassure them that there are a lot of opportunities for making simple mistakes, that's where the real learning begins. You know, you can get very technical, grammar and vocabulary, but it has to be natural. It's like when we learned our first language. Nobody says "past-present perfect," you know. It's just listening and feeling comfortable. (1)

Some teachers expressed their idea of integrating the different skills of listening, speaking, reading, and writing.

> Toda: I think a well-balanced way of teaching English is good. So, not like examination-oriented English, I want to teach English as a means of communication. It would be better if we had such a goal in our department. Right now we separate the curriculum. Some, including native English-speaking teachers, take care of oral communication classes. Others do reading. On the contrary, we should integrate reading, speaking, listening, and writing. (1)

In brief, throughout the interviews these EFL teachers revealed tensions between their individual ideas and the workplace reality. The majority expressed their ideas of communication-oriented English. However, department and workplace elements overpowered individual wishes.

A Hidden Goal. These teachers reported that school norms and values supported a hidden goal of examination-oriented English. Surprisingly, although Mombusho had introduced new guidelines for communication-oriented English in 1994, there were no clear departmental goals, nor was a need for them discussed. Toda commented:

> Toda: Goals? I'm not sure about them. We have not discussed well what we should teach for. For example, we have not talked about what we want to do in oral communication classes. Last year we had a long meeting and agreed that we would like to improve students' reading and writing skills. But we have not talked about goals or objectives in English teaching, not to mention what we want to teach. Therefore, we chose the textbook according to which textbook is easy to teach with, and not according to goals and objectives. So I don't know our goals. (1)

There seemed to be confusion concerning the goals or objectives themselves, not to mention how to teach for them. Inoue termed the situation "chaotic."

> Inoue: One thing is the direct influence of the introduction of mandatory oral communication classes three years ago. And the English required for university entrance exams is changing slightly. So not only Mombusho but teachers are at a turning point with respect to how to teach English and what to teach. We are now finding our way through trial and error. However, we are at a loss to explain the goals and objectives, and to know how much we should incorporate communication into high school English teaching. For example, what kinds of communication skills are necessary for high school students? Is expressing one's own thoughts enough? How about writing? On the other hand, we cannot ignore entrance examinations. The situation seems chaotic right now. (1)

What was worse, teachers perceived a lack of support from other subject teachers and the administration. Sakamoto went on to say that other subject teachers expected EFL teachers to fulfill two goals.

> Sakamoto: Contrary to many schools which aim at preparing students for entrance exams, one of the goals in our department and school has been to take care of students who were weak in English in junior high school. Therefore, we have aimed at having students master basic grammar or basic English. But recently we had to incorporate oral communication classes, and we just started talking about the goals and objectives. We have not spent enough

time discussing the matter yet. But everyone seems to agree that we should put more emphasis on practical English rather than on basic English or basic grammar. However, other subject teachers insist that we should seek two goals at the same time. In other words, we need English for communication and internationalization, along with one for entrance exams so that our school will have a good reputation with respect to the number of students who pass university entrance exams. But it seems almost impossible for us, English teachers, to seek both goals. I think there is a slight difference between what other subject teachers think and what we think, because we have just started to aim at conversation-oriented English rather than basic English or basic grammar. (1)

Regardless of goal emphasis, the teachers agreed that examinations were critical to their teaching. Although none of them favored examination-oriented English, as a group in the department and school they could not ignore it. For example, Yasuda was also a homeroom teacher of Level 3 students. He wanted his students to understand different cultures, but preparing students for university entrance examinations seemed to be a main goal, particularly for Level 3 teachers.

Yasuda: The major goal now is to prepare students for entrance exams. My ideal is to get my students exposed to different cultures in the world. So there is a big gap. (1)

Teachers at other levels expressed similar feelings. Hatano was in charge of the Level 2 students. He stated that as long as university entrance examinations existed, he could not afford to think about other goals.

Hatano: I agree that the purpose of English is developing learners' communicative skills, so being able to get across one's intentions, read, and understand what people say are ideals. . . . It is necessary and is an ideal to be able to speak and listen. But, we cannot ignore university entrance examinations. That's another problem. If entrance exams were removed, we could begin to think about alternatives. (1)

In summary, these teachers took for granted that they should follow the hidden departmental goal of examination-oriented English. Moreover, the departmental goal was supported and emphasized by other subject teachers. Although the new Mombusho guidelines had been introduced, teachers did not discuss goals and objectives in departmental meetings. It seemed that as long as examination-oriented English existed they had no practical need to discuss goals. In fact, subsequent data analysis documented that they continued to ignore the guidelines and to teach in the same way.

A PATTERN OF TEACHING

The Yakudoku (Grammar-Translation) Method. Classroom observation data described these EFL teachers' practices. To the surprise of the researcher, although in their first interviews they expressed their individual ideas about communication-oriented English, a majority of them conformed to an established pattern of teaching with heavy emphasis on grammar explanation and translation. In contrast, in special classes,[2] where they had more freedom to teach and select materials, a minority of teachers tried out their new ideas and developed activities to suit learners' interests and needs. Nevertheless, these new ideas and activities remained marginal and had little impact on instruction in regular English classes. Excerpts from field notes illustrate their classroom actions.

Teachers were asked to recall their successful classes, materials, and activities in the first term. With the exception of two teachers, they had difficulty identifying any successful practices or activities. Teachers seemed to follow a pattern of teaching according to the textbook, unquestioningly, even though they were not satisfied with their practices. Inoue confessed that he could not think of any successful classes, nor did he try.

> Inoue: I don't think I have any successful classes. I didn't try that. Well, we used the textbook of basic grammar in the first term. Each lesson had five key sentences, and to have learners memorize them I gave a quiz at the beginning of the next class. After that, I briefly explained grammar points in the next lesson and had students translate key sentences and try the exercises. If necessary, I added other exercises or had them make simple sentences. I had this kind of pattern. I don't think it is good, but other teachers followed it, too, because we talked about how to go about our lessons. (1)

Inoue followed the pattern used by other teachers. In fact, in his observed class, he went immediately to his routine practice when the class started. As did many other teachers, he had made a handout for his classes. It included a copy of a section from the textbook, key words and phrases, five grammatical points, and a couple of comprehension questions in English. He used this handout and relied heavily on translation and explanation of grammar points. All instructions were given in Japanese. The pattern in his teaching is evident from how he began his class.

> After the greeting, he started the tape recorder and let students listen once to that day's part of the text. Then, he asked students to take out the handout he made for them, and started translation immediately. On the left side of the handout was a copy of the text from the textbook. There were spaces under

each sentence so that students could write in a Japanese translation. The right side of the handout included new words, grammar points, and three comprehension questions in English. He asked each student to read one sentence in English and translate it into Japanese. Inoue gave hints to help the student translate. Then, he explained grammatical points and sometimes told students to underline examples in the text. He gave a model translation so that they could write it down on their handouts. But a minority of them did nothing and remained quiet. He asked another student to read the next sentence and translate it. He repeated this pattern of teaching for about forty minutes in a fifty-minute class. There were many students who had not looked up new words in their dictionaries for their homework. Several students were looking them up in their dictionaries during the class. A couple of students were sleeping. Finally, five minutes before the end of the class, Inoue told the class to take out the textbook. He distributed blank sheets of paper. He directed them to copy that day's text as fast as they could. Sleeping students woke up and all students started. After three minutes, the bell rang, and he collected papers. (Inoue, C-107-10-2)

After class, Inoue told the researcher, "Every Level 1 teacher prepares a similar handout. But, each makes it by himself, because each has his own way of teaching." Surprisingly, despite a difference in materials, other grade level teachers conformed to this pattern of teaching.

Special Classes. Teachers' individual ideas about communication-oriented English were manifested to a more limited extent in special classes for commercial, music, and nursing studies, where teachers did not have to teach for the common exams and thus had more freedom to try out new ideas and materials. Although the majority of teachers could not recall any successful classes or activities in the first term, several teachers recalled successful classes in previous years. For example, Toda compared oral communication classes for a general course with one for a music course he had taught the previous year.

Toda: As for oral communication classes, I cannot tell whether they are successful or not. Japanese teachers took care of listening and spent most of the time using tapes. So what matters is not what to teach but how to teach according to the textbook. When students participate in my class, I feel happy. But in fact, these experiences are rare. Last year I was in charge of the Level 3 music class. When I used activities such as information-gap, games, and interviews, students became enthusiastic. It was fun. (1)

Yasuda succeeded in using English songs for a music class a couple of years earlier, but they did not work well for general classes. As a result, he stopped using them.

Yasuda: As for materials, I used famous songs in a music class a couple of years ago. I prepared material with several words missing. The music class students enjoyed it. After that I tried again for the first year general students. But it did not work well, so I quit using songs. (1)

The first classroom observation data documented Sudo's oral communication class for Level 3 commercial studies students. Sudo was teaching this new class for the first time. Although in his first interview he had expressed his anxiety about how to teach, he collaborated with Brian and tried out many things in his classes. In this observed class, he first tried pair work using material Brian had developed. Then, he used a vocabulary list and gave students a quiz, an activity clearly familiar to everyone. This class depicts his struggle with how to deal with communication-oriented English teaching.

After the greeting, he distributed the handout for pair work to the students. His colleague, Brad, had made the handout. The title of the activity was "Interior Designer." It said, "You are a designer. Choose 8 objects for this model room." He explained the activity in English and told them to work in pairs. Each member of the pair was expected to draw eight objects in the picture and ask the partner about his or her design. But, some students did not work on the activity. They did not seem to understand the directions well. He walked around and explained it in Japanese. He also woke up one student. Students managed to engage in the activity, using both English and Japanese. He spent about ten minutes on this activity and asked one student to collect papers. Then he moved on to the next activity. To my surprise, he told the class to take out the handout with printed English words such as "accessory," "alcohol," "chocolate," and "elevator." They were English loanwords used in Japanese, and about forty of them were listed on the handout. In Japanese he explained to the class the need to pay attention to their pronunciation and stress in English, which was usually different from those used in Japanese. He asked three individual students to pronounce them. He corrected their pronunciation. He asked another student to read and the rest of the class to repeat. Then he told the class to repeat after him. After that, he announced that he would give a quiz. He chose sixteen words and gave the class eight minutes to prepare for the quiz. One student asked him if this quiz would be incorporated into the grade. He replied, "Of course." They worked very hard on it. Sudo walked around. Five minutes before the end of class, he distributed blank sheets of paper and gave ten words in Japanese. Students wrote down the English equivalent. He collected papers, and gave an announcement about the assignment. He told them to record the conversation about summer vacation in pairs or groups and submit the tape. The class was over. (Sudo, C-309-9-30)

The latter half of his class was completely different from the first half. Sudo went back to routine practices. Accordingly, his use of English decreased dramatically in the latter half. After class, the researcher asked him why he had used the loanwords handout.

> Sudo: When students get into an activity, they can enjoy it. But, their abilities are limited and it is not easy for them to communicate in English for the whole hour. So, I have to incorporate materials students can work on easily. (N-9-30)

Sudo found it difficult to keep learners' attention for a whole hour. His practices reflected his interview in which he had reported that on such occasions he had no choice but to go back to routine practices with which learners were familiar. However, he did try out a new activity at the beginning. Previously he had said in his interview, "I am at a loss how to teach this new subject. I am teaching through trial and error" (1). He seemed to be learning how to teach through trial-and-error experiences in collaboration with Brad. In fact, they came up with an idea for assessment, in which students in each group made up a skit and audiotaped the dialogue. They tried this assignment twice in the first term and continued it in the second term with different topics. However, their teaching practices were seldom shared with other teachers or reported in department meetings.

Assessment. These EFL teachers had been using discrete-point tests to assess students for grades. As mentioned before, all general classes in each grade level used common tests to assess students. Although the method of assessment was an issue at this school and had been discussed in every department the preceding year, no conclusion was reached. Consequently, although each grade level in the English department used a different means of assessment, these remained unchanged. Teachers continued to assess students in the same way for the purpose of classroom management and did not assess learners' communication skills. For example, because of the tight schedule, Brad said that it seemed impossible to incorporate oral tests into classes.

> Brad: Short tests, writing tasks, and information gaps. As for interviews, we used them last year. And the reason I did not use them this time was because it is too time-consuming. Especially this year I teach only once a week. It used to be twice a week. So we just don't have time. (1)

During the study year Japanese and native English-speaking teachers exchanged groups once a week in the Level 1 general course oral communication classes. This exchange meant that teachers met with the same class only once per week. When a class was canceled because of a public holiday or a school event, they had less contact with their students. In this situation, it seemed almost impossible to incorporate interview tests without collaboration and communication among teachers.

In addition, teachers were asked to reflect on the outcome in the first term. Surprisingly, several teachers expressed their uncertainty about the outcome, but seemed to teach and assess in the same way. Level 1 teachers had students review and master basic grammar they had been taught in junior high school. Inoue elaborated on "a marathon test."

> Inoue: Before school started in April, to each first-year student we distributed a handout with 60 basic English sentences to memorize. On the first day of school, students sat for a test requiring them to translate into English the Japanese version of these same 60 sentences. About 200 out of 450 students scored below 50 out of 100 points and failed. We gave the test a second time for those who had failed. About 80 more students passed with a score above 60. We discussed what to do next and came up with what was called "a marathon test." Students had to sit for the test again and again until they passed it. Then, by modifying the test many times we managed to have everyone pass it. We noticed that some students didn't understand even the word order of English. I don't think those students can follow the regular lesson. So we needed to work with them individually after the test. (1)

Obviously, these Level 1 teachers set a goal of having all students pass the test. Teachers had to take care of students after school until they could pass the test. Despite this overload, Inoue found some students did not understand even the word order.

Level 2 teachers attempted English sentence memorization tests in grammar classes in the first term. Goto elaborated on this. He stated that students' efforts were assessed but was not sure if they had improved their English abilities.

> Goto: As for my objectives in the first term, they were not that strong. I ended up with normal lessons. One thing we did was an English sentence memorization test. We gave students quizzes every Tuesday and Friday mornings. We were very much worried about the results. However, overall we had good results since lower level students tried hard in memorization tests. For example, those who usually score around 20 scored 50 this time. I am sure they must have gained confidence. Therefore, I think this goal was met in the sense that their efforts were rewarded. However, I am not sure if they have actually improved their English abilities. (1)

Sakamoto, a Level 3 teacher, checked preparation by giving a vocabulary quiz for each lesson. She reported, "in terms of behavioral management and classroom order, the results were good. But in terms of actual learning, I am not sure of the results" (1).

In summary, these teachers reinforced routine practices by using "marathon tests," sentence memorization, and vocabulary quizzes. Although these assessments helped teachers to manage students, they also avoided changing classroom rules, roles, relationships, and results. Thus, when they worked together, teachers continued to follow existing curricula and teaching practices.

Why Teachers Teach the Way They Do. These EFL teachers revealed other potential influences on the way they taught. These included uncertainty about teaching, avoidance of conflict with learners, lack of learner motivation, heterogeneous grouping, and lack of teacher proficiency.

Uncertainty. When asked to define English language teaching and learning, several teachers revealed their uncertainty. For example, Toda confessed that he had not learned how to teach English and had been going about it through trial and error.

> Toda: As to how to teach grammar, I have not learned it yet. I am still studying. I wonder how other teachers teach. The way I understand in my head might be different from the way students understand. I developed my understanding of grammar after I had learned it at my high school. So I wonder if I should teach grammar thoroughly the way I learned it. To be honest, I have not yet learned how to teach English. I have been going about it through trial and error. (1)

Other teachers also expressed their uncertainty about teaching, and about grammar instruction in particular. For example, Brad seemed at a loss with respect to how to teach grammar. Although he avoided direct teaching of grammar for a while, he returned to it. He implied that inductive grammar teaching would work only when students were motivated.

> Brad: I don't know really at this point. In the last few weeks, I have to an extent gone back to a more direct teaching of grammar, which is something that I avoided for awhile. I think students do learn from indirect approaches especially if they are motivated. . . . I think grammar without use is pointless. (1)

In summary, both Japanese and native English-speaking teachers expressed uncertainty and difficulty with teaching in general, and with teaching grammar in particular. Their uncertainty about how to teach seemed to restrict them to their familiar way of teaching.

Conflict Avoidance. It seemed difficult to change learner attitudes or views about English language learning. Several teachers explicitly referred to negative learner attitude and fixed views of examination-oriented English. Sakamoto thought this to be the most difficult problem.

Sakamoto: Well, students were screened in junior high schools before taking high school entrance exams. Students know whether they are good at English or bad, and many have already acquired negative attitudes toward English. . . . I think this is the most difficult problem. . . . I don't think they can enjoy studying English. From this point of view, having oral communication classes in the first year might relieve them of some pain, because the new subject is different. However, again, we often hear from native English-speaking teachers that our students are terribly lacking in basic grammar. Well, students assume from their experiences that learning grammar is boring and uninteresting. Anyway, I think this is a serious problem. I presume that students have acquired pretty strong preconceptions about learning English. (1)

Sakamoto relayed that, for learners, studying English meant studying grammar in uninteresting ways for tests. Hori attempted to use the different material to attract learner interest, only to find that most were uninterested because they felt it irrelevant for the test.

Hori: I usually spend most of the time explaining grammatical points and cannot afford to talk about extra things. To be honest, I want to try it. In a music class I remember using material from a magazine about a remark made by a famous actress. Learner English level is higher than in general classes and some like English very much. Though some were attracted to it, the majority thought it was irrelevant for the test. For them term exams are the most important things. So their concern is to get good marks rather than to learn about topics. (1)

These teachers emphasized the difficulty of changing learners' negative attitudes toward examination-oriented English, and, as a result, toward English in general. It appeared easier to comply with examination-oriented English than to challenge it.

Lack of Motivation. All teachers recognized learner motivation as one of the most critical problems. For example, Goto found it difficult to motivate learners, even with interesting materials.

Goto: Recently, I feel it difficult to motivate learners, even if I use interesting materials. I think it strange that learners shut themselves up in their shells once I try to teach in English. For example, when I gave reading material about a Japanese popular baseball player to the third-year students, they didn't pay attention to it just because it was written in English. I'm sure the story is interesting, but I wonder why reading in English discouraged learners so much. In other words, even if I provide them with interesting materials in simple English, it seems impossible to break their shells. That worries me. So I wonder if I have to teach with different approaches. Although using videos helps interest learners to some extent, how to motivate them and how to make them independent learners who are serious about improving their skills, including speaking and listening, is a difficult problem, I think. (1)

Even in oral communication classes, which are supposed to be fun for students, teachers experienced difficulty. Brad acknowledged that English was not important for many students, and that there was a high wall between them and the actual use of English (see Chapter 4).

> Brad: One of the big things is motivation. . . . And there is a big gap, a big wall, that so many Japanese people think "I cannot speak English, I cannot speak English." And going to class they say "I cannot speak English." . . . And you often hear that Japanese people can't speak English after six years of lessons. There is this wall. (1)

Heterogeneous Grouping. Some teachers gave examples of wide differences in learners' levels of ability. Terada thought the range of abilities limited what mixed classes could achieve.

> Terada: There are some students who really like English and are good at it. I sometimes think it would be better for these students to study in a different class in order to achieve higher goals. I feel there is a limit in mixed classes. (1)

Hori felt sorry for the good students, because they got bored and went to sleep.

> Hori: After all, there is a wide gap between those who are good at English and those who are not. In a class of forty students, I had difficulty knowing how to adjust. I tried to make everyone understand me in the first term. Then, good students got bored and went to sleep. They always prepared for classes. So I thought I was teaching to only poor students who did not like English and did not prepare for classes, while ignoring good students. I felt sorry for good students. Recently I came to realize that I should teach English to those who really want to learn. (1)

Whether students like it or not, English is a required subject. It is worth mentioning that when these teachers said "good students," they meant those who earned good grades on tests. Although they did not say so explicitly, teachers seemed to feel responsible for helping "good students" to improve so that they could pass the entrance examinations of higher-ranking universities.

Lack of Proficiency. While some Japanese teachers alluded to lack of confidence in speaking English, only a minority mentioned lack of proficiency. However, some who had been asked to teach oral communication classes confessed they were poor at speaking. Sudo and Inoue were both teaching oral communication classes for the first time.

Sudo: I am in charge of oral communication classes this year, although I am very poor at speaking. (1)

Inoue: I am fifty-two years old and learned English through traditional approaches. Age might not be a factor, but I have difficulty teaching oral communication classes in some ways. We Japanese are in charge of listening and grammar. So I manage the classes by using tapes, because I cannot speak English fluently. Well, I think I have to learn more about teaching approaches, but it is hard for me. (1)

Due to lack of confidence in speaking, Hori, a novice teacher, was not sure how to teach oral communication. Consequently, he did not use English often. In his regular classes he focused on translation.

Hori: Above all, how to develop learner speaking skills is a problem. But I myself don't use English in my classes so often. I have no experiences studying abroad. So I would be at a loss how to teach an oral communication class if I had to. Therefore, I am concerned with how other teachers are teaching this new subject. Also, in regular classes, I find myself focusing on translation. (1)

Lack of proficiency in English seemed to make it difficult for Japanese teachers to incorporate speaking activities into their classes.

In brief, these teachers were uncertain about specific aspects of teaching and had difficulty changing learner negative attitudes toward English. It seemed to be much easier to avoid conflict and continue to teach according to the textbook to which both teachers and learners were accustomed. Consequently, no matter how vigorously Mombusho promoted communication-oriented English, these teachers seemed to teach according to what would work best in the classroom. In fact, the second and the third data analyses, which included interviews and classroom observations, revealed that their practices did not change much throughout this study. Rather, they intensified their existing practices. Although a few teachers tried out new ideas in special classes, why, as a rule, did they fail to develop their practices? How did they use or not use ideas from workshops outside the school? How did they learn to teach in this context? The next section looks at teacher learning opportunities.

LACK OF TEACHER LEARNING OPPORTUNITIES

This section describes the teacher learning opportunities available for EFL teachers at this school throughout this yearlong study and how these EFL teachers learned to teach and how they developed their beliefs and practices in this school context. Surprisingly, although most teachers reported that they learned how to teach by watching other teachers, there were few opportunities for peer observations. Moreover, the majority of teachers continued to avoid attending workshops offering new ideas (see Chapter 2). As a result, they confessed that their practices did not change. Lack of learning opportunities seemed to be related to scarcity of risk-taking, thus making it difficult for teachers to develop their beliefs and practices in this school culture. Three distinctive cultural themes emerged from data analyses: socialization, scarcity of external interactions, and trial-and-error teaching.

Socialization. To examine what influenced their beliefs about language teaching and learning, teachers were asked where their ideas came from, how they learned about English language teaching, and how they developed their teaching repertoires. Teachers usually cited several sources of learning how to teach. These included preservice programs at universities, in-service workshops, master's programs, watching other teachers, second language learning experiences, and teaching experiences. Most teachers stated that they actually learned from watching other teachers, their own second language learning experiences, and trial-and-error teaching experiences at the school. These sources reinforced their routine practices, enabling them to adapt to the existing curriculum.

Watching Other Teachers. Ten of the fifteen teachers stated that they got ideas from other teachers by observing their classes. Kondo commented on this.

> Kondo: I should get ideas from many different sources, but after all the only way is observing not only English teachers but also other subject teachers. As for workshops, I used to attend them. But now I don't, so unfortunately I don't receive any new ideas from workshops. (1)

Traditionally, the English department provided several opportunities during the school year for peer observation and discussed each observed class in a departmental meeting. In addition, in their first year, novice teachers typically observed experienced teachers. Higuchi reported, "I watched several teachers in the first term" (1). Although novice teachers reported that they learned by watching other teachers, they seemed to adapt to the pattern of teaching. Even if they said they tried different things, they seemed to be struggling within a similar teaching approach based on the yakudoku method. Hori, a novice teacher, tried imitating other teachers' techniques.

> Hori: I learned by watching other teachers and imitating their good techniques rather than from a university. In the first term, I observed about ten teachers. I was impressed with Mr. Terada's reading class. He used

different approaches, using comprehension questions about the passages and not translating all the sentences. (1)

Hori had his class observed by thirteen teachers (ten EFL teachers and three subject teachers). He tried to use a new idea, that of comprehension questions. However, it did not work well. At the departmental meeting the following week, Hori received comments from other teachers who observed his class. The researcher observed Hori's class two days after the meeting.

> Surprisingly, he avoided giving comprehension questions, and moved into translation right after chorus reading. Moreover, three times he asked students to consult the dictionary, when they got stuck in the middle of translating sentences into Japanese. As a result, the flow of the class stopped. About one-third of them had brought dictionaries. The rest of them did nothing. Several students had already checked meanings of new words. They had nothing to do. At the end of the class, Hori said to the class, "We could not finish a lot today, but everyone, please bring your dictionaries next time." The class was over. (Hori, C-102-9-26)

After the class, Hori said to the researcher:

> Hori: I followed Hatano's advice in the department meeting, and tried making students use dictionaries in my classes. Gradually, more students started to bring their own. When I was observed last time, I tried comprehension questions before translation, but it didn't work. So, I skipped it today. (N-9-26)

It was obvious that he was following advice from experienced teachers. Although he attempted using comprehension questions, for him a new activity, so as not to translate the whole text, he subsequently returned to his familiar practices. Keeping classroom order seemed more important than taking the risk of trying out new techniques.

In summary, although teachers had some opportunities for peer observation, it appeared that these opportunities only helped teachers develop or reinforce routine practices rather than helping them learn various teaching approaches.

Persistent Beliefs. In addition to peer observations, teachers seemed to rely on their own second language learning and teaching experiences. The interview data revealed that their second language learning and initial teaching experiences, in particular, remained influential in their approaches to ELT, and that their beliefs remained constant regardless of age or teaching experiences. For example, Sakamoto, a department head, stated that she had been teaching according to her conception of language learning, based on her own second language learning.

Sakamoto: As for teaching method, I have not learned any in particular. After all, the way I teach is based on how I learned English in classes. Another source may be how I studied English on my own. Therefore, I have been teaching according to my vague conception of how we can understand English. I think it is very personal. I don't remember having learned any teaching methods. So I may have preconceptions about the way of teaching. (1)

Kondo said that through his teaching experiences he gradually had changed his teaching practices. However, he stated that he still needed to improve his teaching.

Kondo: I learned by watching other teachers' classes. But I also think I learned by actually teaching. We need actual teaching experiences. However, recently I have come to think that we cannot overestimate experiences. Since the teaching approaches I learned at a university were not helpful at all, I changed my approaches little by little every year by observing learner responses. I used to teach in a very strict way, paying much attention to behavioral management. But I learned through trial and error. In fact, I have come to realize that I need to learn good teaching approaches. (1)

Nevertheless, few teachers reported that they experimented with different approaches. Rather, their initial teaching experiences remained influential. Kobayashi, an experienced teacher, was influenced by his junior high school teacher. He admitted that his teaching approaches were not so different from those he developed when he started teaching.

Kobayashi: I remember my teacher at a junior high school. He was a wonderful teacher. So I imitated his teaching style at first. Then, I developed my teaching skills little by little. First, I tried out his teaching approaches at the cram school when I was a university student. So I improved my teaching skills during these four years. Those experiences became the basis of my teaching style. Basically my teaching approaches are not so different from those days. He was good at teaching reading. As I mentioned, almost everyone mastered reading the textbook. I think he was the one who really got me interested in the study of English. (1)

Yoneda, a vice-principal, confessed that he had been teaching in the same way for more than thirty years without giving much attention to alternatives. He found that his initial teaching experiences were still useful.

Yoneda: First of all, I learned through my teaching practice when I was a senior in a university. Since I went to a teacher training college, I had a six-week practicum. After that I got a job in a junior high school in [city]. I taught there for seven years. I spent all my spare hours preparing for lessons and developing materials. Then, I came to this high school. I thought it would be difficult to teach in a high school. But, in fact, their level of English was low and I could use my teaching approach from junior high school. I have been teaching that way for thirty years without thinking so much about what is a good way of teaching. So basically I learned how to teach from my first seven years of teaching experiences at a junior high school. In those days, there was a district-wide test to check the level of students before they took high school entrance examinations. We worked hard to raise the average score on the test. Not only English teachers but other subject teachers did the same. It was like cramming rather than teaching. Now that way of teaching came under criticism, and the district-wide test was abolished several years ago. (1)

He went on to say that although he watched oral communication classes and found them interesting, his teaching practices did not change. He did not think he could use those new ideas, because they were not compatible with his teaching approaches.

Yoneda: Well, I don't take in any new ideas. Maybe, other teachers of my age don't either. The only source might be watching other teachers. I did observe oral communication classes by native English-speaking teachers three years ago, since oral communication became a new subject at that time. I found them interesting and learned that there were different ways of teaching. However, it was not easy to actually use those new ideas in my classes. (1)

Teachers' beliefs based on second language learning and initial teaching experiences seemed to be persistent. Even though they were introduced to different teaching approaches, teachers seemed to screen them according to their existing beliefs.

In brief, teachers' beliefs appeared immutable; these teachers did not necessarily want to alter their familiar classroom approaches. They seemed to view their initial teaching experiences as useful. Moreover, as discussed above, watching other teachers only reinforced their views, because these teachers shared the same beliefs about English language teaching and learning in this school and department context.

Few External Interactions. In their initial interviews, thirteen out of fifteen teachers readily admitted they had not attended any workshops recently. Surprisingly, there were no government in-service programs provided in 1997. Instead, only two teachers attended informal workshops. Most teachers reported that they were too busy to go or were not offered enough opportunities. For example, Hori, a novice teacher, used to attend Kenkyukai (informal workshops organized by a network of private high school teachers), but is now busy coaching a softball club.

Hori: There are few workshops for English teachers. Mr. Terada took me to Kenkyukai before. But now I am coaching a softball club and can hardly attend workshops. (1)

Some teachers expressed regret that they were unable to attend. Two experienced teachers, Kondo and Sudo, expressed their feelings.

Kondo: I used to go to those workshops for private high school teachers as often as possible. But I have not attended them recently. I hardly have those opportunities now. I know it's not good. (1)

Sudo: Well, I haven't been to any workshops or such. I have a feeling that I should, but I don't have enough time. That's all. (1)

Two other teachers suggested reasons for abandoning workshops. Sakamoto stated that she had not used ideas from workshops.

Sakamoto: I have not been to any recently. I can look for old reports of the workshop in my desk, but have not used those ideas myself. For example, even though some teachers say using English songs is good, I cannot use songs if I am not interested in them . . . unless the teacher really wants to use the idea, he or she won't try it out. (1)

Toda gave a practical reason for not enjoying workshops.

Toda: It is a shame, but I have not attended any workshops for a long time. The most recent one was held by Kenkyukai last June. It was about how to teach by using an English-English dictionary. The instructor was a teacher from [language school]. I thought it was interesting. Maybe it was useful for the particular students in that school, but it was not helpful for me. I have encountered many interesting ideas so far, but in fact, I found most of them not helpful. If I could change the class pattern of my own will, I could try out many things. However, I have to follow the textbook as other teachers do. After all, I have a limited choice. I am not saying this is good or bad. What I want to say is that even though I get some interesting ideas from the workshop, they are not very useful in my classes. (1)

Toda felt it unfortunate that he had not attended any workshops during the current year, but observed that those ideas were not helpful because he had to teach according to the textbook. In contrast, the previous year he had had many opportunities to use ideas from workshops. He went on to explain.

Toda: Last year I had an elective conversation class. It was the only section and I did not have to follow other teachers. As a result, I had to provide materials every time. I attended every workshop desperately to gather materials created by other teachers in different schools. I received some good ideas. But now even in oral communication classes, we use the textbook, and I am just doing

the same as other teachers. So, to be honest, now I feel I am not getting anything useful from workshops. I don't so much enjoy attending workshops. (1)

In summary, most teachers did not seem to be enthusiastic about workshops. All but two had had no recent experiences in workshops, mainly because they did not have enough time or did not feel a practical need to attend.
In fact, Toda lost interest in workshops because he had to follow the pattern
of teaching of other teachers. Two teachers attended informal workshops;
however, they did not report on them nor share new ideas with other teachers in the department. The result corresponds with the survey data, which
indicated few opportunities to discuss goals and new ideas presented through
in-service programs. Consequently, most teachers continued to struggle
without sufficient opportunity to explore new teaching ideas.

Trial-and-Error Teaching. In their second interviews at the end of the third
term, EFL teachers were asked to reflect on their learning opportunities in
the 1997 school year. They continued to report a lack of learning opportunities, communication, and collaboration. A small minority indicated that
they thought their beliefs were evolving through continuous learning and
collaboration.

Continuous Learning. Only two teachers continued to learn through external interactions. They tried out new ideas and felt successful with some of
them. They seemed to have raised their awareness of different perspectives on
language teaching and learning, indicative of evolving beliefs. Terada reiterated that he learned ideas continuously from Kenkyukai (see above). He
developed materials with the help of native English-speaking teachers and
received good response from learners.

> Terada: As I told you before, I received many ideas from Kenkyukai. For
> example, reading strategies such as top-down and bottom-up, comprehen-
> sion questions to understand the gist, and oral introduction in English. I
> arranged those ideas to meet my students' needs and levels. But, above all, I
> really appreciate the help of native speakers. For example, there was a lesson
> in the textbook titled "Superstition." The text introduced a couple of exam-
> ples from English-speaking countries, and took them for granted. But, Brad
> and Tony didn't know them. I decided to interview them about their supersti-
> tions. (Of course it would have been better if my students had interviewed
> them.) Anyway, I then explained to my students what they thought about the
> number 13, for example. Through this activity, students could learn about
> cultures in Canada and Ireland. They really enjoyed it. I found it interesting
> as well. I had attempted to make these kinds of materials before, but didn't
> have enough time. This year I was not in charge of a homeroom, so I could
> prepare many materials. When I was busy, some of them were bad. But, when

I had the time, I could make some good ones and received a good response from my students. (2)

Terada had had more time this year to develop materials because he was not in charge of a homeroom. In contrast with his first interview, he began to consider intrinsic learner motivation to learn English as more important than external goals such as the Standard Test of English Proficiency (STEP).

> Terada: I want my students to study English just because English is fun or they want to know more. For example, I always have my students write comments on my lessons at the bottom of the exam paper. One student wrote that he became interested in English songs and began to listen to some at home. He wanted me to introduce more songs in my classes. Though he may learn English from a different teacher next year, I think he might go to a CD shop to find one of his favorite singers. I think the most important motivation for students to learn English is intrinsic. (2)

Terada also stressed the importance of teaching culture to interest learners. He then returned to the topic of workshops. He stressed the importance of continuous learning.

> Terada: Well, ideas from workshops might not be helpful immediately, but the ideas or strategies we can learn from in-service programs are very important to me. So I occasionally ask new teachers to join me. (2)

When asked where his new teaching ideas had come from that year, Brad reported that he benefited most from his master's degree program.

> Brad: Probably, mostly from my study, really. For example, you know Prabhu. I don't know if he actually did them, but he talked about tasks. So, I did a few things, shape drawing, and calculations. And students really enjoyed that. The point was to get them to do something, to have them think in English to get them to achieve a task in English. Other ideas came from friends, other textbooks, but not too many came from school during this year really. (2)

Brad came to emphasize the role of the teacher as a facilitator. He was asked to describe his understanding of ELT.

> Brad: As for me, information gap is everything in the classroom. Then you have negotiation. If you have negotiation, you can overcome the gap. I think the job of the language teacher is to basically set up the information gap, to provide the raw materials, and be ready to act as a facilitator. (2)

These two teachers reported that they benefited from continuous learning opportunities. When they felt successful in trying out their new ideas, their awareness of different teaching approaches seemed to increase.

Collaboration. A minority of teachers attempted to share their ideas and collaborate with others in special oral communication classes. Sudo reported that he learned about ELT through collaboration with Brad. When he began teaching oral communication classes, he experienced some anxiety.

> Sudo: Well, I taught oral communication classes for the first time this year. I was very apprehensive at first because I myself cannot speak English well. However, while teaching, I have come to realize that being able to speak English well is not enough to teach oral communication classes. I've noticed that we have to prepare many different materials to meet learners' interests and that the most important thing is how to involve learners in the class. Of course, we have to be able to communicate in English, too. I was lucky to be in charge of a small course with Brad and was influenced a lot by him about English language teaching. While working and talking with Brad, we came to the conclusion that we didn't have always to use the same materials. That relieved me. In particular, Japanese teachers think they must teach the same way using the same materials. In principle, the good thing about a private school is freedom in teaching. But in fact this isn't true. I think it's a big problem. Another thing is that we came to share our problems with each other, and I began to warm to him. For example, Brad asked me how to manage the student who always slept during his classes, because the student worked at a part-time job until late at night. I have also noticed that even native English-speaking teachers have difficulty teaching English, and Brad has developed his teaching approaches through trial and error during these four years. When he began teaching, he had trouble with behavior management. He was irritated and sometimes threw chalk at students. But, he came to understand learners' problems and handle matters well with patience. Anyway, I have learned a lot through teaching oral communication classes this year. (2)

He went on to describe the new things he tried out this year. Eventually, he began to hold "this broad image about English language teaching and learning."

> Sudo: As I told you previously, we had our students record their conversation about a certain topic in pairs or groups and hand in their tapes. Other activities included listening to English songs and writing on the topic of "In ten years." Then, I still thought teaching was difficult (laugh). Well, we used to have a set image about teaching English. But, as I said, if we can extend the definition of English language teaching and learning, our old image will change. Then, if we can deal with university entrance exams through this broad image about English language teaching and learning, we all can be happy. But, I think it's possible, although it's not easy. I began to think that

students could go up the stairs by themselves so long as they receive minimal help from us. In other words, we don't have to teach all the time. Instead, we can help them improve their abilities. I began to feel that way recently. I've been teaching in this school for twenty-seven years and came to understand where our students got stuck. All we have to do might be to teach those points and help them move forward. I sometimes feel strongly it might be possible here. (2)

Sudo began to express his certainty about English language teaching. He insisted that teachers should extend their "definition of English language teaching" so that they could have a "broad image."

In summary, these teachers indicated they thought their beliefs about English language teaching and learning were evolving. Nonetheless, given the school culture, almost all teachers shared similar beliefs about the school norms and values, examination-oriented English, students, and other work. Thus, instructional practices remained marginalized in this school context. In fact, the third interview and classroom observation data in the first term in 1998 showed a return to routine practices without discussion of goals or curricula.

Discussion

Freeman and Johnson (1998) have advocated a reconceptualization of the knowledge base of language teacher education. They argue that research on teacher education should account more directly for the school context, the teacher (experiences, knowledge, and beliefs), and practices. However, there has been little research within this tripartite framework with, in particular, documentation of "teacher learning within the social, cultural, and institutional contexts" (397). Using multiple data sources including interviews, observations, a survey, and documents, this study revealed the difficulties inherent in continued professional development given the realities the EFL teachers in this study confront in their working environment. The three research questions highlight what can be learned from this study.

WHAT ARE THE CONTEXT, BELIEFS, AND PRACTICES
OF EFL TEACHERS WHO WORK TOGETHER IN A HIGH SCHOOL?

The data analysis revealed that as they worked together in the school context, these teachers shared beliefs and practices. It was obvious that they struggled with teaching English in their learning environment. Their perceptions of the school and the department were consistent, however, and they maintained their beliefs and practices.

These teachers were occupied with preparation for various school events, recordkeeping, section responsibilities, and so forth. They lacked time to prepare for instruction and talk with other teachers about important teaching issues such as goals and assessment. As a result, even at the start of a new term or new school year, teachers found it much easier to reinforce their routine instructional practices. It is also interesting to note that although Mombusho introduced the new guidelines for communication-oriented English in 1994, teachers avoided discussing goals during the period under study, 1997–1998. Rather, they taught according to their existing curriculum. The findings of this yearlong study indicate that the state guidelines had little impact on the school and departmental context.

Pajares (1992) maintains that "all teachers hold beliefs, however defined and labeled, about their work, their students, their subject matter, and their roles and responsibilities" (314). Research on teachers' beliefs has focused mainly on beliefs about the subject matter, and fails to investigate the interactions with various other types of beliefs, values, and behaviors, which are deeply influenced by the school culture (see Chapter 6). In this study, teachers' beliefs were inferred from what they said and did. The findings revealed that these teachers shared beliefs about school norms and values, English language teaching and learning, students, and other work. In other words, through comprehensive investigation of the relationships among the context, beliefs, and practices, this study showed teachers' beliefs about the subject matter they taught to be only one component in their belief systems. For Pajares (1992), educational beliefs are "teachers' attitudes about education—about schooling, teaching, learning, and students" (314), which, in turn, are part of a teacher's broader, more general, belief system.

Responses from these teachers revealed three critical rules for this particular teaching culture: (1) student management and various noninstructional tasks including homerooms, school events, extracurricular activities, and union affairs took precedence over teaching; (2) communication and collaboration centered on keeping pace with others and getting through the day; (3) for both classroom management and the departmental test, it is particularly important for everyone to teach in the same way. Teachers prioritized these rules because in this teaching culture they felt they were evaluated by other teachers accordingly. In fact, several teachers reiterated that the main criterion for judging a good teacher was the ability to manage students and other work rather than how well he or she taught the subject matter. Furthermore, these teachers mentioned other potential influences on the way they taught. These included uncertainty about teaching, conflict avoidance with students, lack of learner motivation, student discipline, different learning styles, heterogeneous grouping, and their own lack of English language proficiency. Teachers continued to regard these challenges, however, as excuses to rely on their familiar practices. Consequently, they consolidated their educational beliefs.

Repeated measures, including interviews and classroom observations, revealed that regardless of age or teaching experience, teachers conformed to a particular pattern of teaching with heavy emphasis on grammar explanation and translation. The homogeneous teaching pattern supported their belief that classroom order was most important and that mastery of grammar points and translation were necessary for university entrance exams. It was not surprising that even in oral communication classes the main concern was keeping order and keeping pace with other teachers rather than trying out new ideas. Although they had opportunities to develop materials to suit learner needs, teachers found that some learners were unwilling to participate in the activities. As Brad and Tony explained to the researcher, most learners might think oral communication was a fun class and not important for entrance exams. Inasmuch as the school had set no clear goals for communication-oriented English, such presumptions were understandable. Although a few teachers took risks and tried out new ideas in special oral communication classes, their practices were seldom shared with other teachers and had little impact on regular English classes.

HOW DO EFL TEACHERS' CONTEXT, BELIEFS, AND
PRACTICES RECIPROCALLY INFLUENCE OTHER EFL TEACHERS?

As individual teachers were socialized in the teaching culture of the school, they prioritized specific beliefs. Younger teachers adapted their teaching to routine practices, whereas experienced teachers further reinforced their existing beliefs and practices. As teachers grew accustomed to their routine practices, they seemed to be comfortable with their beliefs, which were reinforced. Pajares (1992) affirmed that "People grow comfortable with their beliefs, and these beliefs become their 'self,' so that individuals come to be identified and understood by the very nature of the beliefs, the habits, they own" (318). For instance, experienced teachers such as Yoneda and Kobayashi confessed that their initial teaching experiences were still useful. Even though Yoneda watched oral communication classes and found them interesting, he screened new ideas he found there according to his beliefs. It seemed difficult for teachers to get away from familiar teaching approaches. Consequently, as they worked together, context-specific beliefs prompted them to reinforce

their existing practices. Reciprocally, individual teachers intensified their beliefs and further consolidated the type of the teaching culture in the context.
The findings support those of Kleinsasser (1989, 1993), who demonstrated the
strong relationship between school contexts and teaching practices, and the
reciprocal effects of teachers' beliefs and practices on their school cultures
(see Theoretical Overview above).

Thus, the existing curriculum and teaching according to the textbook were
so familiar and useful in maintaining classroom order that these teachers
continued to teach without considering alternatives. In fact, irrespective
of age or teaching experience, all teachers reported they had been teaching
the same way without any satisfaction. The teaching culture in a particular
school may discourage innovation, and if language learning is highly structured, this approach may be difficult to contest. Citing the work of Habermas
(1971), Schubert (1986) calls Tyler's (1949) perennial analytic paradigm the
dominant curriculum paradigm and identifies its characteristics as follows:

1. posits principles of control and certainty,
2. operates in the interests of law-like propositions that are empirically test-
   able,
3. assumes knowledge to be value free,
4. assumes knowledge to be objectified,
5. values efficiency or parsimony, and
6. accepts unquestioningly social reality as it is. (Schubert 1986, 181)

This view of quantifiable, objective knowledge has far-reaching implications with reference to language teaching. The grammar-translation method
remains popular, Brown (1994) explains, because "it requires few specialized
skills on the part of teachers. Tests of grammar rules and of translations are
easy to construct and can be objectively scored" (53). No matter how vigorously Mombusho attempted to promote communication-oriented English,
these EFL teachers clung to the same curriculum paradigm.

How, then, can teachers be encouraged and helped to transform the established curriculum into one that is innovative? How can they become familiar
with the communicative curriculum proposed by Savignon (1983, 1997) (see
Chapter 6)? How can they further develop their beliefs and practices?

The analysis offers sufficient evidence to substantiate Schubert's (1986)
claim that curriculum improvement entails teacher development. "Teachers
must participate in curriculum improvement proposals because they perceive needs for personal and professional growth and for the growth of
their students. In either case, growth does not accrue from being told what
should be done" (416). Nonetheless, he acknowledges that "The literature of

the curriculum field has too long neglected to give attention to both teachers and students as creators and transformers of curriculum" (422). Similarly, in the area of foreign language teaching, Clair (1998) argues that the standardized curriculum actually limits skill development for many teachers "because they are never given the opportunity to make instructional decisions or taught that decision making is part of their role" (1998, 487; see also Pennycook 1989). And yet, the question remains as to how to empower as curriculum developers teachers who are reluctant to participate in curriculum development.

HOW IS TEACHER LEARNING MANIFESTED FOR EFL TEACHERS
IN THEIR SCHOOL, DEPARTMENT, AND CLASSROOM?

The study revealed that the EFL teachers in this particular context chose not to participate in many teacher learning opportunities. Although they struggled with teaching English in classrooms, individual struggles were not discussed and teacher learning opportunities were avoided. Instead, any type of collective learning that did happen centered on teachers mastering routine practices, keeping pace with others, and learning how to manage students and various kinds of work. Teacher learning and professional staff development were seldom manifest.

Although many teachers reported that they learned how to teach by watching other teachers, there were few opportunities for peer-observations during the yearlong study. Many experienced teachers were reluctant to have their classes observed. And younger teachers who watched other teachers adapted their teaching to the way experienced teachers taught. For example, after he had his class observed and received comments from other teachers, a novice teacher, Hori, quickly adjusted his teaching approach to the yakudoku method. It did not take long, in fact, for less experienced teachers to become socialized in the school culture.

In addition, a majority of teachers continued to avoid attending workshops. So long as they taught the same way according to the existing curriculum, they did not seem to need any new ideas to alter their practices. For example, Toda and Sakamoto reported that they stopped attending workshops because they felt the ideas presented were not useful in their classrooms. The data showed that none of the teachers with more than seventeen years of teaching experience had attended a workshop during the term of this research. With few ideas coming from outside the school, they further consolidated their existing practices according to the established perennial analytic curriculum.

At the classroom level, on the other hand, a minority of teachers teaching primarily special oral communication classes tried out new ideas from workshops and master's degree study, developed materials, and collaborated with one another. They reported that they learned how to teach through trial and error and felt their beliefs were evolving. However, their new practices or ideas were seldom shared. Consequently, individual teacher learning through trial and error resulted in complacency and did not provide a catalyst for teacher learning. Without clear goals, improved communication and collaboration, and support from other subject matter teachers as well as the administration, communication-oriented ELT does not appear to be attainable.

How could individual ideas, freedom, creativity, time for preparation, and learning opportunities for teachers be supported? How could these teachers be encouraged to take risks, collaborate, share their new experiences, and develop their practices and curriculum? Lieberman and Miller (1990) have defined teacher development as "not only the renewal of teaching, but . . . also the renewal of schools—in effect, culture building" (107). In other words, teacher development entails both classroom and school improvement.

Implication

The study advocates the reconceptualization of teacher learning to emphasize teacher learning in school contexts (Darling-Hammond and McLaughlin 1995; Fullan 1991, 1993; Grossman 1992; Lieberman 1995; Little 1993; Smylie 1996). The data revealed the complexity of both teacher learning and the teaching environment. It also became evident that the new guidelines introduced by Mombusho to promote communicative language teaching were mediated by the teachers in the context in which they found themselves. Lacking support for learning, these teachers continued to avoid implementing innovation. This view is reflective of how teachers actually learn to teach. Teachers do not learn by prescribed workshops or new curricula. Rather, as Darling-Hammond and McLaughlin (1995) assert:

> Teachers learn by doing, reading, and reflecting (just as students do); by collaborating with other teachers; by looking closely at students and their work; and by sharing what they see. This kind of learning enables teachers to make the leap from theory to accomplished practice. In addition to a powerful base of theoretical knowledge, such learning requires settings that support teacher inquiry and collaboration and strategies grounded in teachers' questions and concerns. To understand deeply, teachers must learn about, see, and experience successful learning-centered and learner-centered teaching practices. (598)

Teacher learning in schools would provide "occasions for teachers to re-flect critically on their practice and to fashion new knowledge and beliefs about content, pedagogy, and learners" (597). In short, the orientation of lan-guage teaching toward communicative practice requires continuous teacher learning in school contexts as well as support from policy makers and educa-tors. For innovation to happen, we must find ways to help teachers to become lifelong learners in a collaborative environment.

Notes

1. Indicates first interview. Other codes include: (C-107-10-2) classroom observation, Level 1, class 7, October 2; (N-9-30) field notes, September 30.
2. Special classes include both regular and oral communication classes in nongeneral commercial, music, and nursing studies.

4

Zen and the Art of English Language Teaching

KIYOKO KUSANO HUBBELL

My contribution to this collection of perspectives on communicative language teaching is my experience as a part-time teacher of English in private Japanese universities. I cannot claim to speak for all the universities in Japan, but only for those universities where I have taught during the past fifteen years. I began my teaching career in a conversation school when I was a senior in college, and I have been learning and growing ever since.

To begin with, I am uncertain whether the fact that a university would hire a person like me to teach English is a good sign or not. My own university major was not English as a Second Language (ESL), and when I eventually went to graduate school in the United States, I majored in Buddhist studies. But I do have teaching experience in English as a Foreign Language (EFL), twenty years now altogether. Although the focus of my story is language teaching, I would like to reflect a bit on Buddhism because of the great influence my understanding of Buddhist thought has had on my teaching of English.

First, it is said that you cannot really know Buddhism unless you practice it. Knowledge is important, of course, but you cannot claim to be a Buddhist unless you actually use that knowledge in your daily life. There is a parallel here with language. You might have a vast knowledge of English in terms of grammar, rules of usage, and vocabulary, but you cannot say you know English unless you practice it—that is, use it.

Second, Buddhism is essentially teaching. The historical Buddha was a teacher. He sought to teach humankind the truth about our lives with the hope of saving us from the eternal cycle of painful reincarnations. Just as there are different methods and approaches to teaching a language, there are many schools or sects in Buddhism, from the primitive, early schools, and popular Buddhism, to new schools. Most of these sects have appealed to the masses and tried to explain the profound wisdom of truth to laypersons through analogies, metaphors, and symbols, mostly in the form of statues, paintings, and stories. But herein lies a danger. The followers may begin to pray to the statues, believing that truth is found in the physical forms. The means became the end.

In contrast, one sect of Buddhism has not followed this practice. Zen Buddhists use the most direct way of teaching. They do not use formulas, rituals, or chanting. Rather, they believe in living the Buddhist truths in daily life, putting them into practice. They claim that wisdom is not knowledge and that truth cannot be learned but must be experienced. Zen Buddhism has a tremendous appeal to me. And for me teaching a language is much the same. We do not need to be engaged in mimicry, memorization, and pattern drills. Every utterance in the classroom should be genuine, serving the needs of communication. We should not waste our time repeating or memorizing superficial or contrived conversations.

In Zen there is a saying that when a master points his finger at the moon, you should look at the moon, not at the finger pointing to the moon. In some ways too many teachers are looking at the pointing finger. Early on in my teaching career, I began to think that we become too involved with the methods of teaching a language and forget the true goal, that of communication. By focusing on the content and meaning in my students' utterances, and not on the form alone, I can give them the support and encouragement they need to realize their independence as new members of a language community. It was quite natural for me to adopt a communicative approach in language teaching. But of course things do not always go smoothly. I would like to share some problems I face daily both inside and outside the classroom.

For many of my college students who already have been studying English in school for six or seven years, my class is the first where English is used as the language of instruction. The first class usually raises a commotion among the learners. I hear remarks such as "I thought she was Japanese! Can't she speak Japanese?" "This is not supposed to be a conversation class!" and "What is this? A Japanese speaking in English?" I take pride in being able to explain things in English so that even beginning students can understand. But there are some students, usually young men, who *refuse* to understand me for a couple of months. One year I had some students complain to the administration that I, a Japanese, was using *English* in an English class.

At the beginning of the school year I feel it is very important to teach students some "survival English" so that they can cope with the problems they encounter when trying to communicate in class. I give them handouts with standard expressions such as "Please repeat what you said," "What does such and such mean?" and "I don't understand your question. Please explain." I go over the expressions in class and give the students a week to review them, telling them to bring their handouts back to class the following week so that we can use them.

During the next class, while they have the handouts in front of them, I ask them questions and they answer. When they realize that they can actually use some of the expressions on the handout to convey their meaning and to get from me the information needed to answer their questions, the expressions on their faces change. My students begin to realize that these English sentences have power and that they can manipulate their environment by using them. They realize that they have just used English as a means of communication. When this happens, I always think of Helen Keller when she made the connection between the word *water* and the cold liquid running down her hand. But there are always some students who cannot make connections between the printed expressions in front of them and the real situation they are in. For these students, the expressions are merely to be memorized for a pencil-and-paper test, a test they will never take in *my* class.

Many Japanese students have been taught that they have to know the meaning of every word in a sentence or a phrase in order to understand a foreign language. They are not taught to use the strategies that they already use in their native Japanese, that is, to guess the meaning from the context. When the blackboard is full of writing and I am busy in class, I ask a student, "Please erase the blackboard!" and hand him an eraser and point to the dirty blackboard. If he does not move, it is not because he is offended by the request. He just did not recognize the word *erase* and did not understand me. If he is willing to skip over that word, he gets up and cleans the board.

All in all, it seems to be working, because I get a lot of positive feedback from my students. By the end of the term, I read comments like the following. (I wanted the students to be able to express their opinions in the most comfortable way, so the feedback quoted below has been translated from Japanese.)

> Completely different from any class I've ever had!
> I have never expressed my own ideas in English before. Work was always to translate this section, to fill in the blanks or read. It was all passive. In my

career of English education from junior high to cram school there was no teacher who spoke English other than to read the textbooks.

This is the first time that I haven't fallen asleep in English classes!

But, there are other kinds of comments as well, for example:

I don't want to work in groups or in pairs and talk about my private life. I don't talk with strangers.

Evaluating us on raising our hands to speak out in class is not fair. There are shy people, too. You are evaluating our personalities.

We don't speak out in class or express own opinions partially because we are shy. That I don't deny. But there is something bigger among us that hinders us from speaking out. If one has an idea that's different from others' and if he acts on it by expressing it in front of other students, there is tremendous pressure from the class to shut him up because the need for equality in Japan means everybody being the same, looking the same, behaving the same, and thinking the same. It takes an amazing amount of courage and determination and a risk that you might be shunned by the rest of the class when you express your individual self!

These comments show me that there are challenging cultural obstacles to the implementation of communicative language teaching in Japan.

But the problems do not stem only from the attitudes of students. There are problems I face with administrators and colleagues as well. Many Japanese universities treat native speaker teachers of English and Japanese teachers of English differently. Almost all required courses are taught by Japanese teachers, whereas native speakers teach "conversation classes," which are often elective courses with fewer students and for which the students are sometimes screened. Even when required courses are taught by both native speakers and Japanese teachers, we are almost always assigned limited teaching tasks: Japanese teachers are assigned "reading and writing" classes; native speakers are assigned "speaking and listening." This is a familiar pattern in my experience. What is the rationale for this segregation?

I once asked at a faculty and staff meeting if I would be allowed to teach one of the special courses that were strictly reserved for native speaker teachers. My reasons for asking were that these courses were content-based, teaching a subject through the use of English, something that I had already been doing anyway, and that there were fewer students. (I had forty to forty-five students in my class and they had fifteen or twenty, sometimes only five.) The executive committee's answer was no, that these courses were for native speakers. So another Japanese teacher asked, "Would you let us teach those courses if we studied the communicative approach?" "No," the administrators replied, "we don't have a way to assess Japanese teachers' ability in English." The funny thing was that the "native speakers" they had hired to teach these courses included a Romanian, an Austrian, and a Korean. I knew that English was not their native language. What kind of a message does this give to our students? Is it that only foreigners can communicate in English and that Japanese will never be fluent enough to do so?

When I read advertisements for English teachers in newspapers and journals, the English-language version of the ad calls for a person with "native-like" proficiency in English. But the Japanese-language version of the ad for the same position calls for a "native speaker" of English. Am I allowed to apply? Which job description do I trust? Do I waste my time in submitting an application?

My Japanese coworkers sometimes say things that are hard for me to understand. They readily accept the fact that native speakers should teach classes that are different and possibly require higher proficiency. One teacher said, "Oh, it is so wasteful to use native speakers in lower-level classes where students won't possibly understand anything they say. It's like throwing a beginning swimmer into a pool and telling him to start swimming!" Well, I hope that those native speaker teachers would start their students from the shallow end of the pool.

But the need to start from the shallow end of the pool should not be mistaken for intellectual shallowness. A tenured professor of English once told me, "This communicative thing! What those native speakers are doing is kindergarten stuff, like child's play. Pat-a-cake pat-a-cake, or say 'How are you?' and 'How is the weather?' every week." It is questionable how many like-minded professors are willing to converse with others in the language they claim to teach.

Another professor once said to me, "At the university level they should be given material that is university material, readings in philosophy, sociology, and history." But students are not prepared to read in English, so they only translate the philosophy book word by word, and it becomes a riddle and a game.

From all these examples I may come across as a very pessimistic person. In fact, I am not. I definitely feel there is hope. Let me share more candid comments from my students following a year of language learning with a communicative approach:

> I thought I was bad at listening so I had given up from the beginning. But as weeks went by, I found myself understanding well. It was impressive! I also found out English is not an object of study but a means of communication.
>
> Communicating my own opinion in my own words, listening and understanding others' opinions, this is important.

It is fun to make and deliver speeches and express feelings that I have now!

I had this wonderful feeling as I began to understand more and more about other people's thoughts and feelings.

I did not learn expressions in English or linguistic knowledge so much but I think I've discovered my own English.

I want to show who I am or what it is to be myself to others in class.

I want to break the shell around me—take off my armor—and this class has given me a chance to try it.

This final comment from a student is particularly forceful: "Teachers who evaluate us only on paper are lazy. Give us an opportunity for self-expression and that should be reflected in their evaluation of us."

Systems are changing, too. Just last year a university hired me to teach a course that was basically reserved for "native speakers." In my interview with the dean, he said, "I feel the times are changing and Japanese teachers who use English for communication should be given a chance." At another university, I work in a new and progressive department where Japanese and non-Japanese teachers are all regular speakers of English and our responsibilities are exactly the same. Also, the class size is limited to twenty students, compared with forty or forty-five in other schools.

I have highlighted some problems I have encountered while teaching that I believe are important. They challenge me to either adjust my own attitudes and accept my limited role as someone who has power in my own classroom, as we all do, but perhaps not the ability to change the system as it now exists. I see overcrowded classes that work against teacher-student communication. I see teachers who refuse to accept any other way to learn except the way they learned. I see students who are too afraid to express themselves in their first language, let alone in a second language. I see too many university teachers with limited understanding of the communicative approach to language teaching and learning and of the roles of native speakers and Japanese teachers of English.

Having encountered these problems from the beginning of my teaching career, I am determined to learn more about them. I realize that many teachers have encountered similar problems; these problems are not unique to Japan. My reflections based on daily experiences for the past fifteen years of my teaching career may help others facing these challenges.

PART II

Other Contexts

5

The Washback Effect on Classroom Teaching of Changes in Public Examinations

LIYING CHENG

Public examinations have often been used as instruments of control in the school system (Eckstein and Noah 1993; Herman 1992; Madaus 1988; Smith et al. 1990). In most societies, their relationship to the curriculum, teaching, and learning and their effect on individual opportunities in life are of vital importance. The current extensive use of examination scores for various educational and social purposes has made what is called "washback" a distinct educational phenomenon. According to Messick (1996, 241), "washback, a concept prominent in applied linguistics, refers to the extent to which the introduction and the use of a test influences language teachers and learners to do things they would not otherwise do that promote or inhibit language learning" (see also Messick 1992, 1994). There is evidence to suggest that examinations produce washback effects on teaching and learning (Alderson and Hamp-Lyons 1996; Alderson and Wall 1993; Bailey 1996, 2000; Shohamy 2001; Shohamy et al. 1996; Wall and Alderson 1993; Wall 1996).

Consequently, a belief that assessment can promote educational change has often led to top-down educational reform strategies that employ "better" kinds of assessment practices (Baker et al. 1992; Noble and Smith 1994a, 1994b). Currently, assessment practices are undergoing a major change in many parts of the world in reaction to the perceived shortcomings of the prevailing emphasis on standardized testing (Biggs 1995, 1996; Savignon 1972,

1983, 1997). In a paradigm shift, alternative assessment methods have thus emerged in a systematic attempt to measure a learner's ability to use previously acquired knowledge in solving novel problems or completing specific tasks. This change in approach reflects a trend toward using assessment to reform curriculum and improve instruction at the school level (Gipps 1994; Honig 1987; Linn 1983, 1992; Noble and Smith 1994a, 1994b; Popham 1983, 1987).

It is argued that such forms of alternative assessment can be so closely linked to the goals of instruction as to be almost indistinguishable from them. Rather than existing high stakes standardized tests with the inevitable negative consequences, some now advocate linking teaching to proposed alternative forms of assessment. However, such a reform strategy has been criticized by Andrews (1994a, 1994b), for example, as a "blunt instrument" for bringing about changes because the actual teaching and learning situation is clearly far more complex than proponents of alternative assessment suggest. Each element of educational context (school environment, messages from administration, expectations of other teachers, and students) plays a key role in facilitating or limiting the potential for change. This study of the washback effect of public examination change in Hong Kong is situated within this debate.

Hong Kong, where English language teaching is moving toward a task-based approach to curriculum, reflects the apparent worldwide paradigm shift in assessment. For the past two decades, the Hong Kong Examinations Authority (HKEA) has made consistent efforts to bring about positive washback on teaching and learning through changes in major public examination formats. Considerable thought has been given to ways in which the examination process can be used to bring about positive and constructive change in the system (HKEA 1994b).

In accord with the Target-Oriented Curriculum initiative (TOC)[1] in Hong Kong, the HKEA in 1993 introduced major changes to its existing exam in English at the fifth year of the secondary level, or Form 5 (equivalent to the British O level and North American grade 11), known as the Hong Kong Certificate of Education Examination in English (HKCEE). The immediate changes were reflected in an integrated listening, reading, and writing exam, requiring students to perform simulated "real life" tasks, together with an increase in the weighting of the *oral* component. The new *oral* component reflects a dramatic change from the previous *reading aloud and guided conversation* to new task-based *role-play and group discussion*. Both components of the new HKCEE require students to take an active role, participate fully in language interaction, and carry out tasks using different integrated language skills (HKEA 1993, 1994a). The intent of such changes in Hong Kong secondary schools was to improve English language teaching and learning, which has been characterized as centered on the three Ts: test, teacher, and textbook (Morris et al. 1996). The intended washback effect was to influence the teaching of English toward the new philosophy in teaching and learning, moving from noninteractive teacher-dominated talk to more task-based teaching.

Given the importance of public examination qualifications in Hong Kong society, the HKEA inevitably exerts considerable influence on what happens in the senior classes of its secondary schools. Some examples of the positive washback effect of public examinations in Hong Kong are reported in the literature (Andrews and Fullilove 1994; Fullilove 1992; Johnson and Wong 1981). And many major innovations of recent years have been designed with the expectation that examination changes can help classroom teachers promote a better balance between teaching and skill-building on the one hand and examination preparation on the other. However, the nature and the scope of washback effects of public examinations in Hong Kong are still unclear. A search of the literature indicates that washback effects are more perceived or assumed than supported by empirical data (Alderson and Wall 1993; Andrews 1994b; Wall and Alderson 1993).

The goal of the research reported in this chapter was to discover whether and to what extent the change in the public examination to a more task-based and integrated assessment format resulted in change in English language classroom teaching in Hong Kong secondary schools.

Methodology

The Hong Kong Certificate of Education Examination in English is taken by the majority of sixteen-year-old secondary students at the end of their fifth year (Form 5) of secondary schooling. After that, students either proceed to further studies for the sixth year (Form 6) or leave school and seek employment. The 1996 HKCEE was used for the first time in classroom teaching in September 1994 in Hong Kong secondary schools.[2] The first cohort of students sat for the revised exam in May 1996.

The research discussed here was a longitudinal study consisting of three research phases between January 1994 and November 1996. It aimed to capture the changes created by the new 1996 HKCEE from its initial introduction into classroom teaching in 1994 until after the first cohort of students sat for the new exam in May 1996. To some extent the time span of the research both determined and limited those aspects of classroom teaching and learning that could be investigated. During the study, two groups of Form 5 (F5) students studied English using the *same* teaching syllabus, the Syllabus for English (Forms I–V), prepared by the Curriculum Development Council (CDC) (CDC 1982). At the end of the year, however, one group was the last cohort to sit for the "old" HKCEE in 1995; the second group would be the first cohort to sit for the "new" HKCEE in 1996 (Figure 5.1). Even though they were taught using the same syllabus, the fact that they would sit for different exams presumably meant that teachers had to prepare two groups of students in different ways. Therefore, a comparative research methodology was used to investigate both teachers and learners over the two years prior to the first administration of the new 1996 HKCEE. A comparative approach was used to capture the reality, variation, and complexity of changes in day-to-day classroom practice as well as within the local education context as a whole.

A combined research framework, using multiple methods, was used in the study, which emphasized the importance of context, setting, and subject frames of reference. Since context is known to play a role in facilitating or impeding change, the local context as well as the various educational organizations were investigated prior to looking at actual teaching and learning. In an attempt to address the complexity of the phenomenon, the characteristics of policy makers, textbook publishers, teachers, and students were taken into account. Consequently, the study research strategy was one of asking and watching, using both quantitative and qualitative methods, in order to triangulate the various sources of data collected.

In order to understand action and practice, the researchers engaged directly in the local scene, spending sufficient time to interpret action in its specific social context, to gain access to participant meanings, and to show how these meanings-in-action evolved over time. To achieve an understanding of the multiple perspectives of the complex phenomenon of washback, three separate phases of the study looked at the washback effect of this public examination change, first at the macro level (including major parties within the Hong Kong educational context at the time of the public examination change) and then at the micro level (different aspects of teaching and learning in schools). At the micro level, teacher and learner perceptions and attitudes toward the new HKCEE were studied along with classroom behaviors. Owing to the time frame of the research project, learning outcomes were not considered. Since so much change was taking place in schools at the time, especially for students at the senior level of their secondary schooling (Morris 1990), changes in learning outcomes would have taken a longer time to occur and be observed.

Three major research questions were explored in three phases. Phase I examined the strategies the HKEA used to implement the examination change.

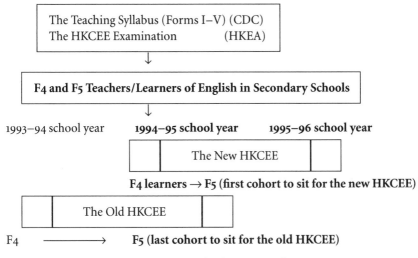

Figure 5.1. Hong Kong secondary school English language teaching.

Phase II explored the nature and scope of the washback effect on teacher and learner perceptions of aspects of teaching for the new examination. Phase III focused on the nature and scope of the washback effect on teacher behavior as a result of the new examination.

Phase I: What strategies did the HKEA use to implement the examination change?

Strategies are operationally defined here as the decision-making process of the HKEA for the new HKCEE. Specific research questions were as follows:

1. What was the rationale for the HKEA to make changes in the HKCEE?
2. What did the HKEA do to help introduce the new 1996 HKCEE into the schools?
3. How did different participants behave in the context of the HKCEE change?

Participants in this study refers to parties or levels of people within the Hong Kong educational context. The existence and/or the nature of the new 1996 HKCEE might have affected their perceptions and attitudes toward teaching and learning. Therefore, this phase of the study looked at the Hong Kong education system as a whole and the reactions of participants within the context of change. These participants included the decision-making organizations such the HKEA, the CDC, and the Education Department (ED); the intervening organizations such as textbook publishers and tertiary institutes; and implementing agents such as principals, department chairs, teachers, and students. To answer the above questions, watching (general observations) and asking (key informant interviews) techniques were employed.

Phase II: What was the nature and scope of the washback effect on teacher and learner perceptions of aspects of teaching for the new examination?

Teacher and learner perceptions are operationally defined as comprehension and understanding of aspects of classroom teaching in relation to the new HKCEE. Aspects of teaching include:

1. teacher reaction to the new HKCEE;
2. teacher perceptions of the rationale and formats of the new HKCEE;
3. teacher perceptions of the extra work or pressures or difficulties in teaching for the new HKCEE;
4. teacher perceptions of the teaching methods, activities, and use of textbooks and exam practice workbooks in the context of the new HKCEE;
5. teacher perceptions of the learning aims and motivation of students, learning strategies, and learning activities they would recommend to their students in relation to the HKCEE; and
6. learner perceptions of teacher talk, medium of instruction, and teaching activities as well as their own learning activities, their use of English inside and outside class, and their motivation and opinions about their English lessons.

These questions were addressed mainly through the use of comparative surveys of teachers and learners over a two-year period.

Phase III: What was the nature and scope of the washback effect on teacher behavior as a result of the new examination?

Teacher behavior is operationally defined as what teachers do in the classroom and includes the following:

1. teacher talk, teaching, and learning activities, and classroom interactions; and
2. teaching materials used in classroom teaching.

Since Phases II and III overlapped, some of the above aspects were looked at through the two comparative surveys as well as through classroom observations. Informing the study of classroom behavior of teachers preparing learners for the new 1996 HKCEE were several research assumptions that used comparisons with the classroom behavior of teachers preparing learners for the "old" HKCEE.

The teacher would assign more practice opportunities to students. A practice opportunity is defined in this study as the opportunity for students to engage in activities for the development of their knowledge about the language and their ability to communicate in the language. If washback does occur, the new 1996 HKCEE would lead to a change from a highly teacher-centered mode of classroom teaching to a more learner-oriented classroom. In this study, practice opportunities are measured by the percentage of class time assigned by teachers for learners to carry out language tasks or activities.

The teacher would assign more class time to learner activities, especially group work such as role-play and group discussion. Such activities would also improve the quality of the learners' talk, help to individualize instruction, promote a positive affective climate, and motivate the learner to learn. Group work provides the kind of input and opportunities for output that enables rapid second language acquisition (see Long and Porter 1985). Also, role-play and group discussions are the two new activities in the oral component of the 1996 HKCEE. If washback occurs, the change of oral formats to role-play and group discussions, as well as the increasing weight of the oral component (from 10 percent in the old HKCEE to 18 percent in the new HKCEE), would lead to the teacher assigning more time for these activities.

The teacher would talk less, and the learners would talk more. This part of the observation would show how much students contribute to classroom interaction. If there is a tendency for students to contribute more and more to classroom interaction, it can be assumed that students take a more active part in learning than before. This is also related to the rationale for the new 1996 HKCEE, especially the increased importance of students' activities such as role-play or group work, which would probably lead to less teacher talk and more learner talk.

There would be more frequent and shorter teacher turns in class. "A turn is defined as off-stream (i.e., discontinuing), introducing something new, or denying/disputing a proposition in a previous turn" (van Lier 1988 cited in Ellis 1994, 579). The rationale of the study of turns lies in the assumption that whether students are actively involved in classroom interaction is largely determined by the turn-allocation behavior of the teacher and turn-taking behavior of the students (see Tsui 1995, 19). This is one area of teaching and learning in which the HKEA intended to promote change by introducing the new HKCEE.

The teacher would use more authentic materials from real-life sources. In this study, "authentic materials" refers to materials taken from real-life sources, rather than textbooks or exam practice books. This assumption was explored at two levels: the type and the source of the teaching materials. The type refers to the material: written, audio, or video. The source refers to whether the materials are pedagogical (main textbook specifically designed for second language learning); semipedagogical (practice exam workbooks) or non-pedagogical (materials originally intended for nonschool purposes).

The three major questions addressed in three phases and using different research methods combined to provide a comprehensive picture of the Hong Kong context at the time when the new 1996 HKCEE examination was introduced. The various methods complemented one another, and data collected from each source were validated between and within methods (Figure 5.2).

Data collection and analysis procedures for both questionnaires were the same. The questionnaires were designed, piloted, and moderated through Phase I of the study and administered twice during the two-year period. Their purpose was to investigate and compare possible teacher and learner perceptual and attitudinal changes in relation to aspects of classroom teaching and learning. The teacher questionnaires were administered to two comparable groups of teachers. Owing to the rapidly changing composition of the teaching profession in Hong Kong, it was not possible to administer the questionnaires for each phase to the same groups of teachers. The learner questionnaires were administered to two cohorts of Form 5 students. Both questionnaires used a five-point Likert scale ranging from 1 ("strongly disagree") to 5 ("strongly agree") on items related to teacher and learner perceptions, and from 1 ("never") to 5 ("always") on items related to teaching and learning activities.

As stated above, the major aim of the parallel surveys was to determine and examine the differences between findings over the two-year period when the HKCEE was changed. The differences of the survey findings were tested for statistical significance using chi-square and independent sample t-tests. A probability index of 0.05 was used as the significance level. While the chi-square test of significance showed the samples to be similar for both teacher and learner surveys, providing a valid statistical basis for comparison, the t-test revealed the differences observed over the two-year period. For comparative purposes, great effort was made to achieve statistical similarity in the samples, for example, the teachers and learners who responded to the questionnaires in both years were from the same sixty schools.

Classroom observations and follow-up interviews provided a closer look at changes occurring in classroom teaching. Procedures for classroom data collection and analysis stressed their cyclical nature and took into consideration the influence of vacations on washback studies.[3] A baseline study of nine teachers and a main study of three teachers teaching over the two years were observed comparatively (see Figure 5.2). No appropriate observation schemes could be found to address the above specific research questions related to teacher and learner classroom interactions in the context of examina-

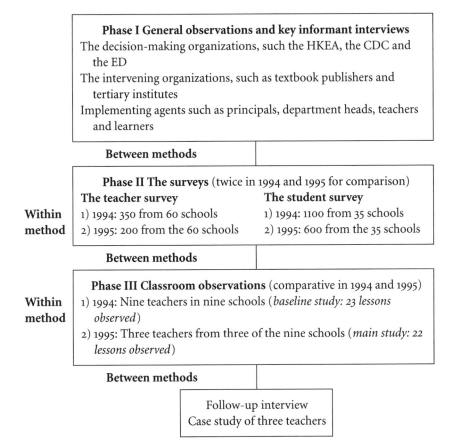

Figure 5.2. Data and method triangulation for the study.

tion change. Therefore, an observation scheme was designed for this study based on two factors: the analysis of the baseline data from Phase I, and an adaptation of Part A of the COLT (Communicative Orientation of Language Teaching) category definitions (Frohlich, Spada, and Allen 1985, 53–56). In order to investigate aspects such as whether the lesson was learner-centered or teacher-centered, how many learning opportunities were provided, and the nature of pedagogical materials used by teachers (real-life materials, main textbooks, or exam practice workbooks), the following five categories were used to describe and code classroom activities:

1. Time: How is time segmented within the lesson as a percentage of class time?

2. Participant organization: Who is holding the floor (talking) during the segments of the lesson as a percentage of class time?
3. Activity type: What teaching and learning activities take up what percentage of class time?
4. Content: What are the teacher and the students talking, reading, or writing about or what are they listening to?
5. Material used: What types and purposes of teaching materials were involved?

The above observation scheme combined field notes and transcription of videotaped episodes of classroom activities at the level of verbal interaction between teachers and students. The data analyses consisted of coding videotaped lessons according to the observation scheme in chunks of time spent on each category to allow an investigation into where and how class time was allocated, and transcribing sample lessons to provide a closer look at the content of those activities within the chunks of class time, both of which required intensive immersion in the data. This scheme also led to the observation and description of the interactions in the classrooms in order to understand how learning opportunities were created in the context of the new 1996 HKCEE.

Research Findings and Discussion

PHASE ONE: THE DECISION-MAKING STAGE OF THE NEW 1996 HKCEE

Phase I of the study consisted of an investigation of the Hong Kong education context at the macro and micro levels. The macro level consisted of decision makers such as the HKEA, the CDC, and the ED as well as intervening organizations such as textbook publishers and tertiary institutions. The HKEA is the development body for the new 1996 HKCEE exam. The CDC is responsible for the teaching syllabus, and the ED is the government's policy-making, supervisory, and quality assurance organization, as well as the agency for recommending textbooks to schools.

The findings showed that the Hong Kong education establishment, including both the government agencies and the intervening organizations, tried to encourage a positive washback effect on teaching and learning. The new 1996 HKCEE is in accord with the major curriculum change, the Target Oriented Curriculum initiated by both CDC and ED, and shares the same underlying theoretical paradigm in teaching and learning as well as in assessment. The actions of these mutually cooperative bodies led to a series of specific support activities from the ED, textbook publishers and tertiary institutions. Textbook publishers, who were informed about the change as soon as the HKEA decided on the new exam, revised textbooks in time for the 1994–95 academic school year before its implementation. In addition, textbook publishers and tertiary institutions organized seminars and workshops before the start of the 1994–95 school year to prepare teachers to teach for the new 1996 HKCEE.

The situation at the micro level was favorable as well. School staffs consciously prepared for the new 1996 HKCEE. At the administrative level, teaching toward the new exam was planned. Teachers also expressed a positive attitude toward the new HKCEE. In the initial survey, 84 percent of the teachers commented that they would change their teaching methodology. As for teaching materials, by the time classes resumed in September 1994, nearly every school in Hong Kong whose students would sit for the new exam was using revised textbooks directed toward the new exam. Teachers were also provided with new auxiliary teaching materials.

To summarize, schools and teachers were prepared for teaching prior to the start of the 1994–95 school year, and the whole education system showed a high level of preparation for the new 1996 HKCEE (see Cheng 1997 for details of the Phase I study). A word of caution needs to be included. Because the findings were obtained through general observations and interviews only after the HKCEE was introduced, the extent to which the new textbooks were actually changed to reflect the theory underlying this public examination change, with its intended washback and curriculum initiative, could not be determined. Only a detailed textbook analysis could answer this question, and such analysis was not a focus of the study.

PHASE II: WASHBACK ON TEACHER AND LEARNER PERCEPTIONS

Phase II investigated the findings from two comparative surveys of teachers and learners in 1994 and 1995.[4] The purpose was twofold: to investigate and describe possible changes in teacher and learner perceptions and attitudes, and to investigate the relationship between these changes and changes in teacher behavior as explored through classroom observations (described in Phase III below).

Teachers reported a positive reaction toward the new 1996 HKCEE over the two years (TQ 3.1). There was a significant change in teachers who welcomed the change, from 30.4 percent in 1994 to 42.7 percent in 1995, whereas there was a decrease in teachers who were initially skeptical about the change, from 38.4 percent in 1994 to 20.2 percent in 1995. In addition, teacher perceptions of both the reasons behind the exam change and the actual format for the change made in the new 1996 HKCEE (TQ 2.1–2.2) were in accord with the intended washback anticipated by the HKEA, suggesting a positive attitude toward the implementation of the new HKCEE.

However, when asked what changes they would like to make in their teaching in the context of the examination change (TQ 2.4), teacher perceptions remained essentially unchanged over the two-year period, even though they acknowledged the changes that had been made in the HKCEE itself (TQ 2.2). Only two items, to put more emphasis on the oral and listening components and to employ more real-life language tasks, were seen to have changed, in keeping with the new exam format. Other items—for example, to adopt new teaching methods and to encourage more student participation in class—remained unchanged. This could suggest teachers' reluctance toward making real changes in the kinds of behaviors that they thought they ought to exhibit, possibly related to practical considerations of teaching when faced with a change in evaluation. For example, during later classroom observations, teachers commented that students did not have adequate English for coping with the new HKCEE. Moreover, even if they express a positive attitude toward change, teachers are often slow to abandon what they have been doing and embrace completely some new philosophy, methodology, or curriculum design (see Chapters 2, 3, and 7).

As to perceptions of the possible difficulties in teaching for the new HKCEE (TQ 2.5), teachers expressed certain concerns. However, those concerns, especially inadequate textbooks and teaching resources and the noisy environment, decreased over the two-year period. In response to whether the new HKCEE had brought extra work or pressure to their teaching (TQ 2.3), the teachers' top worry—preparing more materials for students—decreased over the two years. In contrast, teacher concerns about students' English levels and inadequate practice time emerged. Teacher perceptions of different aspects of teaching for the new exam also changed, suggesting a degree of washback anxiety. The new emphasis on the oral component and interaction showed learners to be weaker in these areas than in the other skills and language elements that had been emphasized prior to the exam change.

Teachers in Hong Kong secondary schools had a lot to say about the selection of textbooks in the context of the new HKCEE (TQ 3.5–3.6). As one of the department heads explained, it was both natural and essential to choose the textbook preferred by teachers; otherwise, they would not enjoy teaching with it. For teachers, an important function of the new textbooks was to provide a structured language program to follow, revealing teacher beliefs about the centrality of the textbook. Initial teacher tensions and concerns over the availability of new teaching materials for the 1996 HKCEE decreased over the two years.

With respect to teacher talk (TQ 3.8), the proportion reportedly remained unchanged, despite the change in exam format. According to teachers, talking to the whole class remained the predominant activity (88 percent of the class time in 1994 and 86 percent in 1995). The teaching delivery mode (TQ 3.2), however, changed from using English only to English with occasional explanations in Chinese in response to the perceived lower level of the students' language proficiency. It may also reflect an increase in classroom discipline problems, with reversion to Chinese for control. When asked about lesson preparation, the teachers reported paying more attention to content than to methods (TQ 3.4 and 3.7).

A washback effect was evident in teacher perceptions of aspects of learning (TQ 2.6 and 2.9). On the one hand, there was a significant increase in teachers' recommendation to their students to learn to jot down better notes and to communicate more in English. This might have been a direct washback effect of Part III of the new 1996 HKCEE, which included an integrated component of listening, reading, and writing. On the other hand, the suggestion to communicate more in English can be related to the increased weighting given to part IV, the oral section of the exam. Moreover, among the recommended learning activities, role-play and group discussion reportedly received an increased amount of attention. Because these two activities are included in part IV (oral) of the new exam, this finding is indicative of a direct washback effect. Giving recommendations to learners, however, is not the same as helping them to develop their skills inside or outside class. This distinction is discussed further below.

PHASE III: A CLOSER LOOK AT THE WASHBACK EFFECT THROUGH
CLASSROOM OBSERVATIONS

Phase III investigated possible washback effects on teacher classroom behavior.[5] The findings consisted of video recordings and transcriptions of classroom observations of a baseline study and main study over more than two years. Only the main study of three teachers, referred to for the study as Ada, Betty, and Cathy, is reported here. The findings are highlighted in terms of participant organization, activity type and content, a comparison of oral lessons, and teaching materials in relation to the research assumptions formulated in the methodology. Inasmuch as there was an increase in the weighting of part IV from 10 percent in the old HKCEE to 18 percent in the new, oral lessons were looked at closely.

In terms of participants and organization (Table 5.1), the interactive patterns of classroom activities carried out in the fourteen lessons (all Form 5 level) by Ada, Betty, and Cathy showed a small increase in class time allocated

Table 5.1 Organization of Lesson Time and Participation,
as a Percentage of Lesson Time

	Whole Class T>S/C	S>S/C	Group Work	Individual	Choral	Total
Ada						
1994 (old)	60	10	22	8	0	= 100%
1995 (new)	61	12	26	1	0	= 100%
Betty						
1994 (old)	41	8	15	15	21	= 100%
1995 (new)	56	8	18	13	5	= 100%
Cathy						
1994 (old)	86	0	5	9	0	= 100%
1995 (new)	68	0	7	25	0	= 100%

to group work for all three teachers, although the degree of increase varied from teacher to teacher. Since group work is one of the required oral activities in the new HKCEE, this increase might suggest a direct washback effect. In contrast, there was a sharp decrease in choral work (required in the old HKCEE, but not in the new), particularly in Betty's lessons, over the two-year period. This finding offers further evidence of a washback effect on classroom teaching from a change in exam.

In terms of activity type and content in classroom teaching, the findings showed an increase in the time spent on learner group work for all three teachers. In preparation for the new 1996 HKCEE teacher talk as a percentage of class time increased, particularly for Betty. This finding was unexpected. The initial research assumptions spelled out in the methodology assumed that there would be less teacher talk. In interviews, Betty stated that the increase was due to the demands of the new exam. She felt she had to spend more time explaining the new examination format in order to make sure that learners were prepared, which most teachers considered their major responsibility; this concern was also noted by Cathy. Cathy was observed explaining throughout an entire lesson how to "conduct" group work. No pattern of change in the percentage of time spent on actual group work was observed in Cathy's lessons, however. This discrepancy illustrates the importance of noting both time allocation and content for each chunk of observed classroom teaching. To some extent, the above findings showed that the new 1996 HKCEE has brought about some changes in teaching. This might well be due to the high-stakes function of this public examination. Yet the resulting changes might not all be positive as intended by the HKEA.

Table 5.2 Teacher Talk and Student Talk During Lesson Time

	Ada		Betty		Cathy	
	1994	1995	1994	1995	1994	1995
Teacher talk (%)	69	44	65	71	89	68
Student talk (%)	31	56	35	29	11	32

Source: Teacher observation.

The oral lessons conducted by the three teachers over the two-year period revealed that teachers tried to use activities appropriate to their understanding of the integrated and task-based approach. The change to the new examination provided them an opportunity to try out new ideas and activities in those schools that afforded them some flexibility. In addition, an overall increase in learner opportunities to participate in oral activities was observed in 1995 for all three teachers. Still, teacher talk remained the dominant classroom activity. This general pattern of teaching did not appear to change significantly, and the main changes lay in differences between the teachers, not for individual teachers (Tables 5.1 and 5.2). Table 5.2 summarizes the lessons of the three teachers observed over the two-year period in term of teacher and learner talk time.

Although working in different schools, the three teachers used the same types of commercially produced textbooks and audiovisual materials. Printed materials also included exam practice workbooks structured following the same four-component format as the HKCEE. In the lessons observed over the two-year period, there was no evidence that teachers made use of authentic materials. For most of the time they relied on the revised examination practice workbooks. In the 1994 lessons, the teachers tended to use past exams. In 1995, however, since no past exams were available, they relied on the commercially produced revised practice workbooks designed especially for the new HKCEE. In this sense, teaching materials in Hong Kong secondary schools can be seen as essentially exam oriented. Heavy reliance on these teaching materials by teachers is further indication of a washback effect of the new HKCEE on teaching content.

Conclusions and Implications

A summary of the findings of this study offers a clearer sense of the process and the nature of washback, involving participants, processes, and products (Figure 5.3) (see Bailey 1996, 264; Markee 1997, 42–47).

PARTICIPANTS

Participants include teachers and students, administrators, material developers, and publishers (those directly connected with the actual teaching and learning), as well as stakeholders in the exam: users of the exam, parents, and the community. In this study, three levels of participants were studied: those who initiated, developed, and implemented the new HKCEE. The combined function of these participants within the Hong Kong education system determined the nature and scope of the washback effect of this new exam. Washback was observed to have effects on some aspects of teaching such as the production of new teaching materials and the incorporation of more role playing and group discussion activities similar to those included in the new exam. But there was no observable effect on teaching methodology. In this sense, washback is seen to be a phenomenon more complex than simply the effect of the exam on teaching and learning. It involves not only participants within the educational context, but a complex process of change within classroom teaching itself. This complexity needs to be taken into consideration in future washback studies.

PROCESSES

Processes include materials development, changes in attitudes toward teaching and learning, changes in teaching methodology, and the use of test-taking strategies. This study focused initially on what happened at the three levels of participants involved with the new 1996 HKCEE, namely, the HKEA, textbook publishers and tertiary institutions, and teachers and learners within the immediate education context during the three years when both the old and the new HKCEE existed simultaneously in the school curriculum. It then focused on the processes of washback in actual classroom teaching and learning both at the behavioral level, by using classroom observations, and at the policy and theoretical or philosophical levels, using both teacher and student surveys (Stern 1989, 210). In a sense, the washback effect being studied was seen as a process as well as a product of the processes involved (Figure 5.3). Viewing washback as a process, research needs to involve a study of classroom teaching and learning, a study of what has been happening in classroom teaching and learning in relation to the exam, and a study of classroom teaching and learning from the perspective of change. Given the complexity of the features of classroom teaching and learning shown here, washback studies need to consider teaching and learning from all these angles.

PRODUCT

Product, which refers both to what is learned in terms of facts and/or skills and to the quality of the learning, was not investigated in this study due

New 1996 HKCEE	Participants	Processes	Products
	↓	↓	↓
Level 1 Decision making level	{ ED HKEA & CDC	*syllabus design*	*new HKCEE*
		↓	↓
Level 2 Intervening level	{ Textbook publishers Teacher educators	*materials development bring about changes in teaching and learning through teacher education*	*new teaching materials*
		↓	
Level 3 School Level	{ Principals Department heads Teachers & Students	*Changes in attitudes toward teaching and learning; changes to teaching methodology; changes to teaching and learning activities*	↓
	⟶	*improved learning outcomes*	

Figure 5.3. Model of the washback effect within the Hong Kong educational context.

to real-time constraints. Product would be a worthwhile focus for further research now that several cohorts of students have taken the new HKCEE. The revised teaching materials and learning outcomes would also both be a worthwhile focus for further research.

The new 1996 HKCEE affected first the perceptions and attitudes of the participants. These perceptions and attitudes, in turn, affected what partici-pants did in carrying out their work. Ultimately, these processes might affect learning outcomes. Though rather simplistic, this is an ideal model of the complex washback process. For example, whether the intended washback effect promoted vigorously by the HKEA has been realized remains in ques-tion. Determining whether all the participant products (e.g., revised text-books) have contributed to the enhancement of learning outcomes would require a longer washback study with different levels and foci.

A phenomenon as complex as washback involves a wide range of variables in teaching and learning that cannot be fully understood through individual studies. Time and resources are needed to allow a pool of researchers to look at different aspects of the phenomenon and bring them together for an over-all understanding within a particular educational context. Analysis should take into account a society's goals and values, the educational system, and the potential effects of its use (Bachman and Palmer 1996, 35). It should also consider aspects of assessment, curriculum, and teaching and learning theories and practices within the educational system. It is impossible to illustrate the washback phenomenon fully within a single model such as the one in Figure 5.3. However, the model can serve as a guide for future washback studies.

The findings of this study of changes in teaching and learning brought about by the new HKCEE appear likely to remain superficial. That is, the ways in which teachers perceive teaching and learning might change, yet they are not likely to influence the ways in which they teach. The change to a new exam has informed teachers about what they might do differently, but it has not shown them how to do it. The washback effect can be fully realized only when all levels of organizations in the educational system are involved. In this sense, there must be a genuine involvement of educators and textbook writers. A change in the final examination alone will not achieve the intended goal. The idea of changing the examination based on an "ideal" assessment model in order to guide teaching and learning toward an "ideal" seems an oversimplification of the teaching and learning situation. To bring about a positive washback effect of the kind intended by the HKEA, the process needs to be redefined and collaboration agreed upon in the areas of teacher education and materials development along with the creation of supportive teaching and learning cultures in schools (see Chapters 3 and 7). Only when all education organizations (participants) work together can substantial changes in teaching and learning be realized. Moreover, the washback effect takes time, and progress may not occur in a straightforward manner.

One outcome of this study is the understanding that washback can influence teaching. In the case of a high-stakes exam, this influence can include implementation of activities similar to those required in the exam. Accountability may have a coercive effect on teaching and learning. However, washback from an exam does not make teachers alter their practice of teaching, such as changing from teacher-dominated talk to the more interactive and task-based teaching intended by the HKEA. Changes in exam format alone cannot revamp the current test-centered, teacher-centered, and textbook-centered English language teaching and learning in Hong Kong secondary schools. One reason is that the HKCEE's increased integrated and task-based activities can show teachers something new, but it cannot in and of itself show or teach teachers how to prepare learners for these activities. Given the lack of subject and professional training of secondary teachers of English in Hong Kong (only 14.2 percent are subject and professionally trained;

19.8 percent are subject trained) (Coniam et al. 1994, 353), it is unlikely that teachers with such limited preparation and qualifications can change the way they teach just because a new public exam has been put into place. They may well lack the knowledge and skills to make the needed changes, even if they have a positive attitude toward the new exam. However, this situation may change as a result of language benchmarks for English language teachers introduced in the year 2000 (see Coniam and Falvey 1997; Coniam and Falvey 1999.) Although references to washback are frequently found in HKEA documents (HKEA 1993; HKEA 1994a; HKEA 1994b), the HKEA did not specify particular areas in teaching and learning that this new examination would influence nor how the intended washback effects in teaching could be brought about. That may be an additional reason why teachers in Hong Kong continue to rely so heavily on textbooks.

Moreover, although the design of exam-related textbooks may be based on information about exam innovations from the HKEA, the final product might be less what innovators view as desirable and more what the publishers think will sell. The competence of textbook writers themselves is an additional cause for concern. In the Hong Kong context, at least, can be seen the rapid production of materials that are very exam specific and represent a limited focus for teachers and learners rather than a broadening of horizons (see also Andrews 1994a; Andrews 1994b). Thus, a washback study that examines the textbook issue in depth would be highly valuable.

In addition, teachers have varying capacity for implementing the mandated assessment reform. In order for instructional improvement through the use of exams to be consistent with cognitive-constructivist beliefs about learning and teaching, the reform should first acknowledge the challenges presented by such conceptual changes. Conceptual change is seldom achieved without attending to the beliefs of those who are the targets of change (in this case teachers and learners) and the environments (schools) in which they function. Not taking these beliefs and conditions into account may well lead to the familiar situation in which the more things change the more they remain the same. Change is everywhere, and progress is not (Fullan 1983).

In order to promote change, Noble and Smith (1994b) pointed out that consistent reform would have to first accept the fact that teacher learning is a process of construction, and that teachers possess diverse interpretations and prior knowledge structures. We have to recognize the need for conceptual change and teacher learning within the context of classroom practice. Any change would require sufficient time and resources for mentoring, peer coaching, intensive seminars, and the like. In addition, an education system should encourage teachers to risk experimentation and failures in the short run. Change requires a sociopolitical context in which teachers feel safe trying out new strategies. However, such an environment is unlikely to be created in an intensive exam-driven culture and society. For teachers to move from a mastery model of content-deliverers to become active constructors of knowledge and co-constructors of learner knowledge involves a fundamental shift in perceptions and practices. This requires a quality and intensity of curriculum and professional development, resources to support the development, and the time to incorporate and refine the changes.

High-stakes exams such as the 1996 HKCEE are not instruments that encourage teacher inquiry or critical thinking about the status quo of teaching and learning. On the contrary, they depend on coercion to create uniformity (see McDonnell and Elmore 1987; McDonnell et al. 1990). If the HKEA expects teachers to change along with their students, school environments conducive to such change must be fostered. But the HKEA cannot be made responsible for implementing all of the changes. In this sense, assessment has a limited effect on teaching and learning. Although the Hong Kong educational context at the macro level is favorable, the actual teaching context at the learner level (school environment, messages from administration, expectations of other teachers, students, and parents) plays an essential role in facilitating or impeding change. In the end, reform is in the hands of teachers. As English (1992) points out, when the classroom door is shut and no one else is around, the classroom teacher can teach almost any curriculum he or she believes is appropriate, irrespective of the various reforms, innovations, and public examinations.

Notes

1. A target-oriented curriculum (TOC) is a curriculum with clear targets and stimulating approaches for lively and effective teaching, learning, and assessment. Better opportunities will be provided for children to learn and to develop their ability to think creatively. Such a curriculum initiative is viewed as the only significant landmark in the post–World War II history of curriculum reform within schools in Hong Kong (Morris et al. 1996).

2. The process of modifying an existing exam syllabus takes approximately eighteen months for the HKEA to complete. Because of the need to give two years' notice to schools, it takes at least three and a half years before candidates actually sit for the new exam. The revision of the HKCEE took place in 1993. The official syllabus was introduced to schools in the 1994–95 school year. Because the first cohort of students sat for the revised exam in 1996, it is referred to as the 1996 HKCEE.

3. Researchers have to be aware of the time of year they observe classrooms. For example, during periods of intensive examination coaching, this coaching will probably

be the only thing observed. Observations should also be avoided between Christmas and the Chinese New Year in Hong Kong, since long stretches of uninterrupted teaching could not be observed between holidays.

4. Findings related to learner perceptions are not included here. For a full report on the learner survey, data collection, and analysis procedures, as well as findings, see Cheng 1998. The teacher questionnaire consisted of three parts. Part one consisted of eight categories of teacher demographic information. Part two consisted of twelve categories (ninety-six items altogether) (TQ 2.1–2.11) dealing with teacher perceptions of aspects of teaching, learning, and evaluation in schools. Part three consisted of eleven categories dealing with teacher reactions to the new exam and aspects of classroom teaching and learning activities related to it (TQ 3.1–3.11). TQ 2.1, for example, refers to Teacher Questionnaire part two, category one, which consisted of ten items.

5. For a full report on classroom observations for both baseline and main studies, see Cheng 1999.

6

National Standards and the Diffusion of Innovation: Language Teaching in the United States

ANA SCHWARTZ

In 1994, U.S. president Bill Clinton signed into law the Goals 2000: Educate America Act. The purpose of this act was to create national curricular standards in the subject areas of math, English, history, and science. These standards were designed to provide high expectations for all learners (Tucker and Codding 1998) and to serve as examples of excellence, an "objective ideal" that all learners can attain (Wiggins 1999).

The first direct involvement of the federal government in the creation of curricular standards, Goals 2000 marked an important turning point in American educational history (Saxe 1999). Education in the United States has been traditionally a state and local concern; issues of curriculum and assessment have been addressed by the states and local school districts, *not* by the federal government. The national curricular standards are voluntary, however; states and school districts can determine the degree to which they follow them in developing curricula. This decentralized system of education poses fundamental obstacles for true and meaningful implementation of the standards, as will be shown here.

This chapter focuses specifically on the U.S. national curricular standards for the foreign languages and issues of their implementation. Implementation issues will be discussed using Markee's (1997) model of curricular innovation, which is based on a "diffusion of innovations" perspective. To understand how and why an innovation is either adopted or rejected requires consideration of the social context in which it is communicated. This perspective will be adopted to illustrate that both the *reasons* for implementing standards and *the consequences* of their implementation will depend on *where* within the social structure (bottom or top) they are advocated and *how* (bottom-up or top-down) they are diffused.

Given its decentralized nature, curricular innovation in U.S. education can result from top-down or bottom-up methods of diffusion, or some combination of the two. The potentially dual nature of innovation can lead to a conflict of interests among members of the U.S. educational system at various levels of its sociopolitical structure (local, state, federal). Before addressing these issues of implementation, however, we need first to review the content and underlying theory of the National Standards for Foreign Language Learning.

The National Standards for Foreign Language Learning

DEVELOPMENT

Foreign languages were not included initially in the Goals 2000 project. Only after considerable lobbying efforts by the American Council on the Teaching of Foreign Languages (ACTFL) and the National Committee on Languages (NCL) did foreign languages become the seventh and *final* area of the school curriculum to receive support from Goals 2000 (Davis 1997). These lobbying efforts resulted from the collaboration of various national foreign language associations, among them ACTFL and the American Associations of Teachers of French (AATF), German (AATG), and Spanish and Portuguese (AATSP). Representatives from each of these organizations served on the board of directors for the National Standards for Foreign Language Learning (NSFLL) project and guided its development.

An eleven-member task force was responsible for the actual writing of the standards. This task force was selected on the basis of two criteria: (1) membership should include representatives from the entire field of foreign language education, and (2) membership should include currently practicing teachers familiar with the classroom environment (Lafayette and Draper 1996). The drafting of the standards was further guided by the project's statement of philosophy:

> Language and communication are at the heart of human experience. The United States must educate students who are linguistically and culturally equipped to communicate successfully in a pluralistic American society and

abroad. This imperative envisions a future in which all students will develop and maintain proficiency in English and at least one other language, modern or classical. Children who come to school from non-English backgrounds should also have opportunities to develop further proficiencies in their first language. (ACTFL 2000, 1)

Based on this philosophy, the project members formulated goals of foreign language education, expressed in terms of curricular goal areas. The task force also included progress indicators to aid in the assessment of learner progress toward the standards as well as learning scenarios to exemplify ways for promoting this progression (Lafayette and Draper 1996).

THE FIVE C'S

The National Standards for Foreign Language Learning were completed in 1995. Eleven standards are organized into five goal areas, known as the Five C's (communication, cultures, connections, comparisons, and communities). Each area consists of two to three standards and sample progress indicators for grades 4, 8, and 12 (see Appendix).

The *communication* goal area addresses learners' ability to use the second language to communicate thoughts, feelings, and opinions in a variety of settings. The three standards listed under this goal area emphasize what learners can *communicate* with the language. The benchmarks for each grade level reflect a gradual increase in the complexity of the context in which learners are expected to communicate.

The *cultures* goal area includes standards that address learner understanding of how the products and practices of a culture shape its perspectives, which in turn are reflected in the language. An understanding of how culture shapes language is of primary importance for language learners.

The *connections* goal area addresses use of the language to learn new content and information beyond the classroom. Learners should use the language as a tool to access and process information in a diversity of contexts. As they use the language in different settings, learners can discover the "distinctive viewpoints that are only available through the foreign language and its culture" (standard 3.2).

The standards included in the *comparisons* goal area are designed to foster learner insight and understanding of the nature of language and culture through a comparison of the new language and culture with the American English language and culture with which they presumably are already familiar. Through such comparison, language learners not only increase their awareness of linguistic features of syntax, morphology, and phonology; they can also develop a more sophisticated understanding of what is meant by *culture* and the factors that comprise it.

The ultimate, overarching objective of the Five C's is the fifth and final goal area, *communities*. Drawing from the knowledge and competence developed in the other four C's, this goal area describes learners' lifelong use of the language, in communities and contexts both within and beyond the school setting itself.

Together the Five C's reflect a focus on what learners can do with the language. They represent a holistic, communicative approach to language learning. This signals a move away from the longstanding pedagogical representation of language ability as consisting of four skills (listening, speaking, reading, and writing) and components (grammar, vocabulary, and pronunciation) (e.g., Rivers 1968) to encourage instead a consideration of the discoursal and sociocultural features of language use (see Halliday 1978; Savignon 1983, 1997). Although the eleven standards are categorized into five goal areas, the development of competence in any one area is intrinsically linked to the development of competence in another.

The NSFLL and Other Representations of CLT

The influence of earlier representations of CLT can be found in the content and pedagogy of the NSFLL. Breen and Candlin (1980), for example, provide principles for designing and implementing a communicative curriculum that coincide well with the structure of the national foreign language standards. According to Breen and Candlin, the content of a communicative curriculum is specified by first designating a selected repertoire of communicative performances that ultimately will be required of the learners. Based on this repertoire, specific competencies assumed to underlie successful performance are identified. For the NSFLL, the performance repertoire is designated by the eleven standards.

Breen and Candlin also discuss the role of teachers as facilitators of communication within a communication-based classroom. Within their framework, the teacher is both a provider and an organizer of resources as well as a resource for communication. Moreover, the teacher acts as an interdependent participant in classroom communication. Similar notions can be found in discussion of the communication standards. Hall (1999), for example, describes the teacher's role as that of facilitator of communicative acts by providing learners with modeling and feedback and directing their attention to important features of communication. (For illustration of the risks inherent in such teacher "attention," however, as opposed to actual classroom practice of communication, see Chapters 4 and 5.)

The content of the NSFLL reflects the communicative curriculum proposed by Savignon (1983). Savignon outlines five curricular components for a communicative classroom: Language Arts; Language for a Purpose; My Language Is Me: Personal Second Language Use; You Be . . . , I'll Be . . . : Theater Arts; and Beyond the Classroom. These components are not separable. They represent clusters of activities or experiences that can be used to promote learner use of the language. Instruction involves a blending of these components, which, in turn, overlap (see Chapter 1).

The intertwined nature of this curriculum is similar to the interrelated and interconnected components of the Five C's. Moreover, three components in particular, language for a purpose, language use beyond the classroom, and personal second language use, relate to curricular objectives of the standards. Similar in objective to the connections goal area, language for a purpose involves activities that encourage learners to use the second language to express, interpret, and negotiate meaning. Language use beyond the classroom involves activities through which learners use the language to interact with second language representatives outside of the classroom, as reflected specifically in the communities standard.

Finally, personal second language use addresses the affective aspects of learning a new language. It includes activities and instructional practices that allow students to express themselves personally through the second language. This notion of personalizing the new language, and in a sense making it one's own, is emphasized through the learner-centered approach of the Five C's (Overfield 1997; Met 1999). Learner experiences serve as the basis of learning within each of the Five C's. For example, through connecting the language with other disciplines (standard 3.1), using the language to gain new perspectives (standard 3.2), and using the language to gain new experiences in a second language community (standards 5.1 and 5.2), learners create their own experiences and develop their own insights. To summarize, the NSFLL appear to be based on a communicative approach to second language learning and teaching with a strong basis in second language acquisition theory and research.

The Indispensable Link Between Theory and Practice

Descriptions of the theoretical underpinnings of the NSFLL are provided in an ACTFL publication, *Foreign Language Standards: Linking Research Theories and Practices* (Phillips and Terry 1999). In this volume, various authors discuss the theoretical models and empirical studies that support the communication, culture, connection, and comparison goals (for a review of the theory for the communities area see Overfield 1997). Since it is beyond the scope of this chapter to discuss each of these areas in depth, attention will be given to Hall's (1999) description of the theories of communicative competence that support the communication goal area. Inasmuch as communicative competence is seen as integral to each of the Five C's, similar theoretical links presumably can be made to each goal area. Indeed, other authors (for example, Overfield 1997; Fantini 1999) make reference to the same theoretical frameworks cited by Hall.

Hall delineates what she perceives to be the theoretical links between the NSFLL and theories of communicative competence. Her analysis begins with a description of what is meant by the terms "communication" and "communicative competence." Communication is described as based on socially constructed "communicative plans." These plans are used to reach communicative goals and involve specific communicative roles. They "function as maps of our sociocultural worlds and contain significant sociocultural knowledge about our communicative activities" (1999, 17).

She traces the term communicative competence to Hymes (1966), noting the well-known contrast of his view of language as social behavior with a Chomskyan concern with individual morphosyntactic knowledge, or linguistic competence. Following brief mention of the familiar frameworks of communicative competence proposed by Canale and Swain (1980) and Bachman (1990), Hall evokes a little-known representation of communicative competence proposed by Celce-Murcia, Dornyei, and Thurell (1995), claiming it to be the most comprehensive, "because it takes into consideration some of the most recent research" (Hall 1999, 20). No research is identified, but the representation itself is subsequently described in some detail.

THE "MODEL" OF COMMUNICATIVE COMPETENCE
OF CELCE-MURCIA AND COLLEAGUES

Citing the "practical needs" of syllabus design and teacher education, and a "belief in the potential of a direct, explicit approach to the teaching of communicative skills" (1995, 6), Celce-Murcia and colleagues offer what they describe as a "pedagogically motivated model with content specifications." In so doing, they expand the Canale and Swain (1980) framework (see Chapter 1) to include actional competence, or "competence in conveying and understanding communicative intent . . . matching actional intent with linguistic form" (1995, 17). Thus, Celce-Murcia and colleagues describe five components of communicative competence: (1) discourse, (2) actional,

(3) sociolinguistic, (4) linguistic, and (5) strategic, with discourse competence at the core. In keeping with the Chomskyan perspective to which Hymes reacted, but in opposition to Halliday (see Chapter 1), they hold to a distinction between performance and competence. They use the term "linguistic" in a narrow sense to refer to sentence-level grammatical form.

Celce-Murcia and colleagues make no claim for the validity of the components they identify. In providing teachers and curriculum developers with an "elaborated checklist" for creating a communicative curriculum, they state as their purpose to provide "a practical guide for teachers," to "achieve a *clear and simple* presentation" (1995, 20, emphasis added). In fact, with its emphasis on simplicity, their proposal fails to adequately capture the dynamic and interactive nature of communicative competence. Unlike the Canale and Swain (1980) and Bachman (1990) frameworks, it has neither appeared in a major professional journal nor drawn the attention of researchers in seond language acquisition or assessment. (For a critique of Celce-Murcia et al. 1995 with respect to the implications drawn by the authors for communicative language teaching, see Thornbury 1998.)

Curricular reform cannot occur in the absence of theory. A look through the history of curricular reform and innovation reveals a continual failure to establish true change when methods and materials are disseminated without an understanding of basic theoretical issues (see Musumeci 1997a; Savignon 1990, 1991; Chapter 10). In the absence of a well-articulated underlying theory, the extent to which the foreign language standards can be said to represent a significant redefinition of curricular goals remains unclear. Liskin-Gasparro has represented the U.S. national standards movement as the "most provocative debate in the history of education reform" (1996, 169) and a fundamental paradigm shift in the area of curriculum. More recently, however, she revisits the efforts within ACTFL in the 1980s to differentiate language "proficiency" from communicative competence and goes on to assert that the proficiency movement that has dominated the American foreign language profession since the publication of the *ACTFL Provisional Proficiency Guidelines* (ACTFL 1982) "*inspired* the national Standard in Foreign Language Learning" (Liskin-Gasparro 2000, 486, emphasis added; see also Chapter 10). If the standards are to promote true and long-lasting reform, the underlying theory, which is the glue connecting the Five C's, must be clarified and conveyed.

We turn now to a consideration of issues regarding the implementation of standards from a diffusion of innovations perspective. This analysis will show that the success of the NSFLL will vary according to the social roles of the participants, or stakeholders, who are potentially affected by this specific curricular reform effort.

The Diffusion of Innovations Perspective: Basic Definitions and Concepts

The purpose of diffusion of innovation theory is to explain and predict the rates of adoption of innovations. This perspective is also used to analyze how innovations are implemented, designed, and maintained by examining certain attributes of the innovation and the social roles of those participating in its diffusion (see Rogers 1995). An innovation is "an idea, practice, or object that is perceived as new by an individual or other unit of adoption" (Rogers 1995, 11). A *diffusion* of innovation is defined as "the process by which an innovation is communicated through certain channels over time among the members of a social system" (10). Thus the major elements of innovation diffusion include (1) the innovation, (2) channels of communication, (3) time, and (4) the social system.

MARKEE'S THEORY OF CURRICULAR INNOVATION

Markee (1997) developed a theoretical framework for understanding innovation in language teaching. By adopting a diffusionist perspective and drawing from the research of multiple disciplines, he suggested how various sociocultural factors interact to influence the implementation of curricular innovation. He defines curricular innovation as "a managed process of development whose principal products are teaching and/or testing materials, methodological skills and pedagogical values that *are perceived as new by potential adopters*" (46, emphasis added).

Thus, it is the perception of newness that defines curricular change as innovation. For example, many consider the Five C's to be reflective of a new and therefore innovative "proficiency paradigm." However, the proficiency paradigm is based on a communicative approach to language learning and teaching that has emerged throughout history under a variety of labels. Early examples of a communicative approach can be identified as far back as the fourteenth century (Musumeci 1997a). Nonetheless, the "proficiency paradigm" is indeed an innovation if those participating in its diffusion perceive it as new.

It is also possible for a single aspect of a curricular innovation (beliefs, materials, or methods) to be perceived as new, and therefore innovative, while other aspects are not. For example, some may perceive the underlying

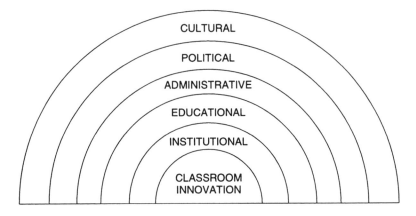

Figure 6.1. The hierarchy of interrelating systems in which innovations have to operate. Reprinted by permission of Oxford University Press from C. Kennedy, "Evaluation of the Management of Change in ELT Projects," *Applied Linguistics* 9, 4 (1988): 332.

model of the NSFLL (CLT) as not new, and something that indeed dates back to the Middle Ages. However, the method (federal government involvement) is indeed new within the context of U.S. educational history. For this reason the NSFLL may be seen as a curricular innovation, since they have at least one component which may be perceived as new.

SOCIAL ROLES AND THE CONTEXT OF CURRICULAR INNOVATION

Participants in an innovation take on different social roles depending on whether they are effecting change or being affected by change. The two major social roles of those effecting change are change agents and suppliers. A change agent is someone who influences others' decisions to adopt an innovation. Change agents are further categorized as being either internal or external. Within curricular innovations, external change agents come from outside the educational system, while potential internal agents include teachers, administrators, and other participants in that system (see Chapter 10). Suppliers facilitate curricular innovation by providing textbooks and other types of materials. The two major social roles played by those being affected by an innovation are those of adopters and clients. Adopters are those individuals who decide to use an innovation. If they have not completed the decision process they are considered potential adopters. Clients are the recipients of an innovation. In the case of curricular innovations, these would be the learners.

Innovations take place within and across different levels of a social structure. Within curricular innovations there are six levels of interrelating subsystems, which are hierarchically arranged and have distinct subcultures. These include classroom, educational, institutional, administrative, and political subcultures (Figure 6.1). As will be seen, the social context from which an innovation is initiated will have a fundamental impact on the method used for its dissemination or diffusion.

Methods of Curricular Innovation

There are a variety of methods adopted for innovation diffusion, which are characterized by the degree to which they represent top-down or bottom-up change. The former refers to change that is mandated from higher levels of the social structure to lower levels (see Chapters 2, 3, 5, and 7). The latter refers to change that is voluntary and works its way up through the social structure. Since the U.S. educational system operates through a combination of top-down and bottom-up processes of change (Davis 1997), curricular innovation can occur through various methods of diffusion.

Three methods of diffusion may be seen as operating in the dissemination of the NSFLL. These three methods are center-periphery, research development and diffusion, and problem solving. The first two are examples of top-down methods and the third is an example of a bottom-up method.

THE CENTER-PERIPHERY METHOD

Within the center-periphery (CP) method of innovation diffusion, the power to promote change lies with a small number of individuals. "The decision makers derive the right to exercise authority based on the hierarchical positions they occupy in a bureaucratically organized institution" (Markee 1997, 63). Change is implemented through means of power and coercion; rewards and sanctions are often used to ensure implementation of the innovation. When this method is employed for curricular innovation, teachers are most often on the periphery and do not share in the decision making.

In terms of the implementation of the foreign language standards, the CP method is most likely to be used when standards are advocated at the political, institutional, or administrative levels as a method to effect change at the educational or classroom levels. For example, a state's political system may institute standards as a method for improving the quality of its schools. To ensure that the standards are implemented, the state may require the administration of certain assessments and offer incentives to the districts that show overall improvements in scores.

This type of implementation can promote change. Research has shown, for example, that state curricular frameworks have a significant impact on local curricular development. These frameworks are often developed to aid schools and districts in designing a curriculum that matches current educational research and development. For example, research on foreign language curriculum in particular suggests that the development and use of ACTFL's proficiency guidelines fostered a shift from grammar-oriented approaches to proficiency-based ones (Bartz and Singer 1996).

However, a CP method, which relies solely on top-down change, is not sufficient for effecting long-lasting reform. Since individual initiative is not fostered and teachers are passive recipients of the innovation, they often do not have an opportunity to develop a full understanding of the innovation (Markee 1997). As discussed earlier, the dissemination of theory along with the method is crucial for curricular innovation. Without the theory, misconceptions regarding the innovation are likely to occur, which will in turn impede its maintenance.

There is substantial evidence suggesting that sole reliance on a CP method of diffusion would be detrimental for true implementation of the standards. As explained above, a CP method of curricular innovation starts typically at the political or administrative level and progresses top-down. However, the U.S. educational system is decentralized. The miscommunication that arises from the agendas of various sectors of the U.S. public educational system is a major obstacle for reform.

Davis (1997) provides an example of reform efforts in the state of Pennsylvania that illustrates how state-level politics can be a hindrance to successful change. In past years, politicians in Pennsylvania worked toward establishing an outcomes-based, minimal expectations approach to curricular development. The Pennsylvania State Modern Language Association (PSMLA) lobbied for several years to have one of the fifty-three outcomes address foreign languages. In 1996, however, newly elected Governor Ridge blocked outcomes-based education in favor of a standards-based, maximum expectations approach. The PSMLA found the standards for foreign languages to be untenable for Pennsylvania school districts, particularly those that did not offer foreign language instruction at the elementary level. Therefore, the PSMLA's struggle to attain state recognition and support for foreign languages was lost with the shift in the state's educational framework.

Davis (1997) also points out that teachers may agree with the underlying pedagogy of the foreign language standards, but that their perceptions of how the standards are being politically instituted may turn them away. He points out the importance of recognizing the multiple identities that individuals carry with them. For example, a teacher may identify herself as a mother, teacher, Latino, and Republican. Therefore, although she may favor "advancing the agenda of her profession via educational reform," her politically conservative leanings may include fears of federally mandated policies and centralized control (155).

Another fundamental limitation of the CP method is the conflict and tension that may result from opposing agendas among different sectors of the educational system. The standards movement has increasingly been seen as a method for instituting school and teacher accountability: "The issue of increased control at the state level with required standards and/or mandated assessments will only exacerbate problems and conflict" (Saxe 1999, 8). This tension is illustrated in Crookes' (1997) description of foreign language teachers' situations in schools. He describes the employment circumstances of teachers as an environment of "alienation." Part of this tension is attributed to the "strong 'accountability' of schools and of teachers to their immediate administrators and to political authorities; [which] in turn results in heavy reporting demands for tests taken . . . as well as day-by-day conformity to a specific page of text" (68) (see also Chapters 3, 5, and 7).

This focus on accountability, testing, and conformity contrasts sharply with the earlier discussion of the theoretical basis behind the foreign language standards. There appears to be an almost complete mismatch between what is advocated pedagogically by the standards and what is emphasized when these same standards are administered and mandated in a top-down fashion. The CP method for implementing standards is characterized by top-down mandated reform, which most likely will result in partial or temporary adoption and/or ineffective assessment practices.

THE RESEARCH DEVELOPMENT AND DIFFUSION METHOD OF INNOVATION

The research development and diffusion (RDD) method of innovation represents another top-down approach to innovation diffusion. This method starts with applied research and development followed by testing and mass production. Within the context of the RDD method it is important to make a distinction between primary and secondary curricular innovations. Primary curricular innovation involves changes in pedagogy, methods, and teaching skills. Therefore, it is considered the heart of innovation. Secondary curricular innovation involves changes in curricular materials, such as textbooks. These are the most tangible and readily observed aspects of an innovation. However, in isolation secondary innovation does not represent true curricular change. Once again, the method and the materials must be accompanied by the underlying pedagogy (Markee 1997).

One of the advantages of an RDD model is the rapid diffusion of secondary innovation through mass production (e.g., textbook publishing). Indeed, many textbooks purportedly reflect a communicative approach to foreign language teaching, suggesting that the underlying theory of the standards has already been widely accepted (see Chapters 5 and 7). Researchers have noted, however, that the innovation resulting from RDD has remained mostly at the secondary level. Classroom research has revealed that many of the textbooks used in foreign language classrooms are replete with trendy jargon that would suggest a communicative approach to language learning. The "communicative exercises" of textbooks are often used to drive entire lesson plans in foreign language classrooms (Savignon 1983; Savignon 1997; Thornbury 1998).

The completion of textbook exercises alone does not constitute true classroom communication, the essential feature of CLT. Classrooms have a discourse culture, which determines how students are to interact with the teacher and one another. The structure of this discourse is most often asymmetrical, with most of the communicative decision-making being done by the teacher. In the foreign language classroom this asymmetrical structure has particular consequence. More specifically, when learners use the second language exclusively through an asymmetrical discourse structure, they may think that the learning of this language is fundamentally different than the learning of the native language (Brooks 1993).

This message is incompatible with the underlying pedagogy of the foreign language standards. Each of the Five C's is designed to convey the message that second language learning, much like learning a first language, involves communication with a purpose. Therefore, although RDD may be effective for disseminating the products of secondary innovation (teaching materials), this does not imply a similar effectiveness in disseminating the products of primary innovation (pedagogy).

There are other limitations of the RDD method of innovation. The change agents often assume that a theoretical rationale is sufficient for promoting adoption, and they are often insensitive to issues of implementation. Furthermore, teachers are most often at the bottom of the hierarchy of this expert-driven change and do not feel that they truly own the products of the innovation (Markee 1997).

Yet through the use of a continual process of research, development, and diffusion, the RDD method by its very nature may overcome the obstacle of inadequate theory dissemination. Change agents for the NSFLL have used research to improve diffusion and development by obtaining feedback from adopters and potential adopters regarding their perceptions, understanding, and use of the standards. For example, Bartz and Singer (1996) distributed questionnaires to various members of the academic community, including teachers, supervisors, and administrators. The questionnaires addressed members' awareness of the standards, their agreement with the content and underlying pedagogy, and the potential for implementation. Several items asked teachers to rate each of the Five C's in terms of its importance and feasibility. The pattern of responses indicated that overall, teachers gave less favorable ratings to the communities goal area, which describes students' lifelong learning and use of the language. Comments on the questionnaires reflected the general impression that this goal area was not practical. One teacher commented that "the goals are unrealistic, especially at the upper levels" (160), and another expressed her view that without study abroad experiences, the average learner would not be able to reach the standards of this goal area.

These responses to the communities goal area would indicate the utility of capitalizing on publishing resources to disseminate information regarding how to attain these standards, even with limited resources. In fact, the major change agency of the standards, ACTFL, has made readily available a description of the standards, as well as progress indicators and sample learning scenarios, through its website (www.actfl.org). Responses to the questionnaire also indicated that teachers did not perceive the standards as new; they felt they were already engaged in such practices. However, inasmuch as the goal of the standards is not to validate current teaching practices but to examine and improve student performance (Phillips 1999), statements such as "My students perform those tasks at high levels of competency" (2) would be more reflective of a true understanding of the objective of the standards. Thus, change agents involved in the dissemination of the innovation should devise ways of encouraging in-depth reflection on the standards. This could be done through the use of workshops and focus group discussions.

In another study, Solomon (1997) distributed surveys to educators in public and private schools to assess their awareness of the NSFLL. Educators in private schools reported less awareness of the standards then those in public schools. Once again, change agents could make use of a variety of channels of communication and publishing resources to reach the targeted audience.

To summarize, the RDD model is limited by its top-down nature. Although it leads to rapid production of the tangible products of an innovation (textbooks, teaching materials), it does not promote pedagogical change. Perhaps if the RDD method is used as a continual, cyclical practice, with research continually informing development, its efficacy can be improved. As will be argued in the next section, however, the RDD method lacks a key component, the active participation of teachers.

THE PROBLEM-SOLVING METHOD OF DIFFUSION

The two methods of diffusion discussed so far, the center-periphery and the research, development, and diffusion approaches, share the limitation of their top-down nature. In both methods teachers remain passive recipients. Although they have responsibility for implementing change, they often do not feel a personal commitment to change. The problem-solving (PS) method, however, involves teachers as both initiators of and collaborators on change. In this case, teachers are internal change agents, who may or may not act with the support of external agents. The bottom-up nature of this method promotes a sense of ownership, which is crucial for the dissemination and true adoption of curricular innovation (Markee 1997).

Yet the PS method faces the major limitation of limited resources. For example, it is difficult for teachers to find time within their tight schedules to engage in professional discussions with others, much less engage in research endeavors. There are not sufficient resources, in terms of money or time, to support teachers' professional development (Crookes 1997; Chapter 3).

Furthermore, teacher-initiated innovation may be blocked by resistance from students and/or their families. For example, teachers have reported student resistance to a communicative approach of language teaching. Because this approach is often not compatible with students' expectations, they may insist on the more familiar direct knowledge-oriented approach (Thornbury 1998; Chapter 7). This lack of support reflects the major obstacle for a PS approach to innovation. The reality of these limitations is clearly reflected in another set of teachers' responses to the Solomon (1997) survey mentioned above. Although the teachers were aware of the standards, they stated that "knowing the best procedures and techniques does not mean there [are] training, conferences or money for implementation" (7).

A COMBINATION OF THE PROBLEM-SOLVING AND THE RESEARCH, DEVELOPMENT AND DIFFUSION METHODS

Within the context of the foreign language standards project it is difficult to draw clear distinctions between the use of RDD and PS methods. As described above, the task force included practicing foreign language teachers. Furthermore, the project involved the voluntary participation of teachers from pilot schools to aid in the research and development process.

This tactic, combining an RDD with a PS approach, may be particularly beneficial for the diffusion of curricular innovation. In fact, the benefits of this combined approach are gaining recognition. There has been a call for a paradigm shift in research approaches that involves teacher-researcher partnerships. This new paradigm, known as action research, "places the development of theory in the hands of the practitioner" (Crookes 1997, 73).

A PS approach enhances RDD because it includes the essential component of implementer ownership. Likewise, the RDD approach enhances problem-solving because it provides support and resources such as research and access to mass media communication channels (e.g., textbook publishing). This is particularly important since innovation through an exclusively PS approach is infrequent and more often discussed as an ideal than a reality (Markee 1997).

Therefore, a collaboration between members of funded research and development projects with interested teachers may be the optimal approach. The following comments from teachers who were involved in a pilot project of the foreign language standards illustrate the benefits of this collaboration:

> The standards provided the impetus to foster communication among the teachers.
> The standards made all three of us teachers sit together and talk. They made us think bigger.
> The standards really helped me and my fellow teachers reflect on our own practice. (Bartz and Singer 1996, 149)

Benefits of a Combined Approach to Diffusion of Curricular Innovation

Research from other disciplines, like school psychology, has shown the importance of teacher interaction for promoting change. For example, a major concern of school psychologists is the improvement of teachers' self-assurance with regard to their ability to use suggested interventions. They address this issue by providing an environment that fosters teacher modeling, discussion, and reflection (Wong 1997). Although a problem-solving approach to innovation includes the essential component of teacher involvement, its effectiveness is often limited by a lack of resources and external support. Therefore, a combination of methods is preferred, as illustrated through examples from the NSFLL project.

For the sake of clarity, the examples in the preceding section were framed in terms of a combination of RDD and PS methods. This is an oversimplification. A broader perspective suggests that the foreign language standards project is actually a combination of all three of the methods of innovation discussed in this chapter. Teacher initiatives for change (problem solving) are supported through the resources of collaborating organizations (research, development, and diffusion). These organizations, like ACTFL, also receive support and resources from federal monies (center-periphery). What allows these three methods to work together is the sharing of an objective, such as the formulation of foreign language standards.

Drawbacks of a Combined Approach to Diffusion of Curricular Innovation

This is not to suggest that the foreign language standards movement represents an ideal collaboration. Although the three change agencies (teachers, professional organizations, and government) share one objective, this does not imply that they share all objectives. For example, a teacher may see the establishment of standards as a means of improving her teaching. She may measure the attainment of this objective through formative evaluations (e.g., authentic assessments) of learner progress. In contrast, a state politician may see the establishment of standards as a means of developing objective measures of the performance of the state's schools. She may measure attainment of this objective through state scores on standardized achievement tests.

Although the teacher and the politician share an overarching goal (improved learner achievement), they may employ different methods in an attempt to attain that goal. At times these methods will be incompatible. Herein lies the major problem in the diffusion of standards. It is not the content of the standards themselves that is controversial but, rather, the methods and purposes for attaining them.

ISSUES OF ASSESSMENT

Many attempts at curricular change have been foiled due to the lack of a corresponding change in method of assessment (Savignon 1983, 1986, 1992, 1997), and issues of appropriate and effective assessment for the NSFLL are far from resolved. Although there is a need to assess learner progress toward the standards, it is important to distinguish standards from standardized tests. Assessment of progress in terms of the standards requires a move away from discrete-point tasks. Assessment needs to be multiple and formative; "Standards are met by rigorous evaluation of necessarily varied student products and performances" (Wiggins 1999).

It has been argued that the paradigm shift reflected in the NSFLL requires a similar shift to authentic models of assessment. Instead of items, authentic assessment includes projects, whose completion is not restricted to a short period of time. Such projects can be used as both summative and formative measures of learner progress. Their completion involves learners' reflection on past performance to improve their future performance (Liskin-Gasparro 1996). If introduction of an authentic model of assessment does indeed represent a paradigm shift, and therefore a curricular innovation, once again the importance of adopting the underlying pedagogy must be emphasized. "Partial adoption of alternative assessment strategies without an underlying paradigm shift in one's view of teaching and learning may jeopardize both the validity and reliability of the assessments" (Liskin-Gasparro 1996, 182; see also Chapter 5).

The above discussion of assessment is included to highlight the fact that the assessment of learner progress with respect to the standards cannot be achieved solely through the use of mandated standardized tests created outside the classroom and implemented in a strictly top-down fashion. Instead, the assessment process needs to include the active participation of teachers who share the underlying theory and pedagogy of the standards, thereby encouraging a bottom-up method of implementation. As with diffusion of the standards themselves, implementation of assessment methods would benefit most from a combination of top-down and bottom-up methods. Here once again, however, although the overarching goal is presumably shared, there remains the inherent risk of miscommunication and conflict when different methods of curriculum and assessment are advocated at different sociopolitical levels of a decentralized system of education.

Appendix: The National Foreign Language Standards Adapted from American Council for the Teaching of Foreign Languages (2000)

COMMUNICATION
Communicate in Languages Other Than English
Standard 1.1: Students engage in conversation, provide and obtain information, express feelings and emotions, and exchange opinions.
Standard 1.2: Students understand and interpret written and spoken language on a variety of topics.
Standard 1.3: Students present information, concepts, and ideas to an audience of listeners or readers on a variety of topics.

CULTURES
Gain Knowledge and Understanding of Other Cultures
Standard 2.1: Students demonstrate an understanding of the relationship between the practices and perspective of the culture studied.

Standard 2.2: Students demonstrate an understanding of the relationship between the products and perspectives of the culture studied.

CONNECTIONS
Connect with Other Disciplines and Acquire Information
Standard 3.1: Students reinforce and further their knowledge of other disciplines through the foreign language.
Standard 3.2: Students acquire information and recognize the distinctive viewpoints that are available only through the foreign language and its cultures.

COMPARISONS
Develop Insight into the Nature of Language and Culture
Standard 4.1: Students demonstrate understanding of the nature of language through comparisons of the language studied and their own.
Standard 4.2: Students demonstrate understanding of the concept of culture through comparisons of the cultures studied and their own.

COMMUNITIES
Participate in Multilingual Activities at Home and Around the World
Standard 5.1: Students use the language both within and beyond the school setting.
Standard 5.2: Students show evidence of becoming lifelong learners by using the language for personal enjoyment and enrichment.

7

Innovative Teaching in Foreign Language Contexts: The Case of Taiwan

CHAOCHANG WANG

From a sociocultural perspective, language phenomena reflect contextual needs, which, together with learner needs, have implications for language teaching. These phenomena pertain to both language use and language learning; the former is a function of an interaction of attitude, function, context, and competence; the latter has to do with language educational systems, institutional practices, and learner beliefs and attitudes. Understanding these components that inform language use and learning is a prerequisite to any pedagogical innovation. To understand English language use and learning within the context of Taiwan, a study delineated a sociolinguistic profile of English use and learning within a four-dimensional framework: attitude, function, pedagogy (Berns 1990), and learner beliefs. Data were both quantitative and qualitative and included teacher, learner, and parent questionnaire responses and interview accounts (Wang 2000).

This chapter presents only a small part of the study concerning teacher educators' perceptions of English language teaching and learning in Taiwan. The interview accounts contribute to a fuller understanding of present day English teaching and learning in Taiwan, where curricular innovation has been both encouraged and challenged. Another reason for presenting this qualitative part of the much larger study is that it provides rich information necessary for in-depth analysis and addresses research questions for which quantitative methods alone are insufficient.

Competent English users are in great demand in Taiwan, where English serves as a link language between people from different cultures and countries as well as a tool for knowledge and information exchange in culture, technology, and business. To raise Taiwanese communicative competence in English, the Ministry of Education of Taiwan (MOE) has made changes in English education policy (Wang 2000). The decision to begin English instruction at the elementary school level in 2001 and eliminate senior high school and college entrance examinations effective in 2001 and 2002, respectively, are among the more important moves in this direction.

In addition, the MOE has published new curricula for English teaching in both junior and senior high schools which exhibit features of communication-based teaching and guide material development and classroom practices. As a result, the textbooks for the junior high schools published in 1998 show great improvement (Chen and Huang 1999). Each book (one per semester) has colorful pictures and short daily-life dialogues. Lessons are arranged according to themes and functions of communication. Speaking and listening skills are the focus of teaching. New textbooks developed for senior high school learners have been in use since fall 1999. Each senior high school maintains the right to select textbooks that fit the needs of learners and teachers. (This parallels the teacher role in textbook selection in Hong Kong described in Chapter 5.)

Changes have also been made in English language assessment, including making examination content practical, interesting, and relevant to learners' daily lives (Chang 1993, cf. Chapter 5). A listening component has been added to junior high school exams, and several years ago a written composition was added to the joint college entrance exam. These changes in test design are intended to have positive effects on English language teaching, leaving more time for listening and writing activities.

Despite the great demand for competent English users and attempts to improve English teaching and learning, however, results have been disappointing. Many who have tried to learn English for years are still not competent in the language (Huang 1995; Liang 1994). English teaching methods have been blamed for learner frustration and disappointment (Huang 1995). According to Ho (1994), two types of teaching approaches can be found in English language classrooms in Taiwan: grammar-translation and communication-based. The former continues to prevail (Ho 1994; Huang 1998; Wang 1999a). Although difficulties in promoting innovative English teaching in many ESL/EFL contexts, including teacher or learner resistance, learning and teaching context, and the educational system, have been documented (Anderson 1993;

Dam and Gabrielsen 1988; Li 1998; LoCastro 1996; Nunan 1993; Sato and Kleinsasser 1999a), research reporting difficulties within the context of Taiwan is sparse (Chen-Wang, Platt, and Stakenas 1999; Ho 1994). The full-scale investigation of the perceptions of teacher educators, high school teachers and learners, and parents, from which the teacher educator interview data reported here were drawn, was undertaken with a view to understanding and facilitating the implementation of innovative communicative approaches to language teaching (CLT).

Although the Taiwanese government has put much emphasis on teaching English for communicative competence and has developed high school curricula with that goal in mind, how this top-down policy is perceived by practitioners and affects English language classroom instruction remains unknown. Thus, the research question to be answered was: How are learner needs addressed in English language classrooms and teacher education programs?

How the Teacher Educators Were Surveyed

Participants in this study were six teacher educators, selected because of their rich experience in training teachers and far-reaching influence in the field of English teaching in Taiwan. At the time of their interviews, they either had been or were currently in charge of the English teacher program in the universities where they were teaching. Five participants were from normal universities; the sixth taught at a university in the central part of Taiwan. They were interviewed individually for about one hour. The teacher educators selected for interviews were unknown personally to the researcher to avoid a "backyard effect."

Following the interview, each teacher educator was asked to respond to a one-page survey about their beliefs regarding English teaching and learning. Two interviewees did not respond to the survey. Then the researcher recorded her impressions in a fieldwork journal at home. The interview data, transcribed verbatim, field notes, and the survey responses were analyzed. Each survey item receiving a score higher than the midpoint (4) was considered one with which the interviewee agreed.

To preserve the validity of the conclusions drawn from the analysis of the interview data, the researcher tried to collect data that were accurate and complete, and the interpretation of data was from the perspective of the teachers interviewed rather than her own. The researcher also paid attention to discrepant data and considered alternative explanations of the phenomena

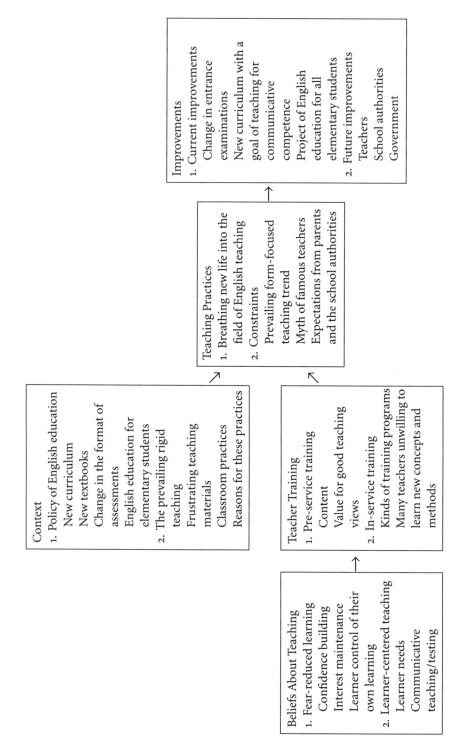

Figure 7.1. Visual model for interview analysis.

Context
1. Policy of English education
   New curriculum
   New textbooks
   Change in the format of assessments
   English education for elementary students
2. The prevailing rigid teaching
   Frustrating teaching materials
   Classroom practices
   Reasons for these practices

Teacher Training
1. Pre-service training
   Content
   Value for good teaching views
2. In-service training
   Kinds of training programs
   Many teachers unwilling to learn new concepts and methods

Beliefs About Teaching
1. Fear-reduced learning
   Confidence building
   Interest maintenance
   Learner control of their own learning
2. Learner-centered teaching
   Learner needs
   Communicative teaching/testing

Teaching Practices
1. Breathing new life into the field of English teaching
2. Constraints
   Prevailing form-focused teaching trend
   Myth of famous teachers
   Expectations from parents and the school authorities

Improvements
1. Current improvements
   Change in entrance examinations
   New curriculum with a goal of teaching for communicative competence
   Project of English education for all elementary students
2. Future improvements
   Teachers
   School authorities
   Government

studied. The researcher used different people and methods to understand teacher educators' views. Seeking feedback about data from participants was also helpful.

Based on analysis of the transcribed interviews, themes that emerged include (1) teaching context, (2) beliefs about teaching and learning, (3) teacher training, (4) practices, and (5) future improvements. The practices of teachers who have completed training in normal universities are influenced by the beliefs of their teacher educators as well as by the training they have received. The current context of English teaching and learning also contributes to their practices, in turn providing teacher educators with insights into what needs to be done to improve high school English teaching. The following descriptive analysis has taken into account the educators' survey responses as well as the researcher's field notes.

The Context of English Language Teaching and Learning

The context of English teaching and learning necessarily affects English language teaching in high school. It is relevant to both current English language educational policy and the prevailing rigidity of English teaching practice.

CURRENT ENGLISH LANGUAGE EDUCATION POLICY

Given recent national gains in international status and the current great demand for English language users in Taiwan, education policy aims to enhance the English language competence of all Taiwanese and increase the number of English users. Recent policy decisions on all levels have affected English learning. One change is a new curriculum for junior and senior high schools published in 1994 and 1995. It clearly states that communication-oriented teaching is a principle for high school textbook writing and classroom instruction. New textbooks for junior high school students featuring activities for communicative language teaching were compiled and published in 1997 and have been in use in junior high schools across the island. New textbooks for senior high school have been in use since fall 1999.

Another encouraging change, according to these teacher educators, has to do with language assessment. A listening component has been added to tests for junior high students. In addition, the current policy of screening students based on results of the joint high school and college entrance exams may be replaced by an alternative selection method that has existed for several years. If this process is adopted, students will be admitted to a senior high school or a university on the basis of teachers' recommendations and scores on tests conducted by individual schools or universities. Furthermore, an evaluation is under way of the feasibility of placement examinations for all Taiwanese conducted by the Language Testing Center. The test would assess any individual's English language competence.

The most ambitious project of all is the nationwide implementation of English education in the fifth grade and above in 2001. The aim is to teach elementary school students to understand spoken English and speak in English. To achieve this goal, three thousand teachers of a total of fifty thousand applicants for elementary certification passed a national examination in spring 1999 and received intensive pre-service training in several universities authorized by the Ministry of Education. The promotion of English education at the elementary level strongly reflects Taiwanese commitment to having children learn English. According to a study participant, most parents nowadays try in every way to prevent their children from entering school with a disadvantage: "Parents do not want their children to be losers at the starting line." The policy of teaching English in elementary school creates an equal opportunity for all children to learn the language. And the demand for more English users and parents' eagerness to have children learn English as early as possible have, in turn, created incentives for improvements in English teaching at all levels.

RIGID TEACHING PRACTICES

The policies and trend of learning English should be encouraging to both learners and teachers. The majority of learners still suffer from the long existent practice of "rigid teaching," however, and have no interest in and motivation for learning English. One teacher expert even asserted that up to two-thirds of learners experience pain and frustration while learning English. Many just give up. Most interviewees agreed that the prevailing teaching system, including both teaching materials and instructional practices, has directly diminished interest in learning and using English.

Materials used in class often frustrate learners, frequently because most reading selections are beyond their comprehension. Sometimes, the textbooks are chosen by individual teachers; typically, they are the same for all learners at the same level in a school. If teaching materials can be categorized into four groups, as one professor observed, those selected for most Taiwanese learners tend to be "frustration materials," compared to other "easy study materials," "independent learning materials," and "instructional materials." What are considered good materials are often those adopted by the "star," or well-known, schools. Problems arise when teachers use them without making adjustments according to their students' level of competence.

Even when materials are made accessible and meaningful for learners or adjusted to their needs, dullness is another characteristic of the language classroom. Most high school teaching is grammar-oriented. Grammar-translation prevails, which makes learning everyday English impossible. Instruction resembles "parrot learning," wherein students make sounds without knowing why. Also common in classrooms is the "Silent Way," as another professor participant expressed it, meaning learner silence. One teacher educator asserted that the current teaching trends are essentially unchanged: "The current trend is teaching the old way but with new textbooks" (cf. Chapter 5).

According to the teacher educators' observations and experiences with high school teachers, classroom practices reflect teachers' lack of knowledge of teaching methods and lack of support from the decision makers and parents, as well as the teachers' own views of teaching. Most English teachers, especially senior high school teachers, are competent English users. Nevertheless, being a good language user does not necessarily make one a good language teacher. "Teachers do not know how or are unable to improve themselves. This is what I have observed when visiting and giving advice to high schools islandwide," reported one educator. Teachers nationwide have no idea of how to improve their teaching and, consequently, are unable to modify their own style. Teaching in a communicative context demands much from teachers, who may not know how to incorporate the related activities. The inevitable result is that they omit the communicative activities suggested in the textbooks and use the time saved for teaching complementary materials in a more "efficient," that is, grammar-translation, fashion.

Parents' expectations concerning efficient learning also contribute to the teaching context in high school. Parents' demand for high test scores, in particular, has burdened teachers. Parents do not necessarily expect teaching to be structured around grammar, but these form-based practices are most efficient for producing immediate results. Parents can also become an obstacle to innovative teaching by consistently questioning the appropriateness of using "easy" materials or student-generated materials for classroom teaching. One professor indicated that parents may cast doubts on the flexible but to them nonroutine approach to the textbooks. Parents want routine so that they know how their children are doing in school. They want standardized answers to questions so that they can check their children's understanding. Given the importance of English language learning in Taiwan, parents' deep concerns about whether the teacher is doing the right thing are understandable.

Lack of support from school administrators is another source of frustration for teachers. Uniformity of teaching outcomes matters greatly. As a result, there is a preference for uniform, or common, textbooks, a common syllabus, and common exams. Teachers of the same level in a school teach with the same textbooks and syllabus and work together to prepare the same tests.

Teachers' own views of teaching have supported form-based instructional practices as well. Many teachers believe in the effect of "traditional" (grammar-based) teaching because that is the way they were taught. For many, it is effective and convenient. According to a professor participant, some teachers consider learners' levels of English ability or intelligence to be too low for them to benefit from more communicative approaches. Other teachers have a high regard for certain techniques in the absence of any particular theory of language teaching. They go to conferences or workshops and are satisfied with only the techniques that they can apply in their classrooms. They cannot generate activities or create contexts for more authentic use of English, as one professor indicated, owing to their lack of sound teaching principles. Another professor also expressed her concern that some teachers so value techniques that they are unable to respect learner needs and individual characteristics. She indicated that many teachers lack a philosophy of teaching. They consider themselves to teach English only as a subject. And even those who show interest in learning new teaching techniques may fall back on familiar ways, and those who are familiar with a variety of techniques may still have difficulty sustaining learner interest and motivation. Beliefs are what underlie the best teaching, which leads, in turn, to the best learning.

Beliefs About Teaching and Learning

There are two main components in these teacher educators' beliefs: fear-reduced learning and learner-centered teaching.

FEAR-REDUCED LEARNING

A common phenomenon about English learning, according to informants, is lack of student motivation. Once students have lost their interest in learning English in junior high school, which provides a basis for gaining English competence in high school and, perhaps, college, further learning often becomes frustrating and fruitless. Good teaching needs to address this problem, and the educators interviewed identified several components that may help: building confidence, maintaining interest, and allowing learners to control their own learning.

Confidence. According to these teacher educators, learners must have confidence in learning English. Three elements may help: accessible materials, spoken English that is comprehensible to them, and their own success in learning. Teaching materials that are too difficult will only perpetuate the frustration that more than half of all high school students experience. Teachers' use of English in class can also be made easier for them to understand. One participant contended that learners must understand the teacher's English; if not, they will resent both the teacher and the English language. Their confidence will also increase with their success in learning. Difficult tests will only discourage most learners. Positive experiences with English learning at the beginning stage often build up confidence and result in ultimate success.

Interest. In addition to confidence in their ability to learn English, learner interest in English needs to be encouraged. Interest will rise when learners know that the goal of learning is language use, when they are provided with everyday examples of English in the classroom instead of bookish English, and when they need not worry about making errors. Students should understand that they are learning the language for communication. A professor participant pointed out that learners lose interest because they are confused about the goal of language learning. This confusion is attributed to the fact that teaching is grammar-focused and teachers are not providing examples of everyday English. He continued, students should understand "Learning language is for use, as opposed to treating it as a decoration or a subject, gaining knowledge, or achieving high grades." An English class conducted primarily in English strengthens students' sense of language use more than one where English is not used for communication. Furthermore, a class that provides everyday English catches learners' interest more than a class with bookish English. Learners will never acquire words such as "ouch" and "whoops" in class unless the teacher uses them authentically. Learners will be more and more interested in English if they are often given frequent opportunities to use English in a learning environment where oral and written communication receive equal emphasis, an environment in which they can try to communicate with peers or adults, orally or in writing, confidently and without fear. A good example, one professor recalled, is that of a teacher who had students in one class write journals and share them with those in another class, who, in turn, wrote their own journals. Real communication takes place when students share and respond to one another. The same is true of oral communication, which can occur between students within a class or between two classes. Language use, according to the educator participants, is the key to raising and sustaining learner interest.

Students need to know when they have made an error, but the teacher's approach to correction may promote or inhibit progress. Two teacher educators consider errors natural and developmental, and they agreed that their correction may easily result in communication apprehension and, thus, hinder attempts to learn. Students need a fear-reduced environment, in which they can communicate without embarrassment or anxiety, to build confidence.

Control. As two professors mentioned, student control of their own learning is another important facet of fear-reduced learning and promotes interest and confidence. This ideal may be difficult to achieve in practice owing to the teacher's need to maintain authority and discipline. Nevertheless, giving students some control is possible. One professor suggested that learners be made responsible for preview tasks before class. Another educator asserted the benefits of having students decide what they are interested in learning and then prepare or generate materials. "Learners can be made responsible for their learning. When a student's sense of responsibility is enhanced, his/her ability will also be strengthened." Students may take charge of their own learning in many ways. Even a song that they like to learn can be developed into a lesson full of lively texts. Teachers should know how to make good use of texts and even create materials with students. The educator continued, "Teachers should be able to create a new text. Teaching materials are not fixed. They can be from any sources, from the learner, the interaction between the teacher and learners, not necessarily from the textbooks." Learners can also set their own pace of learning. One example the same professor provided is that of giving them a long list of books and having them choose among them for extensive reading at their own pace. (For further discussion of learner autonomy, see Chapter 9.)

LEARNER-CENTERED TEACHING

To provide a favorable, fear-reduced learning environment, teaching should be geared to meet learners' communication needs.

Meeting Learner Needs. All professor participants agreed that in terms of curriculum design and classroom instruction, English language teaching should be based on learner needs, which depend on goals, background, and interests. Whereas previously the goal of learning was to achieve accuracy in language use, overall language proficiency now should be valued as much, if not more, than accuracy. The ability to communicate ideas to others is more important than stating grammatical rules. Meeting learner needs also requires accounting for learning background, and teaching materials and tasks/activities should be adjusted accordingly. Remedial instruction can be provided while identifying particularly slow individual learners. As two professors suggested, strategies for meeting learner needs include providing extensive independent learning materials. Learner interest, which also contributes to fear-reduced learning, is another important facet of learner needs. The topics of teaching materials, the types of tasks, and the use of authentic materials should be relevant to learner interests. The teacher's authentic use of English also contributes greatly to learner interest. This requires more frequent use of English rather than Chinese in class, as well as the use of everyday English rather than bookish English, as mentioned above. Three professors stressed the importance of the teacher's English being "standard." They feel that a teacher with "good" pronunciation more easily attracts learners' attention and arouses their interest in learning. (The goal for English language use in Taiwan is Standard American English; see Wang 2000 for discussion.)

Communication-Based Teaching. Communication-based teaching relates to all the elements that contribute to learner-centered teaching. According to the professor participants, it is task-oriented as well as authentic in terms of teaching materials and language use. Tasks designed for communicative teaching encourage interaction in the process of making meaning. A variety of activities with the needed equipment (or props) engage students and promote learning. One professor felt that group tasks, such as drama activities, are especially fruitful. Communicative teaching also entails the use of authentic materials and the use of English in class. Authenticity, according to one professor, is the presentation or the use of real-life English: "Actually, ideal language teaching should go with very, very authentic language materials from which students learn to use English." Authenticity can be realized by using materials relevant to learners' daily life, materials generated from or by them, and the teacher's use of practical English. In spite of the more communicative characteristics of new textbooks, English teachers either lack the ability to provide more natural and context-appropriate English, or they devalue its importance. As a consequence, learners are less likely to use authentic English.

Testing. Even with teachers' best efforts, communicative teaching becomes unfeasible without a change in assessment. According to all teacher educators interviewed, assessment must be improved to promote communicative language teaching. Teaching that adapts to learner differences needs diverse evaluation methods. Both students and their parents will notice mismatches between communicative teaching and traditional standardized discrete-point testing. A professor agreed that the format of assessment should not be limited to pencil and paper examinations. The use of learner portfolios and the teacher's observation of learner interaction in class are a few examples of many ways to evaluate learner achievements. The professor contended that teachers and the administrative staff who stick to common tests for the sake of convenience ultimately sacrifice the benefits of adjusting to learners' individuality.

Teacher Training

The educator participants in this investigation agreed that they have tried to convey their beliefs to prospective teachers and teachers in their classes through pre-service and in-service programs. Pre-service teacher training for prospective high school teachers is mainly through the English teaching departments of three normal universities in Taiwan, situated in the Taipei, Taichung, and Kaohsiung areas. In addition, the Ministry of Education has authorized other universities to provide English teacher education. The difference between English teachers who graduated from normal universities and those from general universities lies in the length of the training period. The former receive four years of training plus a one-year practicum, and the latter, two years of training and a one-month practicum. The pre-service training discussed in the following section is limited to normal universities. In-service training is achieved through different programs designed for current high school teachers. A forty-credit, master's degree–equivalent program in the National Taiwan Normal University has been replaced by a master's degree program similar to those offered at the other two normal universities. These universities also provide various evening classes for advanced studies. In addition, government-supported workshops and seminars are offered, ranging from several days to several weeks.

PRE-SERVICE TRAINING

Based on these professor participants' accounts, not all teachers absorb teacher educators' beliefs about language learning and teaching during their training. To obtain this exposure, a prospective teacher has to go through a four-year training program that emphasizes language skills, teaching methodology, and knowledge of English (e.g., linguistics and phonetics), as well as a teaching practicum in the fifth year. In addition, prospective teachers have to observe actual English classes during the term of training. Most teacher educators agreed that observing real teaching is important for understanding the dynamics of a classroom. One professor indicated that to nurture English teachers, they have trainees start observing classes in their second year of training. Another professor noted that once a prospective teacher enters the program, he or she should start to learn to be a teacher, not only by observing others, but also by volunteering as a teacher assistant.

Most professors said that they communicate their beliefs and the concepts of teaching to teachers in training. They agreed that although methods and techniques do facilitate teaching and learning, correct understanding of teaching is the most important element in a good teacher. Teachers who account for learner needs and attempt to provide fear-free environments better adapt methods and techniques to promote learning. One professor indicated that beliefs associated with effective teaching often lead to correct use of methods and techniques. Generally speaking, the educators are satisfied with what their programs offer to train prospective teachers, with the exception of one participant who felt there was insufficient general training in Taiwan. Much needs to be done to improve teacher training, such as better role models for prospective teachers, more classroom observation, and an additional qualifying examination before one is launched on a teaching career.

IN-SERVICE TRAINING

On-the-job training for teachers is not compulsory. Teachers may choose to participate in the various kinds of training programs described above. Some teachers attend general master's degree programs during the year, and some spend four summers in the programs. Many attend short-term training programs or seminars and workshops sponsored by the MOE or local board of education. According to three of the professor participants, however, most teachers are not interested in learning new ideas about teaching and, therefore, are not willing to try to improve their own teaching. According to one professor's account, many senior teachers see no new ideas in seminars and feel that their listening and speaking does not need improvement because, after all, they can use Chinese to teach English. Although teachers are required to accumulate eighteen credits per year (one hour equals one credit) by attending conferences or seminars/workshops, the requirement is not followed or enforced. Another professor asserted that more than 80 percent of teachers are unwilling to accept new views: "Teachers have no incentives and motivations. Conservatively estimated, more than half or more precisely more than 80 percent of high school teachers do not want to learn new ideas about teaching. They say, 'I've been teaching this way for twenty years. Why should I change?'" In recent years, as a result of the new communicative curriculum for high school English, hundreds of seminars and workshops have been held by the government and publishers all over the island to promote communicative teaching practices. Young faces are most often seen on these occasions; the presence of senior teachers is simply not expected.

Practices

BREATHING NEW LIFE INTO ENGLISH TEACHING

Teachers who complete training at normal universities in Taiwan tend to form their beliefs about teaching during this period. Based on these beliefs, they are generally able to design activities and manipulate techniques and visual aids to create contexts for language use. In addition, they have the ability to speak in English most of the time. One professor interviewee said she has often advised her students to "stick to your beliefs. You should not mistakenly believe that teaching for language use leads to below average test results, and that test-oriented instructional practices result in average or above average scores. You are to breathe new life into the field of English teaching instead of following the trend." Teachers newly graduated from normal universities may well have helped rejuvenate the profession of English teaching. Generally speaking, the teacher educator participants are satisfied with their graduates' practices, given their teaching contexts, which may greatly affect their instruction.

CONSTRAINTS

Perhaps a universal truth is that instructional practices are context-bound. Teachers should be prepared to adapt to learner needs, but context often limits what can be done. According to the participants' accounts, a variety of constraints frustrate many teacher learners: prevailing form-focused teaching, the myth of "famous" teachers (teachers who best prepare students for test-taking), the compulsory use of a common test, materials, and syllabus, and the expectations of both parents and school authorities. (See Chapter 3 for discussion of the Japanese context; for discussion of the same issue within the U.S. context see Savignon and Kleinsasser 1992.)

As the professor participants indicated, the common practices in both senior and junior high school are form-based, with the grammar-translation method most frequently used. Enthusiastic new teachers who are full of high ideals create a vibrant atmosphere. One interviewee shared an observation from a workshop in a new high school that had recruited many young teachers. Several of these teachers demonstrated the communicative instructional practices they applied in their classrooms. Their attempts illustrated the feasibility of teaching in an interactive way. Many other teachers in other high schools with form-based teaching, however, are struggling between the old and the new ways of teaching English. The pressure of keeping up with the common syllabus that requires teachers to cover identical materials for the same examinations may influence them to do their jobs the easier way.

School administrators' emphasis on test results also pushes teachers away from their ideals.

This value placed on test results has also led to the myth of "famous teachers." The "good" teachers, whose students score highest on tests, are often assigned to "first-section" students, considered to be the best students, whereas young teachers are often given "last-section" learners, those whose motivation and interest in English learning quickly vanish. In addition, parents' expectations of immediate learning results often influence administrative decisions.

One professor reported the experiences of newly graduated teachers in public and private schools. A teacher may have some freedom teaching in a public school, especially with first-year students on junior and senior levels. By contrast, newly graduated teachers in private schools, which are often dedicated to raising the proportion of students admitted to good senior high schools or universities and colleges, have even less freedom and may be tremendously frustrated. Overall, whether in a public or private school and with little support from others, young teachers may breathe a new life into the teaching field that may promote a change, or they may be submerged in the mighty torrent of form-focused teaching. Senior teachers, who have attained high prestige, are influential in decision making. The implementation of young teachers' ideal practices may depend on support from not only the school authorities and parents but also senior teachers.

Improvements

Much has been done to meet the demand for competent English users and effective teaching in Taiwan. Current improvements, according to the teacher experts, include the change in entrance examinations, the new curriculum with a goal of teaching for communicative competence, and the islandwide implementation in 2001 of English education in the elementary schools. However, more has to be done to ensure quality teaching and learning in the classrooms. Based on the teacher experts' accounts, further improvements can be stratified into three interrelated levels related to teachers, school authorities, and the government. Each is essential to the success of the other efforts.

Teachers' willingness to make constant changes for the better is what leads to overall advances in English education in Taiwan. Teachers interested in self-improvement seek help from different sources. They try to understand learner characteristics and adapt their teaching to meet learner needs instead of their own convenience. Only with a readiness to learn and improve can teachers implement new teaching concepts and be better able to gain the support of decision makers and parents. In addition to teachers being open to new approaches, the government, the school authorities, and parents must provide resources and support.

School authorities should give individual teachers more freedom in the selection of teaching materials and tests so they can use components that are appropriate for their students. Teachers should also be encouraged to try various instructional practices and be respected for the decisions they make for their students. Furthermore, without the elimination of the "famous teachers" myth, any support for learner-centered teaching tends to be meaningless; teachers remain primarily concerned with producing good test-takers. School administrators need to understand that common exams, which are often discrete-point for the sake of convenience, do not necessarily measure language ability. Therefore, "famous teachers," who are known for their expertise in teaching lexico-grammar and test-taking skills, do not necessarily produce competent language users. Administrators also need to know that teaching for language use takes longer to yield results than the "traditional" way of teaching for accuracy, and that, consequently, more diverse ways of evaluating learning effects should be encouraged. Not only do school policy makers need to know the above, so do parents concerned with teaching and learning "immediate outcomes." School authorities may need to help teachers communicate their views of teaching to parents. Parent workshops, one professor suggested, may help achieve this goal.

Finally, the Ministry of Education should provide more seminars, workshops, and teacher training programs accessible to any English teachers seeking self-improvement. While many forms of encouragement can be given to teachers willing to learn, given the unsatisfactory implementation of the eighteen-credit plan, the MOE should contemplate new ways to reach teachers who are unwilling to explore new concepts and methods of teaching. Much remains to be done to help raise the overall competence of English language use. It requires the ideas and efforts of all concerned: students, parents, administrators, and teachers.

Generally speaking, considerable efforts have been made toward innovative change in English language teaching to meet contextual and learner needs in Taiwan. Nevertheless, progress is slow. From the teacher educators' views of English teaching/learning in Taiwan reported above, summary conclusions can be drawn. Communication-based teaching is being promoted to meet learner needs; however, grammar-based instruction continues to prevail.

Promotion of Communication-Based Teaching

Communication-based teaching is promoted through educational policy and teacher programs. The teacher educators' accounts reveal that current policy in Taiwan encourages teaching English at all levels to develop communicative competence. Arising from external needs, this policy guides teaching in terms of materials development and instructional practices. The goal of promoting English learning for all Taiwanese reflects and directs efforts to meet the increasing demand for competent English users and Taiwanese eagerness for learning English. The project of extending English education to the elementary schools islandwide in 2001 illustrates the relation between policy and context.

Since 1997, nineteen grade schools in Taipei and several in Kaohsiung, the second largest city in Taiwan, have taken the lead by teaching English to third graders and, following the first year of implementation, to students above third grade (Her 1998). In fact, English education in grade school is inevitable because of the long existing and growing trend for parents to send their children to private language institutes or "buhsibans" for an early start in order to better compete with peers. More than one-quarter of elementary schoolchildren in Taiwan are learning English in private language institutes (*China Central News*, April 6, 1999), and nearly three-quarters of elementary schoolchildren in Taipei have studied English in private language institutes (*China Times*, January 6, 2000).

The policy of English education in the elementary schools gives all children the opportunity to learn English. A further example of the widespread interest in promoting English language study is the government's plan to extend English education to all Taiwanese, starting with adults engaged in professions: taxi drivers, hotel and restaurant attendants, ticket sellers and salesclerks in tourism, traffic police, and telephone operators (*Liberty Times*, January 7, 2000). The MOE has also published a new curriculum for English teaching in high school. The new curriculum indicates that the goal of learning English is both for oral and written communication and for cultural awareness. It guides English teaching, materials development, and test design. New textbooks for junior high school students reflect this goal, as do the textbooks selected by individual senior high schools for first-year students. In the area of assessment, a listening component has been added to tests and entrance examinations for individual junior high schools, and a composition component now appears in the English subtest in the joint college entrance examinations.

For all these changes, progress in language classroom practices is slow, a phenomenon seen in other countries with a top-down policy of educational change (LoCastro 1996; see also Chapters 2, 3, and 5). However, the interview data from teacher educators support learner, parent, and teacher questionnaire data showing that teaching English for communicative use is believed to be important (Wang 2000). This suggests that the policy of teaching English for communicative competence in Taiwan is not strictly top-down, but also takes into account needs reflected in Taiwanese attitudes toward English and the attitudes and beliefs about English teaching and learning of all concerned.

According to the teacher educators in this study, communication-based teaching in Taiwan is also promoted through English teacher programs in normal universities. These universities prepare teachers to meet contextual and learner needs through communication-based teaching. The programs feature learner-centered teaching that entails fear-reduced learning. The instructors also believe that the teacher needs to adjust instructional practices to learner characteristics, interests, and competence. The teacher educator survey response findings were consistent with these views. The educators convey their beliefs about promoting quality teaching through both preservice and in-service teaching programs that emphasize language skills, teaching methodology, knowledge of English (e.g., linguistics and phonetics), and real English class observations. They considered that most of their graduates can teach according to the principles learned during their training.

Grammar-Based Instruction Remains Prevalent

Despite educational policies designed to meet contextual needs and the efforts of teacher education programs to promote quality teaching, classroom practices in high school English remain essentially form-based. This study of teacher educators' views includes reports of low learner motivation. The teacher educators' accounts noted the predominance of grammar-focused practices. These findings support those of Wang (1999a, 1999b), who found a mismatch between high school classroom practices and learner needs. The conclusions also corroborate those of Huang (1998), who observed a discrepancy between senior high school students' ideal of learning and their actual classroom experience, as well as those of Chou (1999) which revealed a mismatch between classroom reality and the perceived needs for instructional emphases of two-year college learners as well as those of their teachers.

The prevalence of form-focused instruction is thus clear. The interview analysis in this study shows the majority of high school learners to be frustrated with and afraid of English language learning. They suffer from the practice of "rigid teaching," which is not helped by the continued use of "frustrational" materials and grammar-based instructional practices. However, reports (e.g., Chen and Huang 1999) reveal satisfaction with new textbooks in junior high school and with the resultant classroom practices. In Chen and Huang's study, junior high school teachers report that they like the new textbooks, are changing their teaching methods, and find their students more willing to participate in class. While overall satisfaction with the new teaching materials is quite possible, data concerning learner views and the way teachers use these materials are needed.

Reasons Why Learner Needs Are Addressed the Way They Are

From the teacher educators' accounts, the school context and parents' and teachers' views concerning English teaching seem to perpetuate the prevailing form-based teaching in Taiwan. These factors also contribute to difficulties experienced by new teachers in sustaining communication-oriented teaching.

FACTORS CONTRIBUTING TO FORM-BASED INSTRUCTION

Crucial elements contributing to the school context include the value of teaching outcomes and "famous teachers," as well as lack of support and resources for innovative change. Ho (1994) and Chen-Wang, Platt, and Stakenas (1999) also identify teachers' perceived difficulties in teaching for communication. Ho (1994) suggests that teachers who believe in communication-oriented instruction often feel frustrated with the emphasis on test results and the corresponding grammar-focused teaching. Teacher participants in a study by Chen-Wang, Platt, and Stakenas (1999) reported that language use in teaching was an unrealistic goal in view of constraints such as the restricted test format and insufficient class time for communicative practice.

Parents' concerns about how teachers go about their tasks also contribute to resistance to change. The value placed on immediate learning outcomes and queries about materials or practices may drive teachers away from the new and back to the old approaches. Wachob (1995) has also reported teachers' tendency to adjust instruction to parents' concerns. Although private English institutes for children usually focus on speaking and listening, many parents demand quizzes at every class meeting, and, as a result, Wachob observes, "teaching hours are full of quizzes and exams" (528). Similarly, Chinese parents in a study by Cortazzi and Jin (1996) exhibit zealous concerns about their children's diligence.

In addition to the school context and parents' concerns, teacher views of

English language teaching are most influential in the perpetuation of form-based teaching, especially the grammar-translation method. Some teachers believe in the importance of form-based instruction, and others have no teaching philosophy. They are interested only in techniques and adapt these techniques without consideration of underlying theory.

This finding relating to teachers' views supports that of Chen-Wang, Platt, and Stakenas (1999; see also Chapter 6). However, these authors consider Chinese language learning and cultural practices the best explanation for continued form-based emphasis. They observe that Chinese language learning stresses words and grammar and requires learners to memorize and recite passages in a teacher-centered classroom. In addition, learner silence in the classroom is highly valued. Learners are expected to give their opinions only when asked. Teachers are highly respected for their knowledge, and their role is to transmit knowledge to their students. Cortazzi and Jin (1996) also consider the "traditional" grammar-based method of English teaching to have its root in Chinese literacy education. Discrete practices for learning Chinese are common, and there is usually a fixed order of learning. Students often have to learn Chinese starting with characters, then words and phrases, sentences, paragraphs, and longer texts (183).

Although grammar-based teaching may be culturally situated, it is not particular to Taiwan and other Asian countries. Steele (1996) contends that all language teaching remained essentially grammar-translation until the 1960s. Freudenstein (1996) also indicates that language teaching in Europe has not changed significantly, "One of the main problems is that 40–60 percent of the time available for language instruction is devoted to the teaching of formal grammar . . . and I think that the situation in other European countries and in other parts of the world is not very much different" (45). Therefore, form-based teaching is not limited to Taiwan. To achieve an objective of language use beyond reading and writing, teaching methods must change.

NEW TEACHERS' DIFFICULTIES

Analysis of teacher educators' accounts reveals that they feel graduates from their programs are able to engage in change. Young teachers are willing to learn and improve. Wang's (1998) study of teachers' views about in-service training programs also indicates that young teachers are more involved in learning how to improve their teaching. The teacher educators' views in this study also indicate that teachers who are willing to make changes are often frustrated with the social context in which they find themselves and, as a result, may teach in the easier "traditional" way. In addition to school values and limited support that affect teacher performance, the prevailing grammar-based teaching has become a factor itself. A change becomes impossible without the collective efforts including all involved. The senior teachers who constitute the majority may be more influential in changing the common practice. Finding ways to include all those involved in English language teaching, above all teachers who do not know how and why to change the way they teach, may be among the most important challenges to meeting contextual needs.

Creating a Technical Culture that Encourages Innovative Teaching

Although there are difficulties in averting the prevailing "rigid teaching" and promoting innovative teaching that engages learners in meaning making, it is essential to do so. Much has been done in Taiwan to facilitate the integration of a communicative component in terms of curriculum design, material development, and change in the examination system, but this remains insufficient for satisfactory teaching to occur. This study suggests that teachers need support both from the school and from parents, whose concern for immediate learning outcomes as shown on tests places teachers in a predicament.

When teachers attempt to adopt innovative teaching in the classroom, support from the school, staff, and parents will help sustain their efforts. Implicit in Kleinsasser's (1993) study is the notion that schools may exhibit two main kinds of technical cultures, one culture in which teachers are more certain about their instructional practices and go about their daily tasks nonroutinely, and the other with teachers more uncertain about the effects of their teaching skills and more routine with their tasks. The main variables seem to be teacher collaboration and a concern for teacher learning, as well as fair and helpful evaluation. These variables and others interrelate to form a culture that is either "learning-enriched" or isolated. The more the school environment encourages collegiality and communication, the more teacher learning opportunities there are. Teachers who feel that the evaluation of their teaching is fair are less likely to be frustrated and more willing to exchange ideas with others and involve parents.

Central to a learning-enriched culture for teaching in Taiwan is an atmosphere of teacher cooperation in which teachers enhance instructional skills, explore new teaching practices, and become involved in policy decisions related to quality teaching. However, prerequisite to collegial collaboration is a fair evaluation of teacher performance. The present implicit value placed on "famous teachers" and producing "good students" is detrimental to the trusting environment essential for teacher collaboration.

However difficult the social context makes innovative teaching—and the favorable attitude toward English and need for competent users may make it easier in Taiwan than elsewhere—the crucial element is the teacher, who makes decisions in the classroom and is most effective in persuading those concerned. Evidence in this study indicates that teachers do not know how to teach communicatively or even why they should. Therefore, they need not only methods and techniques but also opportunity to understand major theories and concepts to help them make sense of how and why they teach the way they do (cf. Chapters 5 and 6).

CLT as Guidelines for Developing Context-Dependent Practices

The new curriculum for teaching high school English in Taiwan has a goal of communicative competence in speaking, writing, listening, reading, and culture awareness. Therefore, CLT, which is designed to enhance learners' communicative competence, is more appropriate than other methodologies in developing the ability for "interpretation, expression, and negotiation of meaning" (Savignon 1983, 1991, 1997, 2000). This ability to make meaning is essentially developed through authentic use of English, a view shared by teacher educators in this study.

Teachers concerned with providing opportunities for optimal interactions in the classroom try to discover and meet learner needs, two major steps toward the realization of CLT. Unraveling the overt and the embedded—that is, what learners bring to the classroom and expect from their teachers—promotes meaningful or true communication and, thus, meets learners' communicative needs and raises their interest in learning English.

Finally, and most important for English teachers in Taiwan, CLT sheds light on curriculum design and implementation. As observed by the teacher educators, many teachers do not know how to teach in a communicative way. Instead of always depending on developed techniques and methods, teachers with knowledge of CLT will find inspiration for designing their own methods and materials, contributing to the expansion of communication-based teaching.

Changing Beliefs

Promoting teachers' understanding of language learning theories helps inform their practice. In contrast, the expectation that they will apply received knowledge, methods, and techniques indiscriminately undermines their ability to theorize their practice and inhibits their professional growth. As the results of this study show, teachers who are interested only in techniques and apply them in their classrooms may conveniently fall back on older, easier ways of teaching. Teachers must recognize their leading role in designing teaching practices appropriate to the context constructed by learners and themselves. No less important is their involvement in school change efforts and gaining support from the staff and the administration. Empowerment for such a role comes through constant questioning of one's teaching practices and practical theories and continuously making improvements in teaching (Britzman 1991; Johnson 1995; Zeichner and Liston 1996). Preparing teachers to examine their beliefs about teaching and their actual performance is an indispensable component in any teacher training program if this is to be realized in subsequent teaching practice.

Directions for Further Research

This study has several limitations. The teacher educators in this study have noted the negative impact of the social context on teacher performance and identified its main constituents. Teachers' perceptions of their own work and the social context in which they are situated are crucial for understanding teaching and promoting innovative change. Future research might extend to classroom observation and interviews with teachers for their perceptions about and the factors that influence their performance.

Although the interviews with teacher educators in this study provided rich information about how context and learner needs are addressed, this study did not explore fully the process by which prospective teachers shape their practical knowledge. The teacher educators indicated that they communicate their beliefs and the concepts of teaching to learners. Do the prospective teachers just absorb the beliefs and knowledge their professors convey and form their own practical knowledge? Do teacher beliefs change after training? Further studies should address these questions, perhaps through multiple interviews with teacher educators. Moreover, interviews with teacher learners investigating their views about good teaching before and after training and the ways they construct their knowledge about teaching may be especially helpful for the design of teacher education programs.

8

The Use of Technology in High-Enrollment Courses: Implications for Teacher Education and Communicative Language Teaching

DIANE MUSUMECI

The impact of technology on contemporary academic life is ubiquitous: it clings to the architecture of the academy like the ivy of old. Students register via computer for their classes; professors hold "virtual" office hours when they are available online to their students; e-mail correspondence is commonplace to the point that we refer to the other type as "snail mail." And as institutions of higher learning attempt to cope with rapidly expanding enrollments and diminishing resources, it seems natural that they look to instructional technology for solutions. Distance education and Web-based instruction are changing the very nature of the traditional university, as bytes and modems replace bricks and mortar.

The debate over the future of the university in the digital age is ongoing, and I will not address it here, except to assert that technology will not be eradicated, regardless of how disconcerting the consequences to the status quo (Duderstadt 1997; Jaffee 1998). Nor will I address the multiple ways in which technology has been used to support second language teaching. Warschauer and Kern (2000) have compiled an excellent collection of articles in that regard. My purpose in this essay is to report on a particular use of technology in a foreign language setting in which existing resources could not meet instructional demand and technology was used to increase access, to support communicative language teaching, and to maintain or enhance learning outcomes. Furthermore, the project met these objectives in a way that was satisfactory to both students and instructors as well as cost-effective for the university. The results of the project provide insights into foreign language teacher education in general, and communicative language teaching in particular.

Background on the Spanish Project at the University of Illinois

Spanish is the most widely taught language in the United States other than English. More than three million secondary school students study it each year. However, 94 percent of those do so for less than two years, creating a huge population of "false beginners." When these students seek to continue their study of Spanish at the post-secondary level, colleges and universities lack the resources to support existing, let alone increasing, demand. The Spanish Project at the University of Illinois at Urbana-Champaign (UIUC) was initiated to determine the extent to which technology could redistribute instructional resources to accommodate the demand for Spanish language instruction.

At UIUC, two fifteen-week semesters, one fall and one spring, constitute the regular academic year. The conventional model for teaching first and second year Spanish (and other languages as well) has been to offer classes four times per week in sections of twenty-three to twenty-five students each (according to the Modern Language Association of America recommendations for the ideal class size for foreign language instruction). Graduate students who hold teaching assistantships teach the sections. They receive a tuition and fee waiver in addition to a monthly stipend based on their percentage appointment. (One class per semester is equivalent to a 25 percent appointment; two classes are a 50 percent appointment.) In this conventional model, the graduate student instructor with a 25 percent appointment meets a group of about twenty-four students, four days per week in fifty-minute sessions, for each fifteen-week semester. Under the supervision of a faculty member who directs the language program, the graduate student instructors cover grammar, vocabulary, reading, and communication skills in class. Writing, usually in the form of compositions, is normally done outside of class; and students are assigned homework after each class session. Although the director of the language program specifies the syllabus for the course, the individual instructors are responsible for daily lesson plans, classroom teaching, the grading of homework, exams, and compositions, and record keeping. In Spanish, two examinations—a midterm and a final—are common to all sections of a basic language course. These exams are prepared jointly by the instructors and the course supervisor. In addition, the supervisor prepares two listening comprehension tests, also common to all sections, which are administered and graded by the instructors.

As described, the conventional model for foreign language instruction typically allowed the department of Spanish, Italian, and Portuguese to offer a maximum of sixteen sections of its intensive first semester course for false beginners, Spanish 122, each fall semester, with fewer sections in the spring. That is, each fall the department was able to accommodate an enrollment of 384 students, with anywhere from eight graduate teaching assistants teaching two sections each to sixteen graduate teaching assistants each teaching one section, or some combination thereof. Because the quality and integrity of the graduate program limits the number of graduate students that the department can accept, graduate student instructors are an extremely valuable but limited resource. Thus, the department was never able to meet student demand and simply turned away students after the course was full.

Based on the successful outcomes of earlier technology projects involving the first two semester courses in Italian (Musumeci 1997b) and a fifth-semester Spanish grammar course (Arvan et al. 1998), Spanish 122 and its follow-up course in the basic language curriculum, Spanish 103, were reconfigured to incorporate instructional technology. Instead of meeting four times a week, class meetings were reduced to two. Class instruction focused on communication skills only: oral interaction and negotiation of meaning. In class, students are fully immersed in the second language as they engage in a variety of task-based activities, primarily in the form of in-class surveys, interviews, and jigsaws, identified in their texts as activities for "comunicación" (Van Patten, Lee, and Ballman 1996). The vocabulary, grammar, and reading instruction with accompanying exercises from the students' texts and workbooks were converted, with the publisher's permission, to an online format in Mallard. Mallard, developed by a UIUC professor, is a Web-based application that offers automated grading of exercises, provides immediate feedback on students' responses, allows students multiple attempts to improve their scores, maintains deadlines for the completion of exercises, and automatically submits students' scores to their instructors (along with information regarding the number of attempts required to reach the score and the amount of time spent on each exercise). Writing assignments were also changed from conventional, formal compositions to online conferencing using FirstClass! (a commercially available software). For their online writing, students were grouped by section and were required to make one original post and one reply to another student's post per week, each post consisting of at least one hundred words in Spanish, for a total of sixteen messages per semester.

The redistribution of resources within the new technology-enhanced model increased enrollment capacity in Spanish 122 by 60 percent while it reduced class size from twenty-four students per section to twenty. The change was made possible by changing a 25 percent appointment to include two sections of twenty students twice per week per semester, instead of one group of twenty-four four times per week per semester. As a result, enrollment capacity increased to 640 students in thirty-two sections of Spanish 122 during the fall 1998 semester, with no parallel increase in the number of instructors.

Impact of the Spanish Project on Teaching and Learning

Although the number of hours spent in class was cut in half for students, it did not change for instructors, who were still required to teach four times per week. In exchange for being responsible for more students, however, the instructors' weekly preparations were reduced from four lessons to two and, in fact, since the course supervisor supplied daily lesson plans, were almost completely obviated. The instructors' workload changed in other significant ways as well. While they continued to be responsible for reading students' writing, in the online format instructors were required to respond very briefly once per week only to its content—not to correct it and provide detailed feedback as they had with the compositions. Moreover, they were no longer responsible for grading or maintaining deadlines for the submission of homework assignments since this task was completely automated in Mallard. Finally, the listening comprehension tests were converted to a machine-scored format, as was at least 50 percent of the midterm and final examinations, further reducing the amount of human grading. Paper shuffling was practically eliminated from the course.

As a result of the incorporation of technology in the revised model, the delivery of basic language instruction in Spanish increased enrollment capacity by 60 percent with no increase in instructional staff. That is, in the intensive course for false beginners, instead of eight teaching assistants offering sixteen sections with twenty-four students per section, the same number of instructors offered thirty-two sections with twenty students per section. At the same time, instructor workload was held constant or diminished, in compliance with a contract limit of ten hours per week for a 25 percent appointment. Daily lesson plans reduced the instructors' class preparation to almost zero and computer grading of homework further lightened instructors' responsibilities, as did the use of machine scoring for a significant part of the exams. Nonetheless, the efficiencies produced by the new model would have been worthless without an assessment of learning outcomes.

To that effect, students' performance on the Spanish placement exam, pre- and post-Spanish 122, were compared to determine the increase in scores of those who took the course within the conventional model the previous spring semester and of those who took the course in the technology-enhanced version during the fall. Statistical analyses revealed that students in the technology-enhanced model had significantly higher gain scores than did the students who had completed the course in the conventional way. Comparison of students' performance on the departmental listening comprehension tests and midterm exam revealed no significant difference between the groups. And although the students in the conventionally taught course scored slightly higher on the final exam (a mean difference of five points out of one hundred), subsequent detailed analyses of the exams revealed substantive differences in scoring procedures that compromised the comparability of the results. In other words, the machine scoring of the exams that was introduced under the technology-enhanced model to reduce instructor workload (given the 60 percent increase in the total number of exams to be graded), in conjunction with unpredicted human scoring error in the conventionally taught course, resulted in a more accurate but harsher grading of the exams of the students in the technology-enhanced course. Despite the discrepancy in the final exam scores between groups, there was no significant difference in students' final grades in the course. Thus, the sum of the statistical analyses strongly suggests that students in the technology-enhanced course performed at least as well as or, in the case of the gain scores on the placement exam, better than students in the conventional course.

Implications for Teacher Education: Workload and Satisfaction Issues

The success of the Spanish Project, currently in its fourth iteration, cannot be attributed to any single factor. Certainly, the campuswide support for the project (including supplying the department with high-speed desktop computers and wiring in all of the graduate teaching assistants' offices), the infrastructure of the university as a whole (recently identified as one of the most technologically "wired" in the United States), and the community of learners and teachers at a large, public, research institution contribute in important ways. None of these, however, diminishes the particular role that individual teachers play in the success of any curricular innovation and without whose support the project would have failed. Which features of the project, then, contribute to teachers' satisfaction?

Data from successful technology projects in similar large-enrollment courses in other disciplines on campus that corroborate the Spanish-specific data suggest general contributory factors to instructor satisfaction with technology, as measured by willingness to continue using the technology and overall positive attitudes toward it. It is interesting that the general data identify student satisfaction as perhaps the primary factor in instructor satisfaction. Student questionnaires and focus group interviews conducted within the Spanish Project itself provide important additional insight into students' reactions to the particular use of technology in the language curriculum. Students state that they particularly enjoy the "anytime, anyplace" characteristic of Web-based instruction. They also appreciate the greater flexibility in their course schedules that meeting two, rather than four, times per week allows. The latter is especially intriguing in light of the fact that the University of Illinois is a residential campus. Over 92 percent of the students in Spanish 122 are full-time undergraduates. Fully 76 percent of the students access the online materials from either their room in a university residence hall or from a computing site within their residence hall; an additional 21 percent access the materials from computing sites on campus. Less than 4 percent of the students enrolled in the course reported working online from somewhere other than these locations. It is clear that even students who cannot in any way be considered "commuters" or otherwise typical of distance learning populations still appreciate the ability to work online at their own pace and convenience.

Even more than flexibility, however, these students report that they enjoy the immediate, consistent feedback and the opportunity to resubmit exercises multiple times to improve their scores that Mallard provides. This particular feature of the course could never be reproduced with human graders. Perhaps surprisingly, students also report that they appreciate the deadlines that Mallard maintains for the completion of online exercises: many students report that they would not keep up with the work for the course if it were not for these deadlines. (The grading policy in Mallard can be set according to the course director's preferences. For the Spanish Project, students are permitted to redo exercises an unlimited number of times to improve their scores before a deadline. Once the deadline has passed, Mallard will continue to grade the exercise and provide feedback, but it will not change the highest score received before the deadline, which is recorded automatically in the online grade book.) In addition, students find the online environment nonthreatening; they express relief to be freed from the pressure to perform in front of their teachers and peers and from the resultant embarrassment of making mistakes in public. With regard to online writing, students find it both challenging and purposeful: they see their online writing in Spanish as "real" communication, an opportunity to apply the skills they are learning in class and in their online exercises as they exchange messages with their peers and teachers.

The students were also very clear about what they believe makes for an ideal online component: download times can never be fast enough, servers must never crash, and online exercises must be constructed so that students cannot complete them mindlessly, by guessing, or without understanding why a particular answer is right or wrong.

The investigation of learner satisfaction in the technology-enhanced model is vital to an understanding of instructor satisfaction: unhappy, frustrated, complaining students create a hostile work environment for teachers, whether theoretical justification for the pedagogy exists or not. Nonetheless, student satisfaction is not the sole criterion for instructor satisfaction. Interviews with the instructors in the Spanish Project reveal that they, too, enjoy the flexibility in scheduling that the new model provides. Although they are required to meet two groups of students twice per week, they can often schedule those meetings so that they fall on the same days (for example, Mondays and Wednesdays), giving them two days free from classroom instruction to pursue their graduate studies and research interests. However, as in the case of the students, flexibility is appreciated, but it is not the overridingly satisfying feature of the technology-enhanced model.

More than anything else, instructors appreciate the tremendous reduction in effort that results from automated grading, an advantage that saves them countless hours of routine, mechanical labor. They also enjoy relief from the responsibility of maintaining deadlines for the submission of assignments, a task that the teachers said forced them to play the part of "police officer," a role that undermined a positive relationship with their students. Along the same line, instructors commented on other ways in which their roles changed, from that of information presenter, knowledge supplier, or manager in the conventional course to that of tutor, adviser, or communication coach in the technology-enhanced course. One role that instructors were *not* asked to play in the Spanish Project was that of technical support. A dedicated e-mail address was established to help students solve any problems that they might encounter with the technology. An undergraduate student who had experience with Mallard and FirstClass! was hired on an hourly basis to answer students' e-mails.

It is important to note that not all instructors are pleased with their change in role. Some instructors, especially those who enjoy teacher-fronted instruction and who take pride in their ability to present information in a lively and interesting way, report missing what they consider a satisfying aspect of classroom instruction. Others regret the loss of class time, citing a reduction in the number of potential opportunities for spontaneous teacher-learner interaction. Some students, too, are uncomfortable in the absence of a conventional classroom lecture: they may admit learning more by working online, but they resent that they have "had to teach themselves." Learner autonomy, from the teacher's perspective a successful outcome, may be perceived negatively by the learner. The research of van Esch et al. (see Chapter 9) points out the implications for teacher education in this realm.

Finally, data on instructor satisfaction in the Spanish Project, as well as other UIUC technology projects, are unique in that these instructors do not report the huge increase in instructional effort that is reported in the literature for many technology projects. A distinguishing feature of the UIUC models for the use of instructional technology in high-enrollment courses, of which the Spanish Project is one, is their efficient design. That is, the use of technology is fully integrated into the course; it is not simply an enhancement; it is neither additional nor extraordinary. In each instance, the technology replaces some (but not all) face-to-face instruction with online work. The savings, not only in budgetary resources, but also in instructor effort and students' progress toward the degree, are real. It is easy to see how teachers who already feel burdened with a heavy workload would not adopt technology that is viewed as an "add-on," albeit an enhancement, to what they are currently doing.

Implications for Communicative Language Teaching: Changing Instructional Roles and Expectations

One of the biggest obstacles to change in language teaching practice is teachers' perception that there is not enough time to do what they are currently doing, let alone to do more or to try something different. And, despite research and theory to the contrary, many teachers still feel compelled to spend a large amount of classroom time on the presentation and practice of discrete points of grammar (see Chapters 3 and 7). Communicative language teaching does not advocate the abandonment of instruction in grammar, but it does reframe its role in a setting that must allow students and teachers to interact in the second language (Savignon 1997, 2000). It is also true that a focus on communication takes a great deal of time, as students and teachers formulate and reformulate their messages in the negotiation of meaning. It is with more than a little irony that I admit never having met a language teacher who bewails the fact that communication takes so much class time to be done properly that she does grammar, regrettably, only when there's time left over. The inverse, however, is the rule: the teaching of grammar takes so much time that, regrettably, there is little to none left for meaningful communication. For communicative language teaching to begin to function within the reality of teachers' work environments, teachers first must view the participation in meaningful communication as integral to language teaching, not as an "add-on" or enhancement.

Instructional technology can aid the language teacher by taking over some of her existing responsibilities, more precisely, those tasks that teachers find burdensome or that technology does extremely well. For example, presentation of online materials enjoys tremendous advantages over conventional textbooks, including the incorporation of audio, animation, video, and hyperlinks, all of which can be used to create instructional environments that favor multiple learning styles. Moreover, once the environments have been created they can be easily corrected, revised, updated, and adapted to meet the needs of particular groups of learners. The latter is equally important to the teacher's sense of autonomy (see Chapter 2). In addition, applications like Mallard offer tireless scoring of any predictable student response, along with streamlined course management.

To maintain instructor and student satisfaction with technology, it is absolutely essential that it work as smoothly and transparently as possible. When teachers and students are working asynchronously, support systems must be available twenty-four hours a day, seven days per week. It is also important to realize that the creation of online materials requires theoretical, pedagogical, and technological expertise, creativity, and massive amounts of time; it is best accomplished as a team effort among instructors, designers, and technical staff (Fredericksen et al. 1999). Certainly, no instructor should be expected to create online materials in addition to her or his regular teaching load. In fact, the UIUC data suggest that diffusion of instructional technology beyond an individual teacher is more likely to occur when quality online course materials are already available; that is, when no development is required of the new adopter (Arvan and Musumeci 2000).

Instructional technology initiatives that seek to develop readily accessible, efficient, and inexpensive ways for human beings to interact face-to-face in an online environment will undoubtedly produce tremendous advantages for language learning. A team of researchers at the University of Illinois is working on an application that will allow students and teachers at distant locations to interact online in real time with all-way video and audio. It seems counterproductive, however, to postpone the adoption of any instructional technology in language teaching until it can replicate human interaction. In the meantime, current technology is ready to perform those routine, predictable tasks that take up so much of teachers' time. Teachers will then have the freedom to experiment in the classroom. They will have the time to explore the interpersonal, social, highly nuanced, culturally specific components of language teaching, something that technology may at best someday facilitate, but never provide.

As mentioned in the previous section on teacher education, the changed role of teachers in the technology-enhanced model may be perhaps the most significant factor for teacher education in general and communicative language teaching in particular. In the Spanish Project, the relegation of the presentation of materials and explicit practice in structure, vocabulary, and reading to the online environment has underscored rather than diminished the importance of the teacher's role in the language learning process. In class and in online responses to students' writing, teachers are asked to do what only human beings can do expertly and what is essential to second language acquisition; namely, to express, interpret, and negotiate meaning. In other words, teachers are valued for the uniquely human contribution that only they can make to the language learning process.

The UIUC Model and Other Post-Secondary Foreign Language Environments

The UIUC model was developed to solve the particular needs of a particular institution in a particular cultural context. As such, it may well be generalizable only to similar institutions and contexts with like needs. With modification, however, it may offer potential solutions to problems facing other large-enrollment foreign language courses in quite diverse institutional and cultural settings. One problem that it might address is a class size that cannot accommodate the kind of interaction that communicative language teaching proposes. For example, if the typical class size is sixty students, it might be possible to have the students meet all together for one lecture as preparation for autonomous online practice in grammar and vocabulary, and in three separate groups of twenty to work on communication skills. Of course, the particular teachers, students, and institutions themselves will best determine the applicability or modification of the model for their learning context.

The role of theory and research in teacher education will always be paramount; teachers must be versed in both if they are to make informed decisions regarding appropriate curricula, classroom practice, and materials. To that purpose, a thorough grounding in theory is eminently practical. (For discussion with specific reference to U.S. secondary foreign language innovation, see Chapter 6.) However, for tenets of theory to affect actual classroom practice, teacher education programs must convey how such tenets are applicable in ways that take into consideration the realities of the classroom setting, including class size, demands on resources, and teacher and learner expectations and satisfaction. Technology, managed wisely, may foster language learning both inside and outside the conventional classroom setting through a redistribution of instructional resources in a way that supports communicative language teaching. To do so, however, requires careful consideration of current demands within teachers' work environments, accompanied by an adjustment of those demands upon the introduction of technology, and an investment of resources in teacher education programs.

9

Learner Autonomy and the Education of Language Teachers: How to Practice What Is Preached and Preach What Is Practiced

EUS SCHALKWIJK, KEES VAN ESCH,

ADRI ELSEN, AND WIM SETZ

One afternoon at a university in the Netherlands, the graduate school of education is hosting a secondary school class and their teachers of English and French. In two simulated lessons, the teachers show their audience how they work and learn in their regular foreign language classes. Teacher trainees of English, German, French, and Spanish closely monitor the lessons, which are in many ways different from the language classes they are used to. It is an effort of the graduate school of education to engage the trainees in recent pedagogic approaches.

The instructions given the class are concise but engaging. Subsequently the class starts working and learning in small groups. The various tasks the groups are carrying out seem relevant and challenging. English and French are used frequently in the feedback the young learners give one another. The groups have set their own targets for the lesson and steadily work toward them. Occasionally, the teacher is involved in questions that arise, and at one stage the teacher stops the group work to highlight an important grammar point the groups are struggling with. At the end of the lesson, the groups agree on the individual assignments that have to be finished before the next lesson. Some of the groups consult their semester study guides.

Developing more successful foreign language learners and teachers has never been as exclusively rosy as in this scenario. After the lessons, the teachers and the pupils are interviewed by the teacher trainees. The secondary school pupils agree that some subjects are more suitable for this new pedagogic approach. They feel that it works for English and French, but they are convinced that it will not work for German because that teacher is not the kind of person to give away control. In addition, the class thinks that they will fail all his tests without his explicit grammar teaching. In answer to a question of a Nijmegen teacher trainee, six out of fourteen youngsters say that they would like to have less freedom because they admit they lack the discipline required to work and learn on their own. The remaining eight feel the level of freedom is just right, but they add that teacher instruction and guidance are still very important. They would not like to have more freedom and choice. "Whenever a subject is dealt with by the teacher in front of the class, it is easier to get good marks," some of the young learners claim. The statement does not surprise their teacher of French. "It is a matter of getting used to new ways of teaching. That is why I feel it is important that teachers make explicit why they opt for a particular pedagogic approach. In the Netherlands, we have made our learners dependent on marks and grades, causing them to distrust procedures that differ from the usual. More freedom and responsibility will work only if the learners actually experience that they are becoming better language learners and language users, by making sure the advantages are seen and felt."

In the Netherlands, much effort is put into fostering learner autonomy in young learners so that they become more efficient and successful learners and practitioners in any field, which has resulted in secondary educational reform. Its success largely depends on the willingness and ability of both learners and teachers. If they believe in the reform proposed and are willing to develop the knowledge and skills required, foreign language education is more likely to change for the better. From discussions we have had with teachers, teacher trainees, and pupils, it appears that there is a considerable amount of skepticism with regard to the changes they are facing. As teacher trainers and researchers, we take the skepticism seriously. We accept it as a starting point for research into aspects of learner autonomy in foreign language learning. Our findings help us to incorporate learner autonomy into teacher training and language learning pedagogy.

In this chapter, we first highlight three angles that may help to clarify the present interest in learner autonomy in communicative foreign language learning and teaching. In the first part, we will mention perspectives on self-determination, learning and motivation, and foreign language learning before moving on to a discussion of the specific Dutch context. We then turn to educational practice and report the comments of foreign language teachers, teacher trainees, and pupils on aspects of learner autonomy in foreign language learning and teaching. We conclude with recommendations for initial and postgraduate language teacher training and suggestions as to areas for further research.

Perspectives on Learner Autonomy in Foreign Language Learning

In many industrial countries, secondary education is undergoing change. One of these changes involves the implementation of learner-centered educational models to which the concepts of "learner autonomy" and "learning to learn" are crucial. In the Netherlands, language learners are increasingly expected to acquire and develop attitudes and skills essential for self-direction and self-control in foreign language learning (Simons and Zuylen 1994; Stuurgroep Tweede Fase 1994, 1996). First we wondered about the origins and background of the demand for learners who increasingly feel responsible for their own learning in the society they live in. In a review of literature on the topic, concepts of self-determination soon became prominent. Next, a number of important orientations from educational psychology on learning and motivation attracted our interest. They are useful in exploring concepts of learner autonomy in human learning. Finally, we concentrate on orientations in learning and teaching foreign languages, the home of applied linguistics. These three perspectives shed light on the educational reform in foreign language education taking place in the Netherlands as well as in many other countries around the globe. We will discuss Dutch educational reform in more detail below.

SELF-DETERMINATION IN CULTURE ORIENTATIONS

Every society has its own views and ideas about how it should function. In sociological terms these views and ideas are often referred to as culture orientations. A society may have its own specific culture orientation at a certain point in time, which influences how people think and act in different ways and provides guidelines for their daily actions. As a rule, various culture orientations coexist within a society, but one orientation is typically the most influential for a given period of time. For the Netherlands, Matthijssen (1972) distinguishes four culture orientations that have influenced periods within the past millennia:

The *aristocratic culture orientation.* Its central notion is that the leadership of a state can be entrusted only to an elite of high-ranking people (nobility or patricians).

The *theocratic culture orientation*. Characteristic of a society that considers God the immediate authority and is primarily oriented toward priests ruling as direct servants of God.

The *meritocratic culture orientation*. People derive social status from their individual abilities and achievements.

The *democratic culture orientation*. The direct or indirect government of a state by the people is at the center. The individuals in society decide who rules. The democratic orientation explicitly incorporates a model of self-determination. An important aspect of this autonomy model is that groups and individuals have the opportunity to develop their talents or abilities.

The common factor in the first three orientations is that power in society is outside the reach of ordinary persons. Power is in the hands of select groups of privileged individuals such as nobility and clergy. In the fourth orientation, the individual has social and political status irrespective of ability or achievement. Moreover, interest in the individual is not limited to newly gained social and political status. Societies are concerned with creating opportunities for their members to develop their potential. This aspect of autonomy is most clearly visible in a democratic culture orientation. In Europe as well as in the Americas, the concept of creating opportunities for self-determination has gradually gained acceptance and, in turn, influenced education, as the following historical examples will illustrate.

The nature of education was often passionately debated in light of changing social perspectives, resulting in movements concerned with all forms of education on both national and international levels. In the Netherlands during the seventies, great interest arose in concepts such as learner autonomy within various forms of socially committed project education. Among other things, this interest was a reaction to classic behaviorism. Rejection of behavioristic determinism translated into a general opposition to the establishment and a search for alternatives. An important objection against the established system of education was its one-sided emphasis on cognitive development. For critics, the system of education was too rigid, both because of the strict separation of primary and secondary education and the system of ability streaming and tracking from the first year of secondary education onward. Moreover, links between school learning and the life experiences of the child were generally missing. Among other criticisms leveled were the ineffectiveness of formal education in abolishing social inequality of opportunities and, ultimately, a failure to stimulate and fulfill the needs of learners for independence, responsibility, and participation. (For a summary of these criticisms, see Freire 1972; Illich 1979; Rogers 1983.)

In the early 1980s people lost interest in socially oriented project education in which explicit attention was paid to the social relevance of educational content. Once again, education was profession-oriented and geared toward professional skills and practical thinking. Interestingly, in the 1990s a two-track educational policy emerged in the Netherlands. One track was related to meritocratic utility thinking and was stimulated by business and industry with the important central concepts of selection and restriction of choices. The other track was related to the renewed interest in an autonomy model to empower every individual in society to develop as a human being responsible for social prosperity and welfare. Certain notions of learner autonomy as guiding principles began to attract the attention of policy makers. The elements for a top-down educational reform were in place.

The need for learner autonomy stems from what is in essence a democratically oriented vision of education. Sometimes a more democratic orientation develops as a reaction against a dominant orientation, as was the case with the aristocratic, theocratic, and meritocratic cultural orientations identified above. The meritocratic and democratic culture orientations were among the more influential in the past two millennia. Only the democratic culture orientation incorporates a model of self-determination, and it is this orientation that has increasingly gained influence in Europe within the past few decades. In the Netherlands, it has resulted in an educational reform geared at fostering a learner autonomy that includes both meritocratic and democratic traits.

In the following sections, we will offer two additional perspectives on learner autonomy. We will first review briefly some general theories on learning and motivation and then follow with a summary of developments in foreign language learning and teaching. Together, these three perspectives help to understand current notions of teachers and learners with regard to self-direction in learning how to communicate in a foreign language.

PERSPECTIVES ON LEARNING AND MOTIVATION

A behaviorist perspective on learning dominated educational psychology for decades. Classic behaviorism reflected a strongly deterministic and mechanistic portrayal of man. External regulation of learning behavior left the learner little opportunity for independence and responsibility in his/her individual learning process. Thus, classic behaviorist learning perspectives did not foster learner autonomy. In the 1960s a number of theories of human learning, notably cognitive and constructivist views, were developed in reaction to behaviorist perspectives. More recent versions of these views on learning still resonate in discussions of independent learning. This certainly applies to the renewed interest in the model of direct teaching advanced in the 1980s (Rosenshine 1995). The demonstrated effectiveness of direct teaching seems to account for its renewed popularity, especially in the field of cognitive performance (Rosenshine and Stevens 1986; Good and Brophy 1991).

Humanist psychologists acknowledge that stimulus-response reactions may play a role in learning processes. However, they feel that behavior and experience are primarily initiated by the individual and not exclusively caused by external incentives. Humans have the principal and unique capability to make choices and to distinguish themselves from one another. They assume responsibility for their choices. Humanist psychology thus emphasizes the ways in which learners perceive their environments. In education, humanist psychologists attribute an important role to a learner's thoughts, feelings, and motivation. Two representatives of humanist psychology who have been explicit on educational matters are Maslov (1970) and Rogers (1983).

A behaviorist point of view excluded mental explanations for behavior and changes in behavior. Behaviorists were unable to provide explanations for a great many everyday practical human activities, and this led to the rise of cognitive psychology. Cognitive psychologists saw learning as a process of collecting information and storing it in the brain. Subsequently, they developed an interest in learning strategies. However, the affective aspects of learning generally remained outside their scope of inquiry. In the 1980s, cognitive psychologists focused on metacognition—the question of how aspects of the learning process can be regulated. In research, positive connections were found between metacognitive activities and learning performances (De Jong 1992). There were also indications that the effective use of learning strategies and metacognitive skills could be taught and learned (Baker and Brown 1984; Palincsar and Brown 1984). Within educational circles, research results such as these bolstered the interest in metacognitive aspects of learning as a way to promote learner autonomy.

Social interactionists have approached human learning from yet another perspective, emphasizing that a child grows up in a social world and that learning occurs in part through interaction with others. This continuous interaction allows children to attribute meaning to the world around them. Vygotsky (1978, 1986; see also Wertsch 1985) stresses the importance of language in human interaction. Through language, culture is transmitted, mental processes are made explicit, and human learning can take place. Vygotsky rejected the idea that subject matter can be divided into separate small units that are transferred as isolated knowledge and skills. Subject matter has to be meaningful and be presented in all its complexity. Vygotsky saw an important role for the teacher, who aims the learning process in the right direction and at the same time pays attention to peer and other forms of cooperative learning. By interacting with the learner, the teacher or fellow learners serve as mediators, helping a learner find ways to stay within an area Vygotsky called the zone of proximal development. He defined this zone as "the distance between the actual development level as determined by independent problem solving and the level of potential development as determined through problem solving under adult guidance or in collaboration with more capable peers" (Vygotsky 1978, 86). Applied to foreign language learning, the zone of proximal development refers to the difference between what a language learner can do with help and what he or she can do without guidance. In numerous investigations, the added value of cooperative learning has been convincingly demonstrated. For example, significant results have been measured in the fields of cognitive performance and motivation (Johnson and Johnson 1989; Slavin 1990; Stahl 1995).

Cognitive psychology has contributed significantly to the development of constructivism. Several constructivist theories on learning (e.g., Bartlett 1932; Neiser 1967; Wolff 1994) have in common that every individual uses prior knowledge and experiences to process, store, and retrieve new information in his or her own way. These theories about information processing provide the cognitive underpinning of constructivism. Constructivism has many variants, but they share the claim that human perception is a construct of mental activity in which the environment, "society," or "the other" play essential roles. Learning is considered a continuous process in which learners acquire new knowledge in subjective ways, process it, and locate it in the existing structures of their knowledge, experiences, and beliefs. Learning takes place in the continuous interaction between practical and theoretical knowledge because learners link their practical knowledge to the theoretical knowledge made available to them, and vice versa. In this way learning can be seen as a continual process of construction and reconstruction (Boekaerts and Simons 1995; Lowyck and Verloop 1995).

Let us consider the affective sides of learning in more detail. Discussions on learner autonomy and communicative language teaching have often started from the premise that learners are intrinsically motivated to assume and develop responsibility. In the Netherlands, these aspects came to the fore in the 1990s, when the first experience with learner autonomy was reported by teachers and learners. Teachers in particular indicated that they believed or had seen that many pupils were insufficiently motivated to assume more responsibility for their own learning. The distinction made between intrinsic and extrinsic motivation is helpful here. According to Lens (1993) intrinsic motivation means that learners are motivated because of the activity itself, because they enjoy it or find it rewarding. Extrinsic motivation, in contrast, refers to motivation because of an external reward such as a good grade given by the teacher. The activity itself can be experienced by the learner as pleasant or unpleasant. The notion of extrinsic motivation is related to a behaviorist perspective on learning.

Learner autonomy requires individuals who are primarily intrinsically motivated. The learner should realize that she is the initiator of her own learning behavior (DeCharms 1984; Ryan and Grolnick 1986) and feel responsible for it (Wang 1983). It thus is important that the learner transform her intentions into behavior and can identify and remove at an early stage any obstructions in the areas of action or emotion. Within this framework, Kuhl (1985) uses the notions of action-orientation and situation-orientation. Learners who are situation-oriented waste time in the execution of their tasks as a result of indecisiveness in the orientation stage and volatility in the execution stage. Learners who are action-oriented, on the other hand, take initiative quickly in the orientation stage and persevere in the execution stage.

PERSPECTIVES ON FOREIGN LANGUAGE LEARNING

First, we argued that learner autonomy is closely related to a democratic culture orientation with its inclusion of a model of self-determination. Next, we showed how in learning theories increased attention came to be focused on the learner in the learning process along with affective factors such as motivation. In the Netherlands, some of these insights have been incorporated into theoretical notions of foreign language teaching didactics. Theory tries to provide answers to the question of how learners learn to learn how to communicate in a foreign language. We consider fostering learner autonomy in foreign language learners to be among the most recent developments in communicative language learning and communicative language teaching. The pedagogy of foreign language learning and teaching has undergone numerous changes. We have the distinct impression that, in the Netherlands, traces of past developments will be evident in the beliefs of both teachers and learners on how foreign languages are best taught and learned. A brief survey of these past developments in the field is presented below. The survey moves from an orientation to grammar and translation to the present wide interest in more communicative forms of language learning and teaching, as presented, for instance, by Candlin and Mohr (1978), Neuner and others (1981), and Savignon (1972, 1983, 1997, and Chapter 1).

Despite the development of more communicative approaches to language teaching and learning, traces of the grammar-translation method are still found in language curricula, instructional materials, and lessons. The grammar-translation method was supported by theory, but not by empirical data (Richards 1984; Richards and Rogers 1986). Explicit grammar teaching and translation training do not meet the social need for appropriate communication skills in a foreign language. For many foreign language teachers and learners, translation—along with explicit knowledge, application, and memorization of grammar rules and idioms—is often an objective in and of itself rather than a means to the development of communicative competence. In many respects the familiar direct method is the counterpart of the grammar-translation method. In the direct method, foreign languages are learned and taught in ways similar to the natural way children learn their native language. It mandates considerable listening and reading in the new language before moving on to more spontaneous forms of language use, with less emphasis on grammatical analysis and the memorization of idioms. In early editions of course materials for beginners in the direct method, grammar was kept in the background.

The audiolingual orientation was supported by a behaviorist perspective on learning (Savignon 1983, 1997; Van Els et al. 1984). Structuralists were of the opinion that the structure of oral or written expressions of language could be described in an objective way. Authors published course materials in which new language material was presented in the form of dialogues with a central role reserved for repetition and memorization. Contrastive analysis and pattern drills were also used; there was hardly any explanation of grammar. Audiotapes and visual support were frequently used. In the Netherlands, there are still schools where the language classroom remains as envisioned by the structuralists. In notions of communicative language teaching (CLT), language is seen as a system for the interpretation, expression, and negotiation of meaning (Savignon 1983), with its primary goal interaction and communication. The underpinning theory of learning is that the activities carried out should involve real communication, meaningful tasks, and language that is meaningful to the learner. In CLT, the teacher is the facilitator of the communication process, participants' tasks, and texts. The teacher is the process manager, whereas the learner is a negotiator, an interactor who both gives and receives. The interest in CLT coincided with the formulation of theories on fostering learner autonomy in foreign language learners. We will briefly present some of the more prominent theories that are closely related to the democratic culture orientation referred to above.

According to Holec (1981, 1988), foreign language learner autonomy involves learners who are both willing and able to assume responsibility for their own language learning. They do so by making their own choices of objectives, materials, and process. Similarly, for Little (1994), learner autonomy is a permanent objective in language teaching and language learning. His definition of autonomy seems equally applicable to that of language learning as it fits in with the democratic cultural orientation: the learner has to learn to develop his language learning knowledge and skills independently in order to reach a further stage of autonomy. "Humans are autonomous with respect to a particular task when they are able to perform that task (i) without assistance, (ii) beyond the immediate context in which they acquired the knowledge and skills and on which successful task performance depends, and (iii) flexibly, taking account of the special requirements of particular circumstances" (Little 1997, 94).

Three other aspects of learner autonomy should be stressed. There is the social aspect (Slavin et al. 1985; Kagan 1993; Dam 1994) underlying successful teacher-learner and learner-learner cooperation. In addition, no two learners learn in the same way (Nunan 1987, 1993; Narcy 1994). A fourth aspect of learner autonomy related to the ones above is the learner's orientation toward the learning process. Wolff (1994) explicitly links this aspect to constructivism. In processing information, every learner starts from his or her own prior knowledge and prior experiences in his or her own way. All we perceive in a foreign language is a "construct" of our own mental activities in interaction with the surrounding environment. When focusing on the autonomous student's process, a great deal of attention has to be paid to learning strategies. Related research has resulted in concrete proposals for the learning and teaching of foreign languages (see Naiman et al. 1978; Wenden and Rubin 1987; O'Malley and Chamot 1990; and Oxford 1990).

Together with Rampillon (1994), these principles describe the ideal autonomous foreign language learner: a learner who is motivated, knows his or her own possibilities and limitations and tries to surmount them, formulates his or her own learning targets, initiates the learning process and keeps it going, determines how he or she learns best, keeps track of the subject material, and evaluates his or her learning results to find ways they can be improved. An important condition that has to be met is that the teacher adapt to other roles, namely those of instructor, supervisor, and coach. As Widdowson (1990) justifiably remarks, this does not imply that the teacher no longer directs or "teaches" the learner. More than ever, the foreign language teacher guides learners on their way to responsibility for their own learning process. This can be done by helping students organize and plan their learning and develop new and better modes of acquiring language. The teacher monitors how students learn before, during, and after they carry out tasks, encouraging them to think about how their planning and execution proceeded and the improvements that could be made.

In order for these ideals to become a reality, a number of requirements must be met. Schools have to be organized so that learners can work independently of the teacher, either alone or in groups; study corners, a library, and computers have to be available at all times. Course materials have to be adjusted to principles of learner autonomy. Learning to communicate in a foreign language implies that communication in the foreign language has to be encouraged and instructions for learning tasks made clear. Study guides help increase learner autonomy. Course materials, pedagogical approach, and forms of (self-)evaluation should encourage independence and self-control. Cooperation with others has to be promoted and efficient use made of information and communication technology.

THE STUDIEHUIS CONCEPT IN DUTCH UPPER SECONDARY EDUCATION

How far is this ideal from practice? In various European countries, attempts are being made to realize learner autonomy. We turn now to the gap between theory and practice by describing what has happened in the Netherlands in a period of less than ten years.

The call for learner autonomy became louder and louder early in the 1990s. An example of the plea for learner autonomy and an elaboration of assumed stages of learner autonomy and their related didactic procedures can be found in Simons and Zuylen (1994). Simultaneously, the Stuurgroep Tweede Fase, a steering committee instituted by the government, proposed reforms to reorganize the curriculum for the second stage of secondary education, the so-called upper secondary phase (Stuurgroep Tweede Fase 1994, 1996). The renewed curriculum was to be introduced in schools that had been physically transformed into *Studiehuis,* or "homes of independent study." Along with classrooms, space had to be created for pupils to work individually or in groups, in silence or with the opportunity to collaborate with peers. School libraries were transformed into multimedia information centers. Organizational and pedagogic changes in the second stage were meant to elaborate on a previous educational reform in the first stage of secondary education introduced in 1993.

All secondary schools incorporated the same compulsory core curriculum of fifteen school subjects. In addition, general skill targets were established. In the Netherlands, the first stage is often referred to as basic secondary education. Basic secondary education was introduced to modernize what was commonly taught, to postpone the choice of an eventual profession or concentration of studies, and to raise the general standard of education. The curriculum of the upper levels of general secondary education and pre-university education experienced a number of dramatic changes in 1999. New subjects were introduced, almost doubling the number of examination subjects. Learners were expected to study 1,600 hours a year, considerably raising their work load.

Curricular changes were introduced together with new pedagogic approaches meant to foster learner autonomy in young learners. Publishing companies developed new course materials that appeared either in or just after September 1999, the official year in which the Studiehuis was introduced. The formulation of specific foreign language learning objectives was an important boost for more communicative forms of language learning and teaching. In addition to required courses in Dutch and English, reading courses in German and French were introduced as options along with the general skills courses offered in these two languages.

The Studiehuis concept has the appearance of a conditional sale: learner autonomy was linked to curricular reform. However, final examinations in the Netherlands are still strongly centralized and determine to a great extent what is learned and how it is learned. In addition, these changes were introduced top-down. Government directed the processes of change and left its mark on content and methods.

The problems that resulted were predictable. There was considerable student resistance to the heavy work load and addition of new subjects, a resistance that resulted in a student strike at the end of 1999. Parents resisted as well, in part reacting against the dramatic rise in the cost of course materials. And, finally, many teachers resisted because they felt insufficiently prepared for the content and pedagogy within their recently transformed Studiehuis. In addition, a large-scale investigation by the School Inspectorate into the results of French, German, and English in basic secondary education showed that a number of problems in basic secondary education remained to be resolved. Nearly all the teaching appeared to be carried out at the class level and was dependent on the course materials used; the foreign language was hardly ever spoken by the teacher or learners; there was little communicative language teaching; and computer use was scarce. Only in a small number of cases did the investigators find interesting and varied lessons (Inspectie van het Onderwijs 1999).

Among the various objections leveled against the Studiehuis, the increase in the work load and the new examination requirements along with, to a lesser extent, the pedagogy of learner autonomy, have been particular targets.

Among the articles published on the topic in *Levende Talen* (Living Languages), a journal for teachers of both Dutch and foreign languages, most address the opportunities learner autonomy offers; few mention the problems and pressures caused by the organizational changes. Workshops and refresher courses about learner autonomy are well-attended. Many teachers are looking for new approaches and wish to be trained to promote learner autonomy. A recent evaluation of new didactic approaches for the Studiehuis provided a predominantly positive picture. If instructions and tasks are clear, young learners develop the skills and strategies that help them understand and interpret authentic foreign language materials, even given the current drawbacks: failure of their grammar and idiom training to transfer to the development of communicative skills, and limited access to computers and the Internet.

Views of Teachers, Teacher Trainees, and Secondary School Students

An explanation for the partly faltering implementation of learner autonomy must be found in the conceptions and experiences of the main actors, the teachers, teacher trainees, and secondary learners. We have to take seriously into account the situations in which they find themselves. The following statements from teachers, teacher trainees, and learners were collected in 1999 and 2000 and are taken from research material (the doctoral research of Elsen and Setz) and from training reports by our foreign language teacher trainees. From their statements, we conclude that a considerable number of these teachers and teacher trainees are now recognizing the opportunities created by increasing learners' self-responsibility and self-control. The reconstruction of conceptions has begun, albeit on a restricted scale, and that is gratifying.

Topics covered in this section are (1) increasing learner responsibility, (2) motivational aspects of learning, (3) changing roles of the teacher and pupil, (4) bottlenecks at the introduction of the Studiehuis (5) learning achievement and the culture of marks and grades, and, (6) communicative foreign language teaching.

WORKING THEORIES: WHAT DOES INCREASING LEARNER RESPONSIBILITY INVOLVE?

We quote a teacher of English who implemented the Studiehuis model in upper secondary education for the first time:

> I think it is important to realize that learner autonomy is an objective that is very difficult to achieve. I'll be glad if the majority of the pupils have mastered it by the time they leave school. You see, working independently—on a very clearly specified assignment which has to be finished, needing no one else— they can do that perhaps with a little guidance. But independent learning is

more than that. You receive a survey (from a coherent set of tasks) of what you have to do, when you have to do certain things and how you have to do them, using the material which is, more or less, presented to you. We still have a long way to go, I think.

Self-responsible learning again is another big step ahead. The final target is given but how you will get there and in how much time, that is for you to fill in. Perhaps you may even have to find the necessary materials yourself.

I think that to expect self-responsibility from a [general secondary education] pupil is aiming too high and is not yet under discussion in the framework of the upper secondary phase. We are hesitant about that. We give the pupils the means to get somewhere independently, but the responsibility in great part still lies with us.

This quotation reflects the teacher's wish to remain in charge for the time being. He is very hesitant to pass part of the responsibility for the learning process on to the learners. In addition, he says: "My idea of learner autonomy is guided learning, no, supervised learning [laughs], where the supervision is carried out more and more from a distance: What you do is: always leave the responsibility for their learning to the pupils themselves. Only, before you can do so, you have to remain in charge as a teacher. You have to educate them and guide them in that process."

This teacher of English refers to a distinction among assumed stages of learner autonomy, that is, working without supervision, independent learning, and self-responsible learning (Boekaerts and Simons 1995; Bonset and Mulder 1997). He is familiar with the theory and tries to apply it to his practical knowledge. The distinctions among the three forms of learning can help a teacher to phase in the learners' increasing independence. The distinction suggests that learning how to learn to communicate in a foreign language is a process consisting of stages in which every learner shows a certain amount of independence in all aspects at a given moment. However, we feel that in reality the process is much more differentiated.

MOTIVATIONAL ASPECTS OF LEARNING

In the teachers' quotations above, learner autonomy is seen essentially as a cognitive matter, a matter of knowledge and ability. Affective aspects are left aside. The following observation from a teacher of German addresses this topic:

I wonder to what extent you can incite adolescents—and I don't mean this to be negative!—to want to learn independently and be responsible for it themselves, in the sense of "what do I do and why?" I find that very difficult. . . . But in some way or another it has to be done, I feel. Because if they start studying later, they will be confronted with it too. In their entire further lives as a matter of fact. So I feel it is important. But perhaps we should try to achieve it just for a small portion, perhaps only in the final examination classes.

This illustrates a dilemma reflected in the comments of many teachers interviewed. On the one hand, this teacher seems to be convinced of the importance of learner autonomy. On the other hand, he doubts that adolescents can or even wish to be independent at this phase in their lives.

Yet a number of students indicated that they welcome the increased independence: "It is nice that you can set your own [home]work. If it so happens that one day you don't have enough time for an assignment which has to be finished the next day, you give yourself less homework for once. And the next lesson you will give yourself more homework again. But most of the time you work rather hard during the lesson, because then you don't have that much homework left." Another student pleads for yet more freedom: "I would like to have more freedom in planning. As it is you have to keep exactly to the planning for most subjects. Except for French and Greek; there you don't." Others point to the importance of group checking: "Last year in French class you were really checked quite strictly, so you really memorized your idioms. But if I don't memorize my idioms now for once, my group members skip me. Nothing happens then, so there is actually no real check. In that case you will have to learn really everything for a test. Yes, you really need to have a lot of self-discipline." The participating pupils seemed to appreciate the combination of working on tasks individually and in groups, but they also had some negative comments about group work: "Working in groups is best, but if you really want to learn something, you had better work on a task alone or in pairs. But it has to be with someone you can cooperate well with, so that you both work and don't start talking. But that also has to do with self-discipline. I can easily work in a group of four, but it depends on who are in that group."

A teacher trainee in English speaks of a mixture of freedom and checking:

> It is difficult to draw a certain picture of a pupil, but I think that for present-day pupils it is important to take into consideration that they have their own ideas and their own opinions. As a teacher you don't have to go along with them, but you have to be open and listen to them. The pupils we spoke with were all very responsible and were aware of the fact that school and study are especially important for them. This responsibility does not alter the fact that the pupils need structure and limits. They indicate that they prefer a teacher who is nice, but who also takes care that the work gets done, so the tolerant and authoritarian type.

CHANGING ROLES OF TEACHER AND LEARNER

Moving from the traditional role of ex-cathedra leader toward a role of activator and coach is a gigantic step for many teachers. Teaching strategies adapted to learner autonomy were scarce or nonexistent when the Studiehuis was first introduced. A teacher of English formulates his first experiences as follows:

> The introduction of the upper secondary phase has been an enormous change. Not only for pupils but also for teachers. I had the feeling I was back at school again; all my securities about what I did so well as a teacher had been wiped away. For, with the introduction of the Studiehuis, all of a sudden all these classic skills that I was so used to applying were of little use to me. Now completely different things are asked of me as a teacher.
>
> The first few months it was survival. How do I manage to keep my head above water? You have to structure and start leaving things to the pupils. Otherwise you will go crazy. I have never had such a difficult start of a school year. Really, I have worked for twenty-one years and I have never felt so broken, tired (laughs) after three, four weeks. Honestly. You have the feeling, "I am extinguishing fires but I'm not removing the pyromaniac." I must start dealing with things differently. I must start structuring; I need to acquire an overview. I must want less. I must work more efficiently. So, survival. Fortunately, I have a lot of contact with colleagues. Only recently we exchanged experiences in a workshop one day. You all have the same problems.

In the following remarks, this teacher's indecision and feelings of inadequacy are also felt:

> You get into a sort of role crisis, don't you? On the one hand you still have classes in which you play the traditional role, albeit to a lesser extent than before. I notice that now. And on the other hand you have classes where you are no longer the leader but the coach for two hours a week. And that is difficult. I thought I had prepared quite well for this, had studied the literature, but it was much harder than I thought.
>
> At a certain moment I didn't know any longer what I had to do in such a lesson. You feel that you have to do all kinds of things, but do what and where? On the one hand you are inclined to patronize. And as soon as you realize that, you come to a standstill and you don't do anything at all. I hope to gradually find some sort of balance which is also satisfying to me.

For this teacher, the transition to the new approach has come about very abruptly. In another part of the interview, he indicated that in the past few years very few experiments have been carried out in practice at his school. He feels limited by a lack of know-how and skills important for a learner-oriented conception of tasks. Nevertheless, he is also actively taking steps in order to acquire and master new skills:

I have had a lot of conversations with pupils and I sat with them a lot. Just see what happens and how it happens in the hours for independent work. What do they do and how do they go about it? What goes right and what goes wrong? Where do they get stuck? . . . I think that in my coaching I now increasingly work by way of questioning. That from a stating, prescriptive notion about the teaching profession I am now working more and more by way of questioning just because of the developments of the upper secondary phase. And certainly if it is about gaining insight in the subject matter. I am now trying to do that also in the classes in the upper years that are not included in the upper secondary phase because they started earlier. . . . So having the pupil discover by way of questioning how it has to be done, rather than telling him. At our school we formed small groups with a mentor within every class. I also notice that I'm actually starting to like individual coaching of pupils in their learning process.

For another teacher of English, the transition went much more smoothly. The school where she teaches seized upon the developments around the Studiehuis at a very early stage. These developments connect very well with the direction she wants to take as a teacher:

Matters that have inspired me the last few years are the developments at the Montessori school where I work, the introduction of the Studiehuis, which we have been working on for a number of years, and then, this year, the introduction of the upper secondary phase. In the fifteen years that I have been teaching, we have increasingly grown toward learner autonomy, learning how to learn, and guided learning. I found out that this is what I have always really wanted. I cannot imagine that people have difficulty with this. Perhaps I should say: I can imagine, but they don't know what they're missing. It makes our profession a very satisfying one. It still does, yes. You are involved with the pupils much more closely when you sit next to them and at a level of equality than when you just teach in front of the class.

There are also teacher trainees who are making the change:

At this moment I'm trying as much as possible to get the pupils to work and to take less initiative myself. However, I discovered that this requires a lot of effort on my part. When the pupils are carrying out their learning tasks, I soon get the feeling that I'm losing control. Moreover, it is more difficult for me to assess whether they are working in the right way and get the right results from the lessons.

This is also connected with the fact that I'm teaching lower secondary education classes at the moment. I have three first-year groups and I find that in the beginning they need more guidance and confirmation anyway. Nevertheless I'm trying in these groups as well to make them do more and more themselves and so, instead of directive teaching strategies, I'm applying activating ones. This appears to work well again and again. You can leave more to the pupils than you are inclined to at first. This also goes for the first-year classes.

Not every teacher trainee, however, has reached this point: "The only thing I still have some difficulty with is the upper secondary phase. A great disadvantage is that the pupils miss the explanations very much. Moreover, I think that too much responsibility is given to the pupils. Since they can determine themselves when they do what, apparently it can happen that the teacher has prepared his lesson for nothing. That should not be possible."

There are teachers who indicate that they spend time and energy to create conditions for students to work independently. A teacher of English says that he typically needs a few months to get everything going right.

> If I don't know a class, it usually takes one or two months before I let them go. And then I start with part of a lesson, in which I set them to work on an assignment in groups. I'm mainly busy with making them experience how certain assignments and tasks can be carried out. It's important that pupils know as accurately as possible what they have to know of the English language after they have completed an assignment or a task and how they must and can use that knowledge. For instance, I say to a pupil: "Ask some questions about that piece of grammar. What do you have to know if you don't want to make any mistakes and how do you use what you have learned when communicating with others?" That's something you have to practice a lot, and often. Often I have pupils hear vocabulary. The pupil who is being heard has to use the words in a correct sentence and in the correct context.

With respect to independent learning in groups, a teacher of French emphasizes how the group is constituted:

> In view of good group cooperation it is very important how a group is made up. An example: Alex and Kees are hard workers, but they are easily distracted and they are easily induced to talk. I put them with Marijke and Lieke, who work seriously. . . . In the past I often let pupils choose their own groups. That has hampered me enormously. Thus groups were chosen for reasons of friendship and in these groups they didn't work properly. So, as a rule I don't allow them to choose their own groups, but I explain to them why I choose for a certain formation. In that way they learn how to make that choice themselves later. What is that person good at, what does the other one want, what is he not so good at? That's important for motivation.

Learners notice that a number of their teachers have not yet mastered this new distribution of roles. One of the student participants in our study reported: "They say that you have to work more independently, but in that case I find that it has to be really independent. Take for instance German, we have to attend the lesson in order to work, but he hardly explains anything. And we have to be quiet as a mouse in the lesson, but he goes and talks with pupils about subjects that have got nothing to do with German."

OBSTACLES IN INTRODUCING THE STUDIEHUIS MODEL

Their changing roles require most teachers and learners to adopt new views on learning. Teachers have been and are supported by refresher programs and new pedagogic approaches, but some of these new teaching methods were not available when the Studiehuis was first implemented. This was not the only planning problem. Difficulties also occurred at school and classroom levels, as can be seen in the following comments from a teacher of German:

> We also have a planning problem. We cannot plan as we would like to because too much is asked of the pupils. We just had a report meeting. There we learned, that in 5 VWO [pre-university education and an experimental class of the upper secondary phase] the pupils' work load is too much for them. And you cannot plan when too much is asked of them; then they have to survive. . . . And there is more, however hard it may be. We also have to admit that there are pupils who cannot cope with that level, that level of knowledge. And then it gets even worse, when they have more things to plan. Do you know what I mean? They lose sight of the whole.

Teachers mention a multitude of problems faced by learners during a change from an old to a new system of education. A teacher of English describes how much difficulty he has had in motivating his students.

> As a teacher I spend 30 to 50 percent of my lessons on matters not related to English, but on getting pupils to work. In their schedules, hours are reserved for study. But in the minds of the pupils these are still free periods. A free teaching period means going into town. That was a surprise to me too, disappointing, that even now you have to emphasize that to pupils. On the other hand, pupils complain that they have to do so much at home. In that case I make them face this question: "How much time of the hours for self-study did you spend on your work?" Then they say: "Well, then we went into town and we've been chatting." . . . So it requires from the pupils a considerable change in their thinking process. First we have to make this change. You have to spend forty hours a week on school. Make good use of your time; that's important. Otherwise it gets on top of other things.

A teacher of German mentions skills in learner autonomy and especially learning how to plan as problems that learners encounter:

> Planning, if only we could have achieved that with the pupils. I said could have, because I think we haven't achieved it. If a pupil can deal with that, can do his own planning, then I think we are moving into the right direction. I

think that it does not function well at the moment. The group that can handle this is too small. The fact that most teachers in 5 VWO have abandoned the hours for independent study and for the most part have gone back to class teaching, is a clear sign, isn't it, that it does not function well. We have to do something about that, because this is not right either.

Despite the problems described by teachers, success stories are also reported, as is the case with this teacher of French:

My experience is that groups of pupils can work independently very well. This, of course, makes demands on my instruction and the tasks I want my pupils to carry out. Also, should I be absent, they just start working. They know where to go. They also know very well that if they don't do anything this teaching period they will have to do a lot at home. What I also notice in the group is that when a few pupils are messing around, the rest get annoyed. In that way they correct each other.

I have one group in which the pupils cannot work independently yet. So I check more in that group. I have a look at their written work and listen to their French. Normally I check very little. I think it goes well, because they did well in the tests, so that's all right. Look, we have made agreements. They write down their homework, I won't talk about that but I do have a look at it. . . . When I have a look at it every now and then I get a reasonable idea of how they are doing. I can see that they do that homework well. And if it goes a little less perfectly, I just don't pay any attention to it.

Another teacher observes that in many schools there is great discrepancy between the old approach in the first stage of secondary education, which presupposes a passive, docile attitude in learners, and the new responsibility-oriented approach in the second stage of secondary education: "The mistake is embedded in our system of education. We demand things from pupils, being able to plan, self-responsibility, etc. We should have started with that years ago, in the first stage of secondary education. That is why we are now working in a very structured way on the development of skills like planning, etc., in the second form, and that is going quite well."

LEARNING ACHIEVEMENT AND THE CULTURE OF GRADES

In conversations with students and teachers, it becomes clear that some students assume responsibility for the learning process because they are extrinsically motivated: they want to get good grades. A few students indicate that for that reason they prefer the old style of teaching: "Whole class teaching is convenient. For subjects that are dealt with on a class level I get good grades. If I have too much freedom, I won't do enough. Certain subjects are easier to deal with on a whole class level; large pieces of text and so on. The teacher can simply give a summary. And if there's anything you don't know anymore, you just take your book and read the passage."

These students' teacher has a quite explicit opinion as to the students' orientation toward grades:

> Look, in the Netherlands we are driving pupils crazy for grades. That's something we're all guilty of, because we give grades for everything. So it's logical that pupils are always asking what grade they will get for what they do. The time when grades or marks were not all-important has gone. You can only diminish this orientation toward grades to some extent when you offer a fair number of tests and offer ample opportunities for pupils to get scores they like. I think that the class we are talking about now is less oriented toward grades. You must take into consideration that the pupils in this class make their own tests and actually test one another. If someone gets a low mark they have themselves to blame, for they can also arrange it differently.

An English teacher trainee, with prior experience in teaching, is doubtful about her own approach:

> I, too, have thought for a long time that working together independently automatically leads to learner autonomy, especially because in refresher courses the emphasis mostly was on incorporating working [together] independently into tasks in one's own lesson situation. In my view, this was then presented as being a condition to induce pupils to work independently. However, for quite some time now I've had to acknowledge that working together independently does not necessarily lead to effective and active learning.
>
> For a number of years my pupils have been working together independently a lot. The assignments and tasks are often constructed in such a way that I can make the pupils carry out assignments independently on the basis of oral or written instructions. The method of working on these assignments is often described in detail in order to provide as much clarity as possible to the pupils so that they can start work and keep working. But although the pupils start working independently very well when they receive such assignments, I often find that at the end of the task or the project, the results are disappointing. One way or another the tasks and assignments, however structured and directive, do not result in pupils learning effectively. Apparently the pupils have no insight into what is expected from them at the end of a task or project.

Another English teacher trainee encourages his students to make their learning goals more explicit:

> Summarizing, it may be said that if the pupils are more aware of and better focused with respect to learning goals, this affects the results positively. It is important that the pupils first be taught how. They have to get used to it. As a

teacher you will first have to direct and stimulate the pupils to focus on the learning goals of a task before they can and will be doing that independently. Apart from that, it has a positive effect on the results when pupils are stimulated to think about the relevance of learning goals and when they try to formulate their own learning goals within a task. Thinking about the learning goals of a task and thinking about what they want to learn themselves has, as a result, as the pupils indicated during the experiment, that they work very hard and with great motivation to reach these goals. They work more effectively and more actively.

Some students linked the introduction of the classroom reforms to their grades: "Last year we started with the upper secondary phase for the first time. Well, the teachers didn't know how it worked, we didn't know how it worked. Last year many low grades were given, I think." In the past few decades the orientation toward grades has increased, and this is related to a meritocratic culture orientation. The status of a student is also determined by his or her performance.

LEARNING TO LEARN HOW TO COMMUNICATE
IN A FOREIGN LANGUAGE

We have seen in the commentaries so far that teachers construct and reconstruct their idiosyncratic working theories on aspects of learner autonomy. Most of the teachers we interviewed appeared to be challenged by the idea of increasing the responsibility of language learners for what they know of a foreign language and for what they are able to do with that knowledge. Gradually, the working theories developed are put to the test in experiments and projects in which the learners have to work and learn individually and in small groups. More than ever, teachers discuss their ideas with colleagues and with their learners. Language classrooms that had been closed for years are gradually opening up. Interestingly, we see how teachers' working theories of the widely accepted concept of communicative language teaching (CLT) are defined or redefined. If teachers are asked to state their understanding of CLT, we find interesting parallels with their attempts to define learner autonomy. "Giving a clear definition is difficult for me. In reality each and every person has his own view on what it is to be communicative in a foreign language. More often than not you can only guess what your colleagues' views are. Some are not too communicative in this respect. And if they aren't, it is often hard to find any common denominators you can agree on." Like so many teachers we interviewed, the teacher of English quoted above did not offer a clearly defined working theory. Instead, she alluded to the dilemma between linguistic accuracy and effective communication in a foreign language.

What is being communicative, you tell me. Do you have to get rid of all knowledge of grammar and accept anything your pupil says as long as he or she can put the message across? I don't think so. I feel there should be a proper grammatical base, otherwise they become cruise missiles without any sense of direction. They just haven't got any clue how language works. However, I must admit that whenever I test for effective communication I find it hard to determine when a grammatical error really hampers communication.

Almost every teacher mentioned a grammatical base and knowledge of idioms and phrases often used in the foreign language. Proper verb forms, correct word order, and questions and negations are often mentioned as examples of a grammatical base. For many teachers, this base seems essential for their learners to develop a sense of direction in learning a language on their own. The language teachers are there to make sure they move in the right direction, whatever that may be. Before arriving at a definition not always specified in great detail, more often than not there is evasive action on their part, as can be seen in the following example:

Communicative language teaching? Well, in language education you need a language teacher. I think this teacher should both instruct and stimulate. She may serve as an example, but she may also explain what a communicative exercise is about together with one or more pupils. A next step would be to have pupils work in pairs or in small groups, depending on the class or grade they are in, of course. A certain level is taught, achieved, and practiced with one primary aim in mind. I tend to become a little philosophical now. The most important thing in life is the ability to communicate, in whatever way possible. And of course we as language teachers are the people to teach learners how to communicate in a foreign language. Wasn't it John F. Kennedy who stressed the importance of communication by saying: "Let's communicate or die"? This can be oral or written communication.

These are the words of a Dutch grammar school teacher of English. In her view, the teacher should start by using the foreign language in classroom communication as often as she can. She feels the first three years of grammar school education should be spent on giving learners the grammatical and idiomatic tools to be able to communicate. This is done with the intent that in the final three years of grammar school they learn how to communicate and discuss human values and norms in the foreign language. The link of communicative language teaching with intercultural competence and intercultural learning is very inviting here (Sercu 1995). With such high aims in mind, she tends to distrust any early responsibility given to pupils.

Another teacher seems to have a different frame of mind. His definition of CLT came easily and fast, and looked straightforward:

Communicative language teaching is making sure that whenever one has information another person is interested in, the information is put across, in whatever way possible. Of course, I am talking about real information here. It has to be about things that matter and carry meaning for the people who communicate. That's a drawback of so many textbooks. Very often the subjects they are supposed to talk about are too far removed from what they will ever face in real life. I honestly feel it's no use having two Dutch seventeen-year-olds talk about Victorian English philosophies or about druids. At the beginners' level it is hardly any better. Exercises in textbooks are often too simple and do not have any information gap. "Hello, what's your name?' a pupil asks a fellow pupil he has known for the greater part of his life. The questions and expected answers do not even boost your confidence.

He had come to distrust the effects of rote learning of grammar and idioms and the blind use of course materials. When he started teaching some twenty-five years earlier, he was tutored and supervised by two colleagues who had told him to be wary of whatever seemed "the right thing to do" and to focus on transfer of whatever is taught to actual use of the foreign language. More than other teachers, he was prepared to discuss the merits and long-term effects of the tasks he asks his learners to carry out. He felt that the renewed upper secondary phase with its focus on learner autonomy finally corroborated what he had believed throughout his teaching career. What is it that makes experienced teachers relatively open-minded? If you ask them, none of them mentions teacher training. The teacher in our last quotation was fortunate to have had colleagues that encouraged him to develop and explore his investigating mind in his formative years. Educational and pedagogic change did not take him by surprise.

CONSEQUENCES FOR TEACHER TRAINING

Growing academic interest in learner autonomy influences language learning and teaching. As a result, both teachers and learners increasingly find themselves in situations where language learners are expected to be responsible for and able to direct their own learning. In order to prepare teacher trainees for their future roles, learner autonomy should be fostered in foreign language teacher training.

We have claimed that teacher trainees' subjective educational theories should be the starting point for a training program aimed at teaching them to learn autonomously (Van Esch et al. 1999). We have also claimed that our approach was experience-driven, aimed at a confrontation between teacher trainees' subjective educational theories, their practical knowledge, and other sources of knowledge (see Kelchtermans 1993). This pedagogic principle is based on a constructivist view of learning. Applying this to foreign language teacher training means that every teacher trainee acquires new knowledge in his or her own subjective way, processes it, and locates it in an existing structure of knowledge, experience, and beliefs. Learning takes place through a continuous interaction between practical knowledge and theoretical knowledge. Consequently, learning is an individual process which is different for each teacher trainee. This means that in training foreign language teachers, each teacher trainee's initial situation will have to be considered. Although final requirements must of course be met, goals, subject matter, and methods will have to be fine-tuned to each teacher trainee's possibilities. In turn, this implies that much attention will have to be paid to individual choices and responsibilities in the learning process. This is the only way to ensure that teachers are at least willing and able to continue growing and developing after their initial education. As a result, our tendency to predetermine all subject matter as well as the way it should be processed by teacher trainees has decreased significantly. Previously we had argued that future foreign language teachers should have some insight into their learning processes and be able to make use of them in coaching their pupils properly in autonomous foreign language learning (Van Esch et al. 1996). But the task before us is more complex.

Teacher trainees indicate that they need more information concerning the reforms, as evidenced in this English teacher trainee's comments:

> As preparation for teaching in a second stage class of secondary education, I would like to receive more information on the Studiehuis and the upper secondary phase. I'm thinking of organizational set-up and elaboration, theoretical basis, and practical instruments to realize the change from a class where the teacher is at the center to a class where the learner is at the center. Special attention should be paid to instruments for testing and checking, because during the first week of tests at our school it appeared that the result of the first tests were very poor because, among other things, of lack of immediate checking.

Our analysis leads us to conclude that teachers have an urgent need for support in the implementation of the new approach, provided through both pre-service and in-service training. As teacher trainers we need to increase our knowledge of and insight into learning processes and how these processes can be encouraged. We want to be able to adjust our training pedagogy to the latest developments. Our current research looks into how a teacher obtains insight into the learning process of the learner. What diagnostic activities does the teacher use to establish goals and increments in the learning processes? And how does the teacher take the learning process one step further?

It is too early yet for a final judgment on learner autonomy in the context of foreign language teaching in the Netherlands. But we can draw some preliminary conclusions. The first is that an educational reform such as greater learner autonomy asks for good preconditions and is not helped by a simultaneous change and increased difficulty of content. The second conclusion is that, in spite of resistance from those involved against the Studiehuis, there are no major objections against the principles and the implications of learner autonomy. The third conclusion is that the teacher plays a central part in encouraging learner autonomy and that a positive attitude, good training, guidance, and refresher programs are essential. The fourth conclusion is that adequate course materials and pedagogic approaches along with instruments such as study guides contribute to the successful incorporation of principles of learner autonomy in everyday foreign language learning and teaching. The fifth conclusion is that graduate schools of education have the task of training teachers for new practices and have to carry out research into those practiced. Teacher trainers have to take the teachers' initial situation into account and be prepared to place notions of learner autonomy and foreign language learning in a historic perspective.

PART III

*Language Teacher Education for
the Twenty-First Century*

10

Genres of Power in Language Teacher Education: Interpreting the "Experts"

CELESTE KINGINGER

At the beginning of the twenty-first century, language teacher education shows clear signs of crisis. Following decades of the rapid emergence of second language acquisition as a focus of ongoing research, prominent teacher educators have expressed increasing skepticism regarding the theory-practice dichotomy, a hierarchical distinction that emphasizes the primacy of theory and theoreticians. In rejecting that model, they cite the essentially ideological processes through which theories garner educators' allegiance as well as the paucity of shared values and priorities between teachers on the one hand and theoreticians and researchers on the other. (For examples of this critique, see Clarke 1994; Freeman and Johnson 1998; Kleinsasser 1993; Pennycook 1989; Prabhu 1995; Sato and Kleinsasser 1999a; van Lier 1994; and Chapters 1, 3, 5, and 7.)

Teachers are interested primarily in developing insights for the practice of language instruction in particular contexts, and are often cast as knowledge consumers. Second language acquisition (SLA) researchers, by contrast, see their pursuit as that of gaining knowledge about language acquisition processes that are universal in nature, unaffected by context and relevant to all learners regardless of their particular situation. Thus, for example, the interaction hypothesis of Michael Long (1981) suggests that particular types of social interaction (called "negotiation of meaning") play a crucial role in refining input to the learner, making that input comprehensible and thereby enhancing language acquisition. This hypothesis has become a part of the mainstream approach to language teacher education, and is amply referenced in manuals for language teachers (Lightbown and Spada 1999; Schrum and Glisan 2000). Yet, the theory upon which the interaction hypothesis is based, and to which it is seen to contribute, is not a theory of the social context, one that can be directly related to teaching. Rather, it is a theory of internal representations of second languages, and of the cognitive processes relating features of the linguistic environment to the development of those representations. According to Long, in fact, the social context remains relatively unimportant to the functioning of those processes, and need not be accounted for in theories of second language acquisition: "Social and affective factors, the L2 [second language] acquisition literature suggests, are important but relatively minor in their impact, in both naturalistic and classroom settings, and most current theories of and in SLA reflect that fact" (Long 1997, 319). To question its status as official or received knowledge (Wallace 1991) within approaches to language teacher education, critics need not contest the value of Long's theory within SLA research. A central concern of teacher educators is and must remain the transfer of knowledge from one domain to the other.

Attention must be paid not only to the qualities of such received knowledge but to the stances that teachers are enjoined to adopt vis-à-vis all such knowledge. Without being cast simply as consumers of knowledge that is produced far from the classroom, teachers nonetheless can make good use of access to received knowledge for two reasons. First, received knowledge represents the multiple and diverse "genres of power" (Wells 1999) of language education, genres that eventually come to influence and even to define many features of the teaching context. To deny access to these genres would be as disempowering as to demand unconditional reverence and subservience to them. Second, teachers must learn to mediate between diverse expert and/or powerful discourses, on the one hand, and the particular features of their own practice, on the other (Kramsch 1995a). Such ability to see the same problem through a range of interpretive lenses is a hallmark of reflective practice. In providing access to the genres of power, an important function of teacher education is the inclusion of experience, both in mediating between these genres and in interpreting their value as discursive frames for teaching problems.

Therefore, in this chapter I will show that a primarily pedagogical focus (i.e., emphasis on problems or other topics nominated by teachers) will be tempered and enriched by close reading and analysis of the way these issues are framed in actual texts taken as exemplars of multiple expert discourses. To illustrate with an example of how such multifaceted treatment of a teaching problem might work, I have chosen the classical notion of *error*, with associated concepts such as *focus on form, interlanguage, accuracy*, and *correction*. I will show how this same issue will have multiple meanings within diverse forms of expertise, representing the different sociocultural settings in which these concepts act as mediating tools (Vygotsky 1978; Wertsch 1991, 1998).

Expert Discourses

Given the demand for knowledge firmly grounded in practice, teacher educators have legitimately begun to question the value of the knowledge base for teaching as it is currently formulated. Freeman and Johnson (1998), for example, argue that the knowledge base, having emerged from communities of scholars whose priorities and values are not shared by teachers, "does not articulate easily or cogently into classroom practice" (413). Postmodern critical inquiry (e.g., Kinginger 1998; Lantolf 1996; Prabhu 1995) meanwhile, emphasizes that theories rise to prominence in an essentially commercial process, following successful competition for allegiance in the educational marketplace. This critique argues that the process of gaining teachers' allegiance is based not on the truth or falsehood of the theories. Rather, successful competition becomes fundamentally a question of ideology and the ways in which theories are marketed: "The theories themselves can no doubt be viewed as being ideational in nature, rather than ideological, within their respective disciplines, being attempts to make sense of phenomena within their own disciplines; but their use of language pedagogy to propagate themselves or to gain dominance, sometimes by giving themselves attributes such as truth, authenticity or knowledge of 'real' language for the purpose, makes them a matter of ideology in pedagogy, not unlike commercial ideology" (Prabhu 1995, 66–67).

As critics of the theory-practice distinction have noted (Clarke 1994), the dominant ideology of schooling in most places remains that of technical rationality. According to technical rationalist models, theory building is assigned prima facie superior status and defined as knowledge production, taking place in contexts far removed from classrooms. Teaching is viewed as a delivery system employed in the mere dissemination of knowledge. In this model, both method (Pennycook 1989) and theory operate as top-down directives. The general result is to deprive teachers of skills and to limit the scope of their actions. All such technicist definitions of teaching deny the relevance of local and practical forms of culturally shaped knowledge and downplay the resourcefulness, creativity, and interpretive skill of teachers (Bowers and Flinders 1990). They reject a priori the notion that classroom learning could result in the creation of new and valuable knowledge.

It is reasonable to doubt whether the ways in which some successful theorists portray language learning could become relevant for language teaching. Nonetheless, a strong argument exists for maintaining an inclusive attitude toward the received knowledge of the profession. As Wells (1999) has argued, although respect for and inclusion of local, particular, and context-sensitive forms of knowledge may all but guarantee success, providing access to the genres of power (145) represented within scientific discourse remains a significant task of education. Whether or not expert discourses dovetail well with the personal outlooks of individual teachers, on a larger scale they continue to influence the qualities of officially sanctioned expertise as well as their propagation via the tools of teachers' work: textbooks, curricula, policies, strategic plans, and the like. In sum, even if direct applicability of the knowledge base cannot be asserted, to deny classroom access to the genres of power in favor of local knowledge, folk discourses—or even those insights based solely on reflective teaching—would place teachers and learners at a distinct disadvantage relative to their counterparts who are exposed to the broader ideological context of their education.

Given that the theory-practice distinction and the social hierarchy it engenders are inherently problematic, one way to respond is to change the central role of received knowledge within teacher education courses, beginning with the attitude of supplication that teacher-learners are encouraged to maintain toward expert knowledge and the qualities of their engagement with that knowledge. Rather than cast teachers in the constraining role of knowledge consumers vying to become consumer outlets, teacher educators must recognize and cultivate the value of teachers' own interpretive efforts and their role as producers of context-sensitive, locally relevant knowledge.

A study by Tedick and Walker (1994) demonstrates the need for revision and redesign of teacher education courses. They conclude a report of their research on the education of foreign language teachers with the ironic assertion that teacher education is paralyzed by its very methodology. Most programs tend to fall into one of two categories: either they adhere to one dominant stance from which teacher-learners are advised to evaluate all others, or they are eclecticist programs and present an array of theoretical and/or methodological possibilities with the implied assumption that all approaches are equally valid. Also implicit is an expectation that teachers, like any seasoned veterans of the marketplace, will have learned the knack of selection characteristic of Schön's (1983) reflective practitioner: choosing from among them in a principled way. As Tedick and Walker (1994) observe: "What is missing from all such practices is a sense that all of teaching (a human activity after all) occurs within a social, historical and political context and requires that teachers (and teacher educators) above all consider this context before and while they think about what activities might best meet students' needs" (307). They go on to observe that teachers are left to their own devices as they seek to establish a reasonable and productive relationship between their own context of practice and the form or forms of expertise to which they may be exposed. A major failure of teacher education programs is their lack of emphasis on teachers' own interpretation of expert discourses.

The literature on teacher cognition, meanwhile, emphasizes both the inevitability and the desirability of teachers' interpretive work throughout their careers. Teaching and reflecting on teaching are seen as activities mediated by multiple semiotic tools of diverse origin (van Lier 1996). When teachers encounter a new theory, they do not apply it. They "enter into a dialectical relationship" (Levine 1993, 204) with whatever facets of the new knowledge can cohere within personal outlooks on particular teaching problems (Au 1990; Kinginger 1997). New, integrative understandings emerging from this work are seen as the hallmark of reflective practice (Schön 1983). The benefits of reflective practice emerge from a willingness and capacity to continuously reframe pedagogical questions in productive and informed ways, calling on both received knowledge and knowing-in-action so as to achieve long-term, contextually sensitive enhancement of students' experiences: "Viewing teachers as reflective practitioners assumes that teachers can both pose and solve problems related to their educational practice. Daily, hourly, even minute-by-minute, teachers attempt to solve problems that arise in the classroom. The way in which they solve those problems is affected by how they pose or frame the problem. Reflective teachers think both about how they frame and then how to solve the problem at hand" (Zeichner and Liston 1996, 4–5).

Expert discourses can play a role in teacher education programs, not because they offer solutions to teaching problems but because they provide diverse frames for teaching problems. Recognizing this role of expertise promotes a move from a model emphasizing transmission and application of knowledge to one in which the desired developmental end point is an informed and coherent professional outlook. A major characteristic of this outlook is flexibility in seeing the same pedagogical problem from different perspectives. Instead of asking whether or not teacher-learners understand, have internalized, or can apply theoretical accounts, it may prove more appropriate to explore the extent to which they manifestly profit from evaluating and using competing meanings. Harré and Gilette (1994) posit the existence of broad individual differences, varying limits in the extent to which people can profit from discursive diversity in directing their psychological lives. Significantly, people who are adept at using multiple perspectives have a history of participation in settings where there exists a dialogue between different ways of seeing and interpreting data:

> Some people will be unskilled in balancing competing meanings and submitting themselves to the reflective or challenging scrutiny that leads to revision of character and positionings, and others will be capable of doing that. We would favor the view that certain kinds of discourse facilitate and make available movement and negotiation in relation to the meanings that inform one's behavior. These tend to be found in contexts in which the intersection of discourse and the dialogue between patterns of signification is itself a validated type of activity. If individuals are affirmed and exposed in non-threatening ways to the alternatives presented by different constructions, then one would expect them to develop and be comfortable with the skills of discourse. (Harré and Gilette 1994, 127)

In other words, it is reasonable to expect that through the ongoing process of examining diverse frames for the same pedagogical problem, teachers will gain practical interpretive skill, or wisdom related to the practice of teaching. If the dialogue between patterns of signification includes information about the social and historical construction of received knowledge, they may also develop an awareness of the political and ideological topography of the profession. This, in turn, will assist them in relating productively and selectively to the sources of power that influence teaching contexts.

Example: When Is an Error an Error?

Kramsch (1995a) argues that communication between language educators and applied linguists is characterized by a discourse problem. This problem is generated in part by the rise to prominence of different discourse domains, each with its own distinct social history, signature vocabulary, underlying values, and investment in the definition of professional expertise. The complex and varied professional landscape now presents many opportunities for expanded understanding of language learning. However, "because each discourse domain has its own metaphors, its own categorizations, its own way of relating the parts to the whole, the broadened intellectual agenda now available to language teachers and applied linguists has made it more difficult to communicate across historically and socially created discourses" (46). As Kramsch describes it, the problem is one of mediation between discourse communities: constructs are borrowed and reinterpreted. In that process their meaning is reshaped, appropriately or otherwise, to conform to the sociocultural geography of their new setting.

The following sections of this chapter demonstrate one approach to addressing the discourse problem of competing meanings in the context of teacher education courses, an approach that relies on the critical analysis of pedagogical texts and sociohistorical contexts (Fairclough 1995). In keeping with the increasing validation of teachers' own initial concerns, the first step involves identifying a problem or question that teachers nominate as pertinent to classroom practice, in this case, the status and treatment of learner errors. The approach then involves a definition of discourse and a selection of discourses that intersect in various ways with the teachers' views on the problem. In subsequent work, together with their teacher, the class engages in close reading and analysis of texts representing these various discourses. In contrast to materials for teacher education that are generally characterized by the interpretation and reindexing of expertise on behalf of teachers, this approach places teachers and their students in a dialectical relation with texts that must then be situated with respect to their social history and ideological foundations.

Most beginning teachers receive without critical analysis the notion that non-native forms in language production signal a source of difficulty for learners. Thus, they have a responsibility for developing a reasonable stance toward such "errors." When they turn to the professional literature, however, they find no easy answers. An indication of the sheer variety of interpretations in the literature is to be found in Morissey's (1992) analysis of the conceptual metaphors (Lakoff and Johnson 1980) in influential texts for error. Morissey examined texts representing so-called structural/behavioral, generative/cognitive, and functional/interactional approaches to language teacher education. Her findings reveal that although the texts she studied include numerous common metaphors, they also present significant differences and occasional contradictions.

For example, whereas in some cases error is unnatural (Palmer 1964: "unnatural dialect unknown to native speakers," 18), in others, error is natural (Krashen and Terrell 1983, "speech errors must be accepted as a natural part of the acquisition process," 143). In addition, error is wrong in the three approaches Morissey studied (e.g., in Brooks 1960, "like sin" and "quite simply immoral," 56 and 168). Also, throughout the literature, error is a defect, a failure, missing the target, and harmful. Elsewhere, in the functional-interactional approach, error is acceptable, a learning and teaching aid, and even desirable (in Hymes 1979, "what to grammar is imperfect, or unaccounted for, may be the artful accomplishment of a social act," 8).

Turning now to the analysis of discourses related to this pedagogical problem, in a plenary address at the annual meeting of the American Association for Applied Linguistics, Cazden (1998) offered a useful commentary on the transformation of the term "discourse." Within linguistics, orthodox discourse analysis has traditionally concerned itself with the structural organization of naturally occurring samples of language use. In recent years, however, following Gee (1990), the term has come to refer to broader categories of socially situated meaning, "constellations of repeated meanings" (Stubbs 1996, 158, cited in Cazden 1998, 12) or "ways of understanding" (Cazden 1998, 11) that emerge from histories of participation in particular kinds of institutionally sanctioned language use, and that are linked to explicit or implicit ideological stances. Used in this way, discourse is connected to a particular group of people who share a common history, a signature vocabulary, and a set of values. Cazden therefore categorizes approaches to discourse along two lines: those that are principally concerned with naturally occurring language use, which she terms Discourse 1, and those that analyze "ways of understanding," Discourse 2.

In parallel with Fairclough (1995), Cazden notes that there is rich potential in studying the interaction between Discourse 1, traditionally the purview of linguistics, and Discourse 2, traditionally the focus of social theory. These two categories in fact constitute a dyadic system, wherein the two forms of discourse are mutually constitutive: ways of talking both construct ways of understanding and are engendered by them.

In the categorization proposed by Kramsch (1995a, 1995b) and adapted here, there are four primary discourses (in the broader, socially situated sense of the term) that are commonly invoked in discussions of foreign language teaching in the United States. (The term "discourse" with a small d will be used to denote broad, socioculturally generated "ways of meaning"—Gee's "Discourse" or Cazden's "Discourse 2." The term "text" will refer to the samples of writings used as illustrative examples.) They are indexed in the discussion below by the following convenient (albeit inadequate) shorthand descriptors: modernist/scientific, modernist/utilitarian, instructional discourses, and the discourse of critical pedagogy. In surveying the professional landscape, teacher educators find that each distinct discourse adopts its own approach to the problem of errors in accordance with its ideological underpinnings. Inasmuch as every person has allegiance to and history of many different sources of identity, it is inadvisable to identify individuals as representatives of discourses. Rather, it is possible to demonstrate and encourage teachers to analyze how specific texts signal their belonging to the historical flow of particular streams of discourse. The examples below illustrate the selection and interpretation of sample texts.

MODERNIST/SCIENTIFIC DISCOURSE

Modernist/scientific discourse adheres to the values and methods of modern science, tracing its roots to the change of mind that occurred in the seventeenth century when, following Descartes, medieval humanist scholarly approaches were set aside in favor of abstract rationality (Toulmin 1990). Henceforth, rather than examine local, timely, and particular realities, serious scholarship would focus on discovering that which is universal, timeless, and general. The rules of logical scientific argumentation largely supplanted the prior focus on rhetoric and on personal authority. Epistemological pedigree, in the form of who said what to whom and when, was replaced by a scientificist system in which the truth could be accessed in texts by anyone capable of reading them correctly. Texts could be unpacked, and their pure meaning unveiled, by anyone properly equipped to do so.

For language acquisition researchers to participate in this discourse, it is necessary that they believe in abstract, universal truths about human behavior that follow the laws of nature and that can ultimately be discovered through rigorous application of experimental method. Scholars studying cognitive processes of language acquisition therefore emphasize the importance of objective scientific inquiry, and of progress toward greater knowledge of the truth about acquisition processes.

Thus, for example, in *Second Language Learning: Theoretical Foundations* (1994), Sharwood Smith provides the following precise definitions of the technical term "error":

> *Error* (see also "deviant form," "interlanguage"). An error signifies a deviation from the standard norms, understood to be the learner's target. The negative connotation of the notion of error makes it an undesirable term in IL [interlanguage] research but many still use it, as a convenience.
>
> *Deviant form* (see also "developmental pattern"). An interlanguage form which deviates from the native equivalent and which may either be a random occurrence or form part of a pattern of development.
>
> *Developmental pattern.* A non-native structural pattern (form/construction) which deviates from the native equivalent but which is not a random occurrence but forms part of a pattern of development as observed by second language researchers within a given well-defined structural area like negation or wh-question formation.

Interlanguage. The systematic linguistic behavior of non-native speakers of a given language, normally understood to be what is produced in natural situations of language use where the focus is on conveying meaning and not on the formal correctness of utterances. (Sharwood Smith 1994, 198, 199, 200)

As is characteristic throughout modernist/scientific discourse on language learning, errors in this instance are neither good nor bad. The "negative connotation" of the term renders it ill-suited as a tool in the search for truth, a search conducted through a dispassionate examination of empirical facts, with no associated value judgment. Errors are empirical facts. They may be "deviant" with respect to the "target" (see Chapter 1) but they are also, crucially, "systematic" and "part of a pattern of development." Properly categorized errors (that is, those that are correctly read) constitute evidence for these patterns, which in turn are assumed to be indicative of universal truths about language acquisition.

MODERNIST/UTILITARIAN DISCOURSE

Like modernism in general, the utilitarian facet of modernism traces its ideological roots to the European Enlightenment, hence to the origins of individualism and egalitarianism (Scollon and Scollon 1995). Utilitarianism has achieved prominence in commerce-oriented corporate discourses around the world. In the United States, where effectiveness is increasingly equated with personal life fulfillment (as is anecdotally suggested by the overwhelming popularity of Covey's bestselling *The Seven Habits of Highly Effective People,* 1989), utilitarianism exists in harmony with common sense. It is based on the ethical principle of utility, that society exists in order to produce the greatest happiness for the largest number of people. Utilitarianism also presumes that humans are logical, rational economic beings, that the free individual is the basis of society, and that the key to greater production (hence progress toward greater happiness for more people) is technology and invention.

The utilitarian aim of formal schooling is to maximize the efficiency with which progressive knowledge (a commodity) is distributed for cumulative accretion via lessons dispensed in discrete measured quantities. With the emergence of institutionalized schooling within the broader utiliarian society came devaluation of nonformal learning; forced separation of working and learning contexts; emphasis on quantification of both physical and human attributes; and, of course, the conception of the student mind as a vessel to be filled with knowledge, through the purposeful act of teaching.

In the U.S. language teaching context, utilitarian discourses are closely as-

Table 10.1. Assessment Criteria—Speaking

Proficiency Level	Accuracy
Superior	No pattern of error in basic structures. Errors virtually never interfere with communication or distract the native speaker from the message.
Advanced	Understood without difficulty by speakers unaccustomed to dealing with non-native speakers.
Intermediate	Understood, with some repetition, by speakers accustomed to dealing with non-native speakers.
Novice	May be difficult to understand, even for speakers accustomed to dealing with non-native speakers.

Source: Swender 1999, 31, cited in Schrum and Glisan 2000, 174.

sociated with policy and public relations, simultaneously emphasizing both a view of language acquisition as product and the importance of quality control in the form of "priorities," "standards," "accountability," and "performance objectives" (see Chapter 6). Because of its affiliation with the public discourses of government, commerce, and industry, U.S. language teaching borrows many of its forms from these sources. These are also the sectors from which the institutions engaged in language education receive funding for research, classroom education, and curriculum development,

In utilitarian discourse on language teaching, language competence is a product that can be gauged through objective measurement of its effectiveness. Such a definition is implicit, notably, in the American Council on the Teaching of Foreign Languages' Oral Proficiency Guidelines (1986). In the early 1980s, national efforts to improve the practicality and applicability of language teaching in the schools had led to an effort to translate this scale of speaking ability from the form used within governmental and military language training contexts to a form suitable for secondary and post-secondary education. The result was a descriptive scale ranking three aspects of speaking ability (function, content, and accuracy) from "novice" to "superior" levels. The descriptors of "accuracy" contain reference to the learner's errors.

Promoters of the guidelines and related national standards (ACTFL 1996; see Chapter 6) are concerned with the image of effectiveness projected to the public by the language teaching profession. They emphasize measurement of discrete quantities of competence and the quality of the final product of instruction. The guidelines focus on the degree to which learner language displays "accuracy" with respect both to the "basic structures" of the language and to the judgment of native speakers. An error, therefore, is a defect in the product that reduces its effectiveness but (presumably) can be improved through closer attention to the production process.

INSTRUCTIONAL DISCOURSES

Instructional discourse is action-oriented, reflecting the immediate "hands-on" needs of those who directly intervene in the organization of the classroom. Teachers and teacher educators highlight specific, practical skills and outcomes, and the techniques for attaining them in the classroom. This is the discourse of educators who are confronted on a daily basis with various dilemmas in creating an environment to optimize classroom work and production: how to organize material, what and how to teach, tips for the practical solution of common problems predictably encountered in the field, and how to evaluate progress toward attainment of goals. Taking the goals and their validity as a given, instructional discourse directly assists the teacher immersed in the classroom with suggested activities, best practices, and case studies to expedite classroom processes.

Issues that may be complex subjects of long-term inquiry within the other discourses, such as the nature and significance of social context, or the natural processes of interlanguage development, become practical problems requiring an immediate solution. In instructional discourse, therefore, errors present a task for the teacher. In this genre, writers steadfastly maintain their conviction that teacher intervention makes a difference and can always be improved through effort and attention to classroom techniques.

One way in which the development of grammatical competence is frequently addressed is in terms of error correction, that is, what the instructor should do about students' production of non-native forms. In the following example, from *Teaching French: A Practical Guide* (1988), Rivers addresses teachers directly on the subject of error correction during autonomous oral interaction:

> The best approach during interaction activities is for the instructor silently to note consistent, systematic errors (not slips of the tongue and occasional lapses in areas where the student usually acquits himself well). These errors will then be discussed with the student at a time when the instructor is helping him to evaluate his success in interaction, with particular attention to the types of errors which hinder communication. The instructor will then use his knowledge of the areas of weakness of a number of students as a basis for his emphases in instruction and review. In this way, we help students focus on what are problem areas for them as they learn from their mistakes. (Rivers 1988, 55)

Note that the emphasis here is on assisting students in the efficient production of error-free language, based on the assumption that conscious, well-organized work in the classroom will ultimately lead to group learning. The text borrows selectively from the other discourses. In enjoining the teacher to note systematicity in learners' errors, it uses a category from scientific discourse. The text emphasizes the quality of learner production not in terms of meaning, intentionality, or broader cross-cultural understanding, but in terms of distracting errors ("errors which hinder communication"). In furthering this aspect of the instructor's role in achieving the greatest good for the largest number of students, the text again borrows from utilitarian discourse. The overall problem, however, is framed in pragmatic terms as the individual student's responsibility to "acquit himself well," and the teacher's overriding observation, understanding, and orchestration of learning in support of that goal.

THE DISCOURSE OF CRITICAL PEDAGOGY

Kramsch notes the rising prominence of a fourth discourse, the "discourse of critical pedagogy, cultural criticism and postmodern thought" (1995a, 47), of scholars in the social sciences and humanities. In an effort to understand the connections between language learning, sociocultural history and identity, this discourse concerns itself with such questions as the extent to which the profession meets its stated larger goals of educating for peace, communicative competence, intercultural understanding, and awareness of the social meaning of language. Experts who align their work with the discourse of critical pedagogy are expressly adhering neither to the rigors of modernist science nor to the rationalized production orientation of utilitarianism. Rather, they are working to recover a humanist approach that values reasonable conduct in scholarship over strict application of abstract rationalist method, that asks and answers questions in a contextually sensitive way, and that admits as evidence a full range of sources excluded from experimental research: ethnographies, case studies, life histories, and stories.

An example of a critical approach to "error" can be found in Tomas Graman's (1988) essay on the application of Freire's pedagogy to the study of second languages:

> The students in ESL and foreign language classes in the United States suffer from an abuse of professional authority that denies the value of their ideas and interlanguage constructions. Many teachers and administrators refer to much of these students' language as inferior, as gibberish, or as "mindless ungrammatical chatter" (citing James, 1985). In the Freirean sense, however, "mindless chatter" results not from the language's lack of standard or native-

like grammar, or from any aspect of the form of the language, but rather from the absence of meaningful content.

 The most important thing is that words be genuine and that their aim be to understand and name some element of the world relevant to them. The criteria of grammaticality and pronunciation, on the other hand, ignore the importance of the transforming experience involved in constructing language. Teachers who focus on the form of the language are emphasizing what Freire calls the "sonority of words" in a way that subordinates what students say to how they say it. For Freire, the point is to focus on the meaning that learners construct. This is the essence of the transforming power of the learning experience. (Graman 1988, 438)

The definition of "error" that emerges from this text is, once again, significantly different from those presented by the other texts. In claiming value and relevance for student's construction of meaning, and calling for teachers' attention to the transforming experience this involves, Graman suggests that focus on form represents a kind of social and political repression, draining the classroom of significance, while alienating students and silencing their voices. The error is no longer merely an interesting empirical fact, nor it is a defective product requiring intervention by the teacher. Instead, the error is a sign of the learner's struggle to appropriate genuine words, and a marker of changing identity.

Applied linguists and language teachers can understand one another not so much by informing one another of their expert research, or of their professional teaching practices, but by engaging together in an intellectual exploration of the historical and social forces that have shaped their respective discourses (Kramsch 1995a, 56).

 The above analysis of representative texts of diverse origin yielded an array of discursive frames through which to view a specific pedagogical problem, the "error." As responses to teachers' concerns, these discursive frames may be seen to "apply," each in its own way, to different contexts in teachers' work. These include, for example, forming reasonable expectations for students' grammatical competence, advocating for language learning in the public arena, selecting strategies for focus on form in the classroom, and interpreting the meaning of language use and development.

 Other pedagogical problems might readily be addressed in a similar manner. These problems include the "negotiation of meaning," the role of the teacher, the identity of the learner, and, of course, the meanings of "communicative competence." Within the context of U.S. foreign language teaching, for example, one impediment to understanding the construct of communicative competence as it was initially framed is the way in which it is translated by and for teachers within utilitarian discourse that values individually owned and quantifiable deliverables. This transformation of the construct makes sense within the general outlines of American utilitarianism, Taylorism, and pragmatism, and the history of their profound influence upon schooling. Teachers and administrators in the United States relate with singular enthusiasm to a vocabulary that translates and objectifies the results of their efforts into a product comprehensible to the taxpaying public (Kramsch 1995b). Yet this process of interpretive translation also obscures the fundamentally "dynamic," "relative," and "interpersonal" nature of communicative ability (Savignon 1997) as well as the long-term sociocultural processes of its development and its relationship to the broader goals of education in the humanities. In all cases, close examination of the texts used in professional discussion of a given construct illuminate the diverse interpretive themes surrounding its use.

Such emphasis on the multiplicity of available meanings may seem to suggest an encroachment of the unprincipled eclecticism so prevalent in teacher education. However, the stance advocated here assumes that the principles of teaching are not the province of teacher educators alone, nor are they to be found only in teacher preparation materials. Rather, it is the responsibility of each individual teacher to develop a coherent and informed yet flexible professional outlook of his or her own, through collaborative engagement with professional resources including authoritative texts, colleagues, learners, and teacher educators' history, culture, and context. One important role of teacher education is to provide access to discourses in such a way that teachers can situate their meaning with respect to their own practice and to the genres of power influencing language education. Close reading of representative texts demonstrates the intricate relation between language use and ways of meaning. This in turn allows teachers to grasp how constructs come to make sense—a particular kind of sense—within the discourses of their origin, and to examine how the values and priorities of a given discourse overlap or diverge from their own and those of their students, institutions, and cultures.

Epilogue

SANDRA J. SAVIGNON

In the preface to this volume I stated my purpose to be that of bringing together a collection of initiatives, projects, and activities to showcase some of the best work being done in places around the world to make communicative language teaching (CLT) an attainable goal. My efforts as editor were directed at reflecting the contextualized nature of CLT by preserving the unique perspective of individual authors in the particular context that they describe.

Three chapters on Japan, individually and in concert, record the reality of CLT in that vibrant English language teaching setting. Nearby Hong Kong, a region that has known considerable political and social transformation in recent years, boasts a strong contingent of applied linguists and language teaching methodologists. Within this setting, an award-winning doctoral dissertation has carefully documented the influence of a change in public examinations on the classroom teaching of English. And in yet another Asian setting, a group of respected teacher educators offer their views on the challenges that must be confronted in terms of teacher attitudes and beliefs if Taiwan is to meet the increasing demand for competent English users. Curricular and materials revisions and the early introduction of ELT at the elementary school level, while significant, are insufficient to bring about the needed change.

Within the United States, where education reform has remained a focus of national debate for some time, curricula and assessment are not directly regulated by a centralized ministry or department of education. Rather, a set of National Standards for Foreign Language Learning (NSFLL) established by a coalition of professional language teacher organizations represents the hoped for, if elusive, goal of CLT. At the university level, a combination of technological innovation and increasing pressure to hold down costs while competing for student enrollment has enhanced the attraction of computer-aided instruction (CAI). A thoughtful account of one such context highlights the implications for teacher education and foreshadows the impact of innovations yet to come. A third chapter by an American educator looks at theoretical and practical issues in language teacher education from the perspective of postmodern critical theory. In advocating teacher empowerment and showing us how to read different discourses critically and set them in a framework for reflection and discussion, she underscores the theme of culture- and context-specific knowledge that is central to this collection.

Learner autonomy is essential to language education in continental Europe, where communicative competence in three languages or more is often the norm. The free flow of people and knowledge within the European Union itself has increased both the need and the opportunity for language learning and led to experimentation with an array of programs that place new demands on both learners and teachers. The implications for language teacher education are far reaching.

Taken together, the chapters in this collection have looked at language teaching contexts in Europe, Asia, and the United States. Although each is significant in its own right, they are by no means representative. If we are fully to appreciate the dynamic and contextualized nature of language teaching in the world today, we must hear from voices in South Africa, in Tunisia, in Israel, in Egypt, in Germany, in Russia, in China, in Costa Rica, in Brazil, and elsewhere. Each has a story to tell.

I noted also in the preface the challenge I faced in setting an organizational framework for the texts once they had all been completed. My decision was somewhat arbitrary. Alternatively, I could have settled for divisions based on research methodology, or the way of knowing represented in individual chapters. Or I could have established a sequence consisting of theoretical background followed by program implementation and then ongoing research and adaptation. The various contributions might even be viewed in kaleidoscopic fashion, like brilliant multi-layered bits of glass that tumble about to form different yet always intriguing configurations.

Quite independent of the sequence in which they are read, each text records an instance of language teaching and learning as observed from a particular vantage point. From these records, four themes emerged that reflected language teaching and language teacher education more generally.

1. Throughout the chapters, the highly contextualized nature of CLT is underscored again and again. It would be inappropriate to speak of CLT as a teaching "method" in any sense of that term as it was used in the twentieth century. Rather, CLT is an approach that understands language to be inseparable from individual identity and social behavior. Not only does language define a community; a community, in turn, defines the forms and uses of language. The norms and goals appropriate for learners in a given setting, and the means for attaining these goals, are the concern of those involved.

2. Directly related both to the concept of language as culture in motion and to the multilingual reality in which most of the world population finds itself is the futility of any definition of a "native speaker." The term came to prominence in descriptive structural linguistics in the mid-twentieth century and was adopted by language teaching methodologists to define an ideal for language learners. Attention was given to discerning what was termed "integrative" motivation, the desire to be like or to be accepted by a particular cultural group. More recently, British and American promotion of English as a global language has been aided by lingering notions that "authentic" use of English somehow requires the involvement of a "native" speaker.

3. The richness of the data found in many of the texts, including surveys and interviews with teachers, is striking. As is true within the social sciences more generally, we are increasingly aware that in our attempts to discern system or rationality, we have been led to focus on certain observable patterns while at the same time disregarding all that defies classification. Just as the implementation of CLT is itself highly contextualized, so too are means of gathering and interpreting data on these implementations. When I shared the chapters in their prepublication format with a group of graduate students in applied linguistics, many of them at the doctoral level, I was pleased by their response to one text in particular. They liked the account by a Japanese teacher of how she relates the communicative teaching of English to precepts of Zen Buddhism. Many found her narrative to be "novel" and "refreshing." For an Argentinean woman it "represented CLT not only as a theoretical ideal but also as something highly adaptable to the realities of many different settings." She found it annoying that "CLT has primarily been depicted from a Eurocentric or North American point of view."

4. The role of language tests in language teaching is overwhelming. Time and again, assessment appears to be the driving force behind curricular innovations. In many settings, demands for accountability along with a posi-

tivistic stance that one cannot teach that which cannot be described and measured by a common yardstick continue to influence program content and goals. Irrespective of their own needs or interests, learners prepare for the tests they will be required to pass. High-stakes language tests in many settings determine future access to education and opportunity. They may also gauge teaching effectiveness. And yet, tests are seldom able to adequately capture the context-embedded collaboration that is the stuff of human communicative activity. A critical reflexive analysis of the impact of tests on language teaching practice, then, would seem a good place to enter into a consideration of how language teaching practices in a given context might be adapted to better meet the communicative needs of the next generation of learners.

References

Adams, R. S., and D. Chen. 1981. *The Process of Educational Innovation: An International Perspective.* London: Kogan Page/UNESCO Press.

ALC. 1996. *Eigo Kyoiku Jiten* (Handbook of English teaching education: Survey on oral communication). Tokyo: ALC Press.

Alderson, J. C., and L. Hamp-Lyons. 1996. TOEFL preparation courses: A study of washback. *Language Testing* 13, 280–297.

Alderson, J. C., and D. Wall. 1993. Does washback exist? *Applied Linguistics* 14, 115–129.

American Council on the Teaching of Foreign Languages. 1986. *ACTFL Proficiency Guidelines.* Yonkers, N.Y.: ACTFL.

——. 2000. Executive summary of standards for foreign language learning: Preparing for the twenty-first century. www.actfl.org/htdocs/pubs/download.htm.

Anderson, J. 1993. Is a communicative approach practical for teaching English in China? Pros and cons. *System* 21, 471–480.

Andrews, S. 1994a. The washback effect of examinations—Its impact upon curriculum innovation in English language teaching. *Curriculum Forum* 4, 44–58.

——. 1994b. Washback or washout? The relationship between examination reform and curriculum innovation. In D. Nunan, V. Berry, and R. Berry, eds., *Bringing About Change in Language Education.* Hong Kong: Department of Curriculum Studies, University of Hong Kong.

Andrews, S., and J. Fullilove. 1994. Assessing spoken English in public examinations—Why and how? In J. Boyle and P. Falvey, eds., *English Language Testing in Hong Kong*. Hong Kong: Chinese University Press.

Arvan L., and D. Musumeci. 2000. Instructor attitudes with the SCALE Efficiency Projects. In J. Bourne, ed., *On-line Education*. Nashville: Center for Asynchronous Learning Networks.

Arvan, L., J. C. Ory, C. Bullock, K. K. Burnaska, and M. Hanson. 1998. The SCALE Efficiency Projects: A preliminary report. *Journal of Asynchronous Learning Networks* 2, www.aln.org.alnweb/journal/jaln_vol2issue2.htm.

Au, K. H. 1990. Changes in a teacher's views of interactive comprehension instruction. In L. C. Moll, ed., *Vygotsky and Education: Instructional Implications and Applications of Sociohistorical Psychology*. New York: Cambridge University Press.

Bachman, L. 1990. *Fundamental Considerations in Language Testing*. Oxford: Oxford University Press.

Bachman, L. F., and A. S. Palmer. 1996. *Language Testing in Practice*. Oxford: Oxford University Press.

Bailey, K. M. 1996. Working for washback: A review of the washback concept in language testing. *Language Testing* 13, 257–279.

———. 2000. *Washback in Language Testing*. Princeton, N.J.: Educational Testing Service.

Baker, E., P. Aschbacher, D. Niemi, and E. Sato. 1992. *Performance Assessment Models: Assessing Content Area Explanations*. University of California, Los Angeles, Center for Research on Evaluation Standards and Student Testing.

Baker, L., and A. L. Brown. 1984. Metacognitive skills and reading. In D. Pearson, M. Kamil, R. Barr, and P. Mosenthal, eds., *Handbook of Reading Research*. New York: Longman.

Bartlett, F. C. 1932. *Remembering: A Study in Experimental and Social Psychology*. Cambridge: Cambridge University Press.

Bartz, W. H., and M. K. Singer. 1996. The programmatic implications of foreign language standards. In R. C. Lafayette, ed., *National Standards: A Catalyst for Reform*. Foreign Language Education Series. Lincolnwood, Ill.: National Textbook Company.

Berns, M. 1990. *Contexts of Competence: Sociocultural Considerations in Communicative Language Teaching*. New York: Plenum.

Biggs, J. B. 1995. Assumptions underlying new approaches to educational assessment. *Curriculum Forum* 4, 1–22.

Biggs, J. B., ed. 1996. Testing: To educate or to select? *Education in Hong Kong at the Cross-Roads*. Hong Kong: Hong Kong Educational Publishing Company.

Boekaerts, M., and P. J. R. Simons. 1995. *Leren en instructie. Psychologie van de leerling en het leerproces*. Assen: Van Gorcum.

Bonset, H., and H. Mulder. 1997. Leren leren in de nieuwe tweede fase. *Levende Talen* 525, 670–677.

Bowers, C. A., and D. J. Flinders. 1990. *Responsive Teaching: An Ecological Approach* to *Classroom Patterns of Language, Culture and Thought.* New York: Teachers' College.

Breen, M., and C. Candlin. 1980. The essentials of a communicative curriculum in language teaching. *Applied Linguistics* 1, 89–110.

Briscoe, C. 1996. The teacher as learner: Interpretations from a case study of teacher change. *Journal of Curriculum Studies* 28 (3): 315–329.

Britzman, D. P. 1991. *Practice Makes Practice: A Critical Study of Learning to Teach.* Albany: State University of New York Press.

Brooks, F. B. 1993. Some problems and caveats in "communicative" discourse: Toward a conceptualization of the foreign language classroom. *Foreign Language Annals* 26, 233–241.

Brooks, N. 1960. *Language and Language-Study: Theory and Practice.* New York: Harcourt, Brace.

Brown, H. D. 1994. *Teaching by Principles: An Interactive Approach to Language Pedagogy.* Englewood Cliffs, N.J.: Prentice-Hall.

Browne, C. M., and M. Wada. 1998. Current issues in high school English teaching in Japan: An exploratory survey. *Language, Culture, and Curriculum* 11, 97–112.

Burns, A. 1990. Focus on language in the communicative classroom. In G. Brindley, ed., *The Second Language Curriculum in Action.* Sydney: National Center for English Language Teaching and Research.

Byram, Michael. 1997. *Teaching and Assessing Intercultural Communicative Competence.* Clevedon, England: Multilingual Matters.

Canale, M. 1983. From communicative competence to communicative pedagogy. In J. C. Richards and R. W. Schmidt, eds., *Language and Communication.* London: Longman.

Canale, M., and M. Swain. 1980. Theoretical bases of communicative approaches to second language teaching and testing. *Applied Linguistics* 1, 1–47.

Candlin, C. 1978. *Teaching of English: Principles and an Exercise Typology.* London: Langenscheidt-Longman.

Candlin, C., and P. Mohr. 1978. Form, Funktion und Strategie. Zur Planung kommunikativer Fremdsprachencurricula. In *Kommunikativer Englischunterricht. Prinzipien und Uebungstypologie.* Munich: Langenscheidt-Longman.

Carter, K. 1990. Teachers' knowledge and learning to teach. In W. R. Houston, ed., *Handbook of Research on Teacher Education.* London: Macmillan.

Cazden, C. 1998. The meanings of "discourse." Paper presented at the Annual Meeting of the American Association for Applied Linguistics, Seattle.

Celce-Murcia, M., and D. Larsen-Freeman. 1999. *The Grammar Book.* Boston: Heinle and Heinle.

Celce-Murcia, M., Z. Dornyei, and S. Thurrell. 1995. Communicative competence: A pedagogically motivated model with content specifications. *Issues in Applied Linguistics* 2, 5–35.

Chang, W. C. 1993. English subtests of the Taiwan and Taipei joint high school entrance examinations in the last three years: Issues of current junior high school

English language teaching. In *Proceedings of the First International Symposium on English Teaching*. Taipei, Taiwan: Crane.

Chen, C., and J. Huang. 1999. An evaluation of the new version of junior high school EFL teaching materials based on the communicative theory model. In *Proceedings of the Sixteenth Conference of English Teaching and Learning in the Republic of China*. Taipei, Taiwan: Crane.

Chen Wang, L., E. Platt, and R. G. Stakenas. 1999. A countenance model for EFL program evaluation: A Taiwanese example. In *Proceedings of the Sixteenth Conference of English Teaching and Learning in the Republic of China*. Taipei, Taiwan: Crane.

Cheng, L. 1997. How does washback influence teaching? Implications for Hong Kong. *Language and Education* 11 (1): 38–54.

——. 1998. Impact of a public English examination change on students' perceptions and attitudes toward their English learning. *Studies in Educational Evaluation* 24, 279–301.

——. 1999. Changing assessment: Washback on teacher perspectives and actions. *Teaching and Teacher Education* 15, 253–271.

Chou, L. Y. 1999. English instructional innovation in southern Taiwan's two-year junior colleges of technological and vocational education system: A needs assessment. Ph.D. diss., Pennsylvania State University.

Clair, N. 1998. Teacher study groups: Persistent questions in a promising approach. *TESOL Quarterly* 32 (3): 465–492.

Clark, C. M., and P. I. Peterson. 1986. Teachers' thought process. In M. C. Wittrock, ed., *Handbook of Research on Teaching*. 3rd ed. New York: Macmillan.

Clarke, M. 1994. The dysfunctions of the theory/practice discourse. *TESOL Quarterly* 28 (1): 9–25.

Coniam, D., and P. Falvey. 1997. Introducing English language benchmarks for Hong Kong teachers: A preliminary overview. *Curriculum Forum* 6 (2): 16–35.

——. 1999. Setting standards for teachers of English in Hong Kong—The teachers' perspective. *Curriculum Forum* 8 (2): 1–27.

Coniam, D., S. Sengupta, A. B. M. Tsui, and K. Y. Wu. 1994. Computer-mediated communication and teacher education: The case of TELENEX. In N. Bird, P. Falvey, A. B. M. Tsui, D. A. Allison, and A. McNeill, eds., *Language and Learning*. Hong Kong: Institute of Language in Education.

Cortazzi, M., and L. Jin. 1996. Cultures of learning: Language classrooms in China. In H. Coleman, ed., *Society and the Language Classroom*. New York: Cambridge University Press.

Council of Europe. 1996. Common European framework of reference for language learning and teaching: Draft 1 of a framework proposal. Strasbourg: European Committee.

Covey, S. 1989. *The Seven Habits of Highly Effective People: Restoring the Character Ethic*. New York: Simon and Schuster.

Creswell, J. W. 1998. *Qualitative Inquiry and Research Design.* Thousand Oaks, Calif.: Sage.

Crookes, G. 1997. What influences what and how second and foreign language teachers teach? *Modern Language Journal* 81, 67–79.

Crystal, D. 1997. *English as a Global Language.* Cambridge: Cambridge University Press.

Curriculum Development Council. 1982. *The Syllabus for English (Forms I–V).* Hong Kong: Hong Kong Government Printer.

Dam, L. 1994. How do we recognize an autonomous classroom? *Die Neueren Sprachen* 93, 503–527.

Dam, L., and G. Gabrielsen. 1988. Developing learner autonomy in a school context: A six-year experiment beginning in the learner's first year of English. In H. Holec, ed., *Autonomy and Self-Directed Learning: Present Fields of Application.* Strasbourg: Council of Europe.

Darling-Hammond, L., and M. W. McLaughlin. 1995. Policies that support professional development in an era of reform. *Phi Delta Kappan* 76, 597–604.

Davis, J. N. 1997. Educational reform and the Babel (Babbel) of culture: Prospects for the standards for foreign language learning. *Modern Language Journal* 81, 151–163.

De Jon, F. P. C. M. 1992. *Zelfstandig leren: Regulatie van het leerproces en het leren reguleren. Een procesbenadering.* Academisch Proefschrift, Tilburg: Katholieke Universiteit Brabant.

DeCharms, R. 1976. *Enhancing Motivation in the Classroom.* New York: Irvington.

——. 1984. Motivation enhancement in educational settings. In R. E. Ames and C. Ames, eds., *Research on Motivation in Education.* Vol. 1, *Student Motivation.* New York: Academic Press.

Duderstadt, J. J. 1997. The future of the university in an age of knowledge. *Journal of Asynchronous Learning Networks* 1, www.aln.org.alnweb/journal/jaln_vol1issue 2.htm.

Eckstein, M. A., and H. J. Noah. 1993. The politics of examinations: Issues and conflicts. In M. A. Eckstein and H. J. Noah, eds., *Secondary School Examinations: International Perspectives on Policies and Practice.* New Haven: Yale University Press.

Eisner, E. 1991. *The Enlightened Eye: Qualitative Inquiry and the Enhancement of Educational Practice.* New York: Macmillan.

Ellis, R. 1985. *Understanding Second Language Acquisition.* Oxford: Oxford University Press.

——. 1994. *The Study of Second Language Acquisition.* Oxford: Oxford University Press.

——. 1997. *SLA Research and Language Teaching.* Oxford: Oxford University Press.

English, F. W. 1992. *Deciding What to Teach and Test: Developing, Aligning, and Auditing the Curriculum.* Newbury Park, Calif.: Corwin Press.

Fairclough, N. 1995. *Critical Discourse Analysis.* New York: Longman.

Fantini, A. E. 1999. Comparisons: Towards the development of inter-cultural competence. In J. K. Phillips and R. M. Terry, eds., *Foreign Language Standards: Linking Research Theories and Practices.* Chicago: National Textbook Company.

Firth, A., and J. Wagner. 1998. SLA property: No trespassing! *Modern Language Journal* 82, 91–94.

Firth, J. 1937. *Tongues of Men.* London: Watts. Reprint 1964, London: Oxford University Press.

Fish, S. 1980. *Is There a Text in This Class?* Cambridge, Mass.: Harvard University Press.

Foss, D. H. 1993. Elementary mathematics methods: A cultural scene in the teacher preparation act. Ed.D. diss., Memphis State University.

Foss, D. H., and R. C. Kleinsasser. 1996. Preservice elementary teachers' view of pedagogical and mathematical content knowledge. *Teaching and Teacher Education* 12 (4): 429–442.

Fox, C. A. 1993. Communicative competence and beliefs about language among graduate teaching assistants in French. *Modern Language Journal* 77 (3): 313–324.

Fredericksen, E., A. Pickett, K. Swan, W. Pelz, and P. Shea. 1999. Factors influencing faculty satisfaction with asynchronous teaching and learning in the SUNY learning network. Paper presented at the Sloan ALN Summer Workshop, University of Illinois at Urbana-Champaign, August 16–18.

Freeman, D. 1996. The "unstudied problem": Research on teacher learning in language teaching. In D. Freeman and J. C. Richards, eds., *Teacher Learning in Language Teaching.* Cambridge: Cambridge University Press.

Freeman, D., and K. E. Johnson. 1998. Reconceptualizing the knowledge base of language teacher education. *TESOL Quarterly* 32 (3): 397–417.

Freire, P. 1972. *Pedagogy of the Oppressed.* Harmondsworth: Penguin.

Freudenstein, R. 1996. Foreign-language teaching after the year 2000. In J. E. Alatis, C. A. Straehle, M. Ronkin, and B. Gallenberger, eds., *Georgetown University Round Table on Language and Linguistics 1996.* Washington, D.C.: Georgetown University Press.

Frohlich, M., N. Spada, and P. Allen. 1985. Differences in the communicative orientation of language classrooms. *TESOL Quarterly* 19, 27–56.

Fullan, M. G. 1983. *The Meaning of Educational Change.* New York: Teachers College, Columbia University.

——. 1991. *The New Meaning of Educational Change.* New York: Teachers College Press.

——. 1993. *Change Forces.* Bristol, Pa.: Falmer.

Fullilove, J. 1992. The tail that wags. *Institute of Language in Education Journal* 9, 131–147.

Gee, J. P. 1990. *Social Linguistics and Literacies: Ideology in Discourses.* Bristol, Pa.: Taylor and Francis.

Gipps, C. 1994. *Beyond Testing.* London: Falmer Press.

Glaser, B., and A. Strauss. 1967. *The Discovery of Grounded Theory: Strategies for Qualitative Research.* Chicago: Aldine.

Glesne, C., and A. Peshkin. 1992. *Becoming a Qualitative Researcher.* New York: Longman.

Golombek, P. 1998. A study of language teachers' personal practical knowledge. *TESOL Quarterly* 32 (3): 447–464.

Good, T. L., and J. E. Brophy. 1991. *Looking in Classrooms.* New York: HarperCollins.

Graman, T. 1988. Education for humanitization: Applying Paolo Friere's pedagogy to learning a second language. *Harvard Educational Review* 58, 433–448.

Grossman, P. L. 1992. Teaching to learn. In A. Lieberman, ed., *The Changing Contexts of Teaching* (91st yearbook of the National Society for the Study of Education, Part 1). Chicago: University of Chicago Press.

Guba, E. G., and Y. S. Lincoln. 1981. *Effective Evaluation.* San Francisco: Jossey-Bass.

Habermas, J. 1970. Toward a theory of communicative competence. *Inquiry* 13, 360–375.

———. 1971. *Knowledge and Human Interests.* Boston: Beacon Press.

Hall, J. K. 1999. The communication standards. In J. K. Phillips and R. M. Terry, eds., *Foreign Language Standards: Linking Research Theories and Practices.* Chicago: National Textbook Company.

Halliday, M. A. K. 1978. *Language as Social Semiotic: The Social Interpretation of Language and Meaning.* Baltimore: University Park Press.

Halliday, M. A. K., and R. Hasan. 1976. *Cohesion in English.* London: Longman.

Harré, R., and G. Gilette. 1994. *The Discursive Mind.* Thousand Oaks, Calif.: Sage.

Her, K. 1998. Tower of Babel. *Free China Review* 48 (7): 4–15.

Herman, J. L. 1992. Accountability and alternative assessment: Research and development issues. CSE Technical Report 384. University of California, Los Angeles, Center for Research on Evaluation Standards and Student Testing.

Ho, H. L. 1994. The cultural meaning of English language teaching in Taiwan: A phenomenological study. *English Teaching and Learning* 18, 23–35.

Holec, H. 1979. *Autonomy and Foreign Language Learning.* Strasbourg: Council of Europe.

———. 1981. *Autonomy in Foreign Language Learning.* Oxford: Pergamon Press.

———. 1988. *Autonomy and Self-Directed Learning: Present Fields of Application.* Strasbourg: Council of Europe.

Hong Kong Examinations Authority. 1993. *Hong Kong Certificate of Education Examination 1996—Proposed English Language Syllabus.* Hong Kong: Hong Kong Examinations Authority.

———. 1994a. *Hong Kong Certificate of Education Examination 1996—English Language.* Hong Kong: Hong Kong Examinations Authority.

———. 1994b. *The Work of the Hong Kong Examinations Authority—1977–93.* Hong Kong: Hong Kong Examinations Authority.

Honig, B. 1987. How assessment can best serve teaching and learning. *Assessment in the Service of Learning: Proceedings of the 1987 ETS Invitational Conference.* Princeton, N.J.: Educational Testing Service.

Horwitz, E. 1988. The beliefs about language learning of beginning university foreign language students. *Modern Language Journal* 72, 285–294.

Huang, S. C. 1998. Senior high school students' EFL learning beliefs: A site study. In *Proceedings of the Seventh International Symposium on English Teaching.* Taipei, Taiwan: Crane.

Huang, S. C., and S. F. Chang. 1994. Taiwanese people's attitudes toward requiring EFL course at elementary schools: The opinions of the Taiwanese students at Indiana University, Bloomington. ERIC Document Reproduction Service No. 396–535.

Huang, Y. K. 1995. Developing your students' communicative competence: Some practical ideas for classroom teachers. In Chi-Fan Lee, ed., *Selected Papers from the Ninth Conference on English Teaching and Learning in the Republic of China.* Taipei, Taiwan: Crane.

Hymes, D. 1966. Why linguistics needs the sociologist. Paper presented at the annual meeting of the American Sociological Association, Miami Beach.

——. 1971. Competence and performance in linguistic theory. In R. Huxley and E. Ingram, eds., *Language Acquisition: Models and Methods.* London: Academic Press.

——. 1979. On communicative competence. In C. Brumfit and K. Johnson, eds., *The Communicative Approach to Language Teaching.* Oxford: Oxford University Press.

Illich, I. 1979. *Deschooling Society.* Harmondsworth: Penguin.

Inspectie van het Onderwijs. 1999. *Onderwijsverlag.* Utrecht: Inspectie van het Onderwijs.

Jaffee, D. 1998. Institutionalized resistance to asynchronous learning networks. *Journal of Asynchronous Learning Networks* 2, www.aln.org.alnweb/journal/jaln_vol2issue2.htm.

Jakobovits, L. 1970. *Foreign Language Learning: A Psycholinguistic Analysis of the Issues.* Rowley, Mass.: Newbury House.

James, D. 1985. Toward realistic objectives in foreign language teaching. *ADFL Bulletin* 16 (2): 9–12.

Johnson, D. W., and R. T. Johnson. 1989. *Cooperation and Competition: Theory and Research.* Edina, Minn.: Interaction Book Company.

Johnson, F., and C. L. K. L. Wong. 1981. The interdependence of teaching, testing and instructional materials. In J. Read, ed., *Directions in Language Testing.* Singapore: Regional Language Center.

Johnson, K. E. 1994. The emerging beliefs and instructional practices of preservice English as a second language teacher. *Teaching and Teacher Education* 10 (4): 439–452.

——. 1995. *Understanding Communication in Second Language Classrooms.* New York: Cambridge University Press.

Kachru, B. 1992. World Englishes: Approaches, issues, and resources. *Language Teaching* 25, 1–14.

Kagan, S. 1993. *Cooperative Learning*. San Juan Capistrano, Calif.: Resources for Teachers.

Karavas-Doukas, E. 1996. Using attitude scales to investigate teachers' attitudes to the communicative approach. *ELT Journal* 50 (3): 187–198.

Kelchtermans, G. 1993. De professionele ontwikkeling van leerkrachten basisonderwijs vanuit het biografisch perspectief. Academisch proefschrift, Katholieke Universiteit Leuven.

Kern, R. 1995. Students' and teachers' beliefs about language learning. *Foreign Language Annals* 28, 72–92.

Kinginger, C. 1997. A discourse approach to the study of language educators' coherence systems. *Modern Language Journal* 81, 6–14.

——. 1998. Language program direction and the modernist agenda. In L. K. Heilenman, ed., *Research Issues in Language Program Direction*. Boston: Heinle and Heinle.

Kleinsasser, R. C. 1989. Foreign language teaching: A tale of two technical cultures. Ph.D. diss., University of Illinois, Urbana-Champaign.

——. 1993. A tale of two technical cultures: Foreign language teaching. *Teaching and Teacher Education* 9 (4): 373–383.

Kleinsasser, R., and K. Sato. 1999. Japanese LOTE inservice teachers' views and actions concerning communicative language teaching (CLT): Multiple data sources and practical understandings. Paper presented at the AILA '99 Tokyo Twelfth World Congress of Applied Linguistics. August 3.

Kleinsasser, R. C., and S. J. Savignon. 1991. Linguistics, language pedagogy, and teachers' technical cultures. In J. E. Alatis, ed., *Georgetown University Round Table on Language and Linguistics, 1991*. Washington, D.C.: Georgetown University Press.

Kramsch, C. 1995a. The applied linguist and the language teacher: Can they talk to each other? In G. Cook and B. Seidlhofer, eds., *Principle and Practice in Applied Linguistics*. New York: Oxford University Press.

——. 1995b. Embracing conflict versus achieving consensus in foreign language education. *ADFL Bulletin* 26, 6–12.

Krashen, S., and T. Terrell. 1983. *The Natural Approach: Language Acquisition in the Classroom*. Hayward, Calif.: Alemany Press.

Kuhl, J. 1985. Volitional mediators of cognition-behavior consistency: Self-regulatory processes and action versus state orientation. In J. Kuhl and J. Beckman, eds., *Action Control: From Cognition to Behavior*. Berlin: Springer-Verlag.

Kumaravadivelu, B. 1993. Maximizing learning potential in the communicative classroom. *ELT Journal* 47 (1): 12–21.

Kyoikukateishingikai. 1987. Yochien, shogakko, chugakko oyobi kotogakko no kyoikukatei no kaizennitsuite (Report by the Council on the School Curriculum). Tokyo: Mombusho.

Lafayette, R. C., and J. B. Draper. 1996. *National Standards: A Catalyst for Reform.* ACTFL Foreign Language Education Series. Lincolnwood, Ill.: National Textbook Company.

Lakoff, G., and M. Johnson. 1980. *Metaphors We Live By.* Chicago: University of Chicago Press.

Lamb, M. 1995. The consequences of INSET. *ELT Journal* 49 (1): 72–80.

Lange, D. L. 1990. A blueprint for a teacher development program. In J. C. Richards and D. Nunan, eds., *Second Language Teacher Education.* Cambridge: Cambridge University Press.

Lantolf, J. 1996. Second language acquisition theory building: Letting all the flowers bloom. *Language Learning* 46, 713–749.

Lantolf, J., ed. 2000. *Sociocultural Theory and Second Language Learning.* Oxford: Oxford University Press.

Lee, C. 1996. *Native Speaker.* Berkeley: Berkeley Publishing Group.

Lee, O., and S. J. Yarger. 1996. Modes of inquiry in research on teacher education. In J. Sikula, ed., *Handbook of Research on Teacher Education.* 2nd ed. New York: Simon and Schuster.

Lee, R. W. 1993. Perceptions of a beginning teacher: Exploring subjective reality. Ed.D. diss., Memphis State University.

Lens, W. 1993. *Studiemotivatie: Theorie voor de praktijk op school en thuis.* Leuven: Universitaire Pers Leuven.

Levine, J. 1993. Learning English as an additional language in multilingual classrooms. In H. Daniels, ed., *Charting the Agenda: Educational Activity After Vygotsky.* London: Routledge.

Li, D. 1998. "It's always more difficult than you plan and imagine": Teachers' perceived difficulties in introducing the communicative approach in South Korea. *TESOL Quarterly* 32, 677–703.

Liang, T. 1994. Teaching English can be fun and effective. In *Proceedings of the Third International Symposium on English Teaching.* Taipei, Taiwan: Crane.

Lieberman, A. 1995. Practices that support teacher development: Transforming conceptions of professional learning. *Phi Delta Kappan* 76, 591–596.

Lieberman, A., and L. Miller. 1990. Teacher development in professional practice schools. *Teacher College Record* 92 (1): 105–122.

Lightbown, P., and N. Spada. 1993. *How Languages Are Learned.* Oxford: Oxford University Press.

——. 1999. *How Languages Are Learned.* 2nd ed. New York: Oxford University Press.

Lincoln, Y. S., and E. G. Guba. 1985. *Naturalistic Inquiry.* Beverly Hills, Calif.: Sage.

Linn, R. L. 1983. Testing and instruction: Links and distinctions. *Journal of Educational Measurement* 20, 179–189.

——. 1992. Educational assessment: Expanded expectations and challenges. CSE Technical Report 351. University of Colorado at Boulder, Center for Research on Evaluation Standards and Student Testing.

Liskin-Gasparro, J. 1996. Assessment: From content standards to student performance. In R. C. Lafayette, ed., *National Standards: A Catalyst for Reform*. Foreign Language Education Series. Lincolnwood, Ill.: National Textbook Company.

——. 2000. Proficiency movement. In M. Byram, ed., *Routledge Encyclopedia of Language Teaching and Learning*. London: Routledge.

Little, D. 1994. Learner autonomy: A theoretical construct and its practical application. *Die Neueren Sprachen* 93, 430–442.

——. 1997. Language awareness and the autonomous language learner. *Language Learning* 6 (2–3): 93–104.

Little, J. W. 1993. Teachers' professional development in a climate of educational reform. *Educational Evaluation and Policy Analysis* 15 (2): 129–151.

LoCastro, V. 1996. English language education in Japan. In C. Hywel, ed., *Society and the Language Classroom*. New York: Cambridge University Press.

Long, M. 1981. Input, interaction and second language acquisition. In H. Winitz, ed., *Native Language and Foreign Language Acquisition*. Annals of the New York Academy of Science 379. New York: New York Academy of Science.

——. 1997. Construct validity in SLA research. *Modern Language Journal* 81, 318–323.

Long, M. H., and P. Porter. 1985. Group work, interlanguage talk, and second language acquisition. *TESOL Quarterly* 19, 207–228.

Lowyck, J., and N. Verloop. 1995. *Onderwijskunde: Een kennisbasis voor professionals*. Groningen: Wolters-Noordhoff.

Madaus, G. F. 1988. The influence of testing on the curriculum. In L. N. Tanner, ed., *Critical Issues in Curriculum: Eighty-seventh Yearbook of the National Society for the Study of Education*. Chicago: University of Chicago Press.

Maley, A., and A. Duff. 1978. *Drama Techniques in Language Learning*. Cambridge: Cambridge University Press.

Mallard. www.ews.uiuc.edu/Mallard

Markee, N. 1997. *Managing Curricular Innovation*. New York: Cambridge University Press.

Maslov, A. H. 1970. *Motivation and Personality*. New York: Harper & Row.

Masumi-So, H. 1981. Nihongo Kyojuho no Jittai (An investigation of Japanese teaching methods in the Melbourne area). *Journal of Japanese Language Teaching* 45, 89–104.

Mathison, S. 1988. Why triangulate? *Educational Researcher* 17 (12): 13–17.

Matthijssen, M. A. J. M. 1972. *Klasse-onderwijs: Sociologie van het onderwijs*. Deventer: Van Loghum Slaterus.

Maxwell, J. A. 1996. *Qualitative Research Design*. Thousand Oaks, Calif.: Sage.

McDonnell, L. M., and R. F. Elmore. 1987. Getting the job done: Alternative policy instruments. *Educational Evaluation and Policy Analysis* 9, 133–152.

McDonnell, L. M., L. Burstein, T. Ormseth, J. M. Catterall, and D. Moody. 1990. Discovering what schools really teach: Designing improved coursework indicators. Prepared for the Office of Educational Research and Improvement, U.S. Department of Education.

Mercer, N. 1994. Neo-Vygotskian theory and classroom education. In B. Stierer and J. Maybin, eds., *Language, Literacy, and Learning in Educational Practice.* Clevedon: Multilingual Matters and Open University.

Merriam, S. B. 1998. *Qualitative Research and Case Study Applications in Education.* San Francisco: Jossey-Bass.

Messick, S. 1992. The interplay between evidence and consequences in the validation of performance assessments. Paper presented at the annual meeting of the National Council on Measurement in Education, San Francisco.

———. 1994. The interplay of evidence and consequences in the validation of performance assessments. *Educational Researcher* 23, 13–23.

———. 1996. Validity and washback in language testing. *Language Testing* 13, 241–256.

Met, M. 1999. Making connections. In J. K. Phillips and R. M. Terry, eds., *Foreign Language Standards: Linking Research Theories and Practices.* Chicago: National Textbook Company.

Mombusho. 1989a. *Chugakko Gakushu Shido Yoryo* (Curriculum Guidelines for High School). Tokyo: Mombusho.

———. 1989b. *Kotogakko Gakushu Shido Yoryo* (Curriculum Guidelines for Middle School). Tokyo: Mombusho.

Morissey, M. M. 1992. Metaphors second language teachers live by: A conceptual metaphor analysis. Ph.D. diss., Purdue University.

Morris, P. 1990. Teachers' perceptions of the barriers to the implementation of a pedagogic innovation. In P. Morris, ed., *Curriculum Development in Hong Kong.* Faculty of Education: Hong Kong University Press.

Morris, P., et al. 1996. Target oriented curriculum evaluation project: Interim report. INSTEP, Faculty of Education, University of Hong Kong.

Musumeci, D. 1997a. *Breaking Tradition: An Exploration of the Historical Relationship Between Theory and Practice in Second Language Teaching.* New York: McGraw-Hill.

———. 1997b. *SCALE progress report: Italian 101–102.* w3.scale.uiuc.edu/scale/courses/Y2Results/ital101.htm.

Naiman, N., M. Frohlich, H. Stern, and A. Todesco. 1978. *The Good Language Learner.* Toronto: Toronto Institute for Studies in Education.

Narcy, J. P. 1994. Autonomie: Evolution ou révolution? *Die Neueren Sprachen* 93, 442–454.

National Standards in Foreign Language Education Project. 1996. *Standards for Foreign Language Learning: Preparing for the Twenty-First Century.* Yonkers, N.Y.: Author.

National Standards in Foreign Language Education Report. 1996. *National Standards for Foreign Language Learning: Preparing for the Twenty-first Century.* Lawrence, Kan.: Allen Press.

Neisser, U. 1967. *Cognitive Psychology.* New York: Appleton.

Neuner, G., M. Kruger, and U. Grewer. 1981. *Uebungstypologie zum kommunikativen Deutschunterricht.* Berlin: Langenscheidt.

Noble, A. J., and M. L. Smith. 1994a. Measurement-driven reform: Research on policy, practice, repercussion. CSE Technical Report 381. Arizona State University, Center for the Study of Evaluation.

——. 1994b. Old and new beliefs about measurement-driven reform: "The more things change, the more they stay the same." CSE Technical Report 373. Arizona State University, Center for the Study of Evaluation.

Nunan, D. 1987. Communicative language teaching: Making it work. *ELT Journal* 41 (2): 136–145.

——. 1993. From learning-centeredness to learner-centeredness. *Applied Language Learning* 4, 1–18.

——. 1993. *The Learner-Centered Curriculum*. Cambridge: Cambridge University Press.

Ogasawara, L. 1983. Problems encountered in applying linguistics to the teaching of English in Japan. In J. E. Alatis, H. H. Stern, and P. Strevens, eds., *Georgetown University Round Table on Languages and Linguistics, 1983*. Washington D.C.: Georgetown University Press.

O'Malley, M. J., and A. U. Chamot. 1990. *Learning Strategies in Second Language Acquisition*. Cambridge: Cambridge University Press.

Overfield, D. M. 1997. From the margins to the mainstream: Foreign language education and community-based learning. *Foreign Language Annals* 30, 485–449.

Oxford, R. L. 1990. *Language Learning Strategies: What Every Teacher Should Know*. New York: Harper Collins.

Pacek, D. 1996. Lessons to be learnt from negative evaluation. *ELT Journal* 50, 335–343.

Pajares, M. F. 1992. Teachers' beliefs and educational research: Cleaning up a messy construct. *Review of Educational Research* 62 (3): 307–332.

Palincsar, A. S., and A. L. Brown. 1984. Reciprocal teaching of fostering and monitoring activities. *Cognition and Instruction* 1, 117–175.

Palmer, H. E. 1964. *The Principles of Language Study*. London: Oxford University Press.

Paulston, C. 1974. Linguistic and communicative competence. *TESOL Quarterly* 8, 347–362.

Pennycook, A. 1989. The concept of method, interested knowledge, and the politics of language teaching. *TESOL Quarterly* 23 (4): 589–618.

Phillips, J. K. 1999. Introduction: Standards for world languages, on a firm foundation. In J. K. Phillips and R. M. Terry, eds., *Foreign Language Standards: Linking Research Theories and Practices*. Chicago: National Textbook Company.

Phillips, J. K., and R. M. Terry, eds. 1999. *Foreign Language Standards: Linking Research Theories and Practices*. Chicago: National Textbook Company.

Piepho, H. E. 1974. *Kommunikative Kompetenz als Übergeordnete Lernziel des Englischunterrichts* (Communicative Competence as a General Learning Goal in English Instruction). Dornburg-Frickhofen, Germany: Frankonius.

Piepho, H. E., and L. Bredella, eds. 1976. *Contacts: Integriertes Englischlehrwerk für*

Klassen 5–10 (Contacts: Integrated English Series for Grades 5–10). Bochum, Germany: Kamp.

Popham, W. J. 1983. Measurement as an instructional catalyst. In R. B. Ekstrom, ed., *New Directions for Testing and Measurement: Measurement, Technology, and Individuality in Education.* San Francisco: Jossey-Bass.

———. 1987. The merits of measurement-driven instruction. *Phi Delta Kappa* 68, 679–682.

Powell, R. R. 1997. Teaching alike: A cross-case analysis of first-career and second-career beginning teachers' instructional convergence. *Teaching and Teacher Education* 13 (3): 341–356.

Prabhu, N. S. 1995. Concept and conduct in language pedagogy. In G. Cook and B. Seidlhofer, eds., *Principle and Practice in Applied Linguistics.* New York: Oxford University Press.

Preston, D. 1981. Ethnography of TESOL. *TESOL Quarterly* 15, 105–116.

Rampillon, U. 1994. Autonomes Lernen im Fremdsprachenunterricht—ein Widerspruch in sich oder eine neue Perspektive? *Die Neueren Sprachen,* 93, 455–466.

Richards, J. C., and T. S. Rodgers. 1986. *Approaches and Methods in Language Teaching.* Cambridge: Cambridge University Press.

Richardson, V. 1994. Conducting research on practice. *Educational Researcher* 23 (5): 5–9.

———. 1996. The role of attitudes and beliefs in learning to teach. In J. Sikula, ed., *Handbook of Research on Teacher Education.* 2nd ed. New York: Simon and Schuster.

Richardson, V., P. Anders, D. Tidwell, and C. Lloyd. 1991. The relationship between teachers' beliefs and practices in reading comprehension instruction. *American Educational Research Journal* 28 (3): 559–586.

Rivers, W. 1968. *Teaching Foreign Language Skills.* Chicago: University of Chicago Press.

———. 1988. *Teaching French: A Practical Guide.* Lincolnwood, Ill.: National Textbook Company.

Rogers, C. 1983. *Freedom to Learn for the 80s.* New York: Merill.

Rogers, E. M. 1995. *The Diffusion of Innovations.* 4th ed. London: Macmillan/Free Press.

Rokeach, M. 1968. *Beliefs, Attitudes, and Values: A Theory of Organization and Change.* San Francisco: Jossey-Bass.

Rosenholtz, S. J. 1989. *Teachers' Workplace.* New York: Longman.

Rosenshine, B. 1995. Advances in research on instruction. *Journal of Educational Research* 88, 262–268.

Rosenshine, B., and R. Stevens. 1986. Teaching functions. In M. C. Wittrock, ed., *Handbook of Research on Teaching.* New York: Macmillan.

Ryan, R. M., and W. S. Grolnick. 1986. Origins and pawns in the classroom: Self-report and projective assessments of individual differences in children's perceptions. *Journal of Personality and Social Psychology* 50, 550–558.

Sato, K. 1997. Foreign language teacher education: Teachers' perceptions about communicative language teaching and their practices. Master's thesis, Centre for Language Teaching and Research, University of Queensland.

Sato, K., and R. C. Kleinsasser. 1999a. Communicative language teaching (CLT): Practical understandings. *Modern Language Journal* 83 (4): 494–517.

——. 1999b. Multiple data sources: Converging and diverging conceptualizations of LOTE teaching. *Australian Journal of Teacher Education* 24 (1): 17–33.

Savignon, S. 1971. A study of the effect of training in communicative skills as part of a beginning college French course on student attitude and achievement in linguistic and communicative competence. Ph.D. diss., University of Illinois, Urbana-Champaign.

——. 1972. *Communicative Competence: An Experiment in Foreign Language Teaching*. Philadelphia: Center for Curriculum Development.

—— 1974. Teaching for communication. In R. Coulombe, R., J. Barré, C. Fostle, N. Poulin, and S. Savignon, *Voix et visages de la France: Level 1 Teachers' Guide.* Chicago: Rand-McNally. Reprinted in *English Teaching Forum* 16 (1978): 2–5, 9.

——. 1983. *Communicative Competence: Theory and Classroom Practice*. Reading, Mass.: Addison-Wesley.

——. 1990. In second language acquisition/foreign language learning, nothing is more practical than a good theory. In B. Van Patten and J. Lee, eds., *Second-Language Acquisition and Foreign Language Learning*. Oxford: Multilingual Matters.

——. 1991. Communicative language teaching: State of the art. *TESOL Quarterly* 25, 261–277.

——. 1992. This is only a test: What classroom tests tell learners about language and language learning. In E. Shohamy and A. Walton, eds., *Testing and Evaluation: Feedback Strategies for Improvement of Foreign Language Learning.* Washington, D.C.: National Foreign Language Center.

——. 1997. *Communicative Competence: Theory and Classroom Practice.* 2nd ed. New York: McGraw-Hill.

——. 2000. Communicative language teaching. In M. Byram, ed., *Routledge Encyclopedia of Applied Linguistics*. London: Routledge.

Savignon, S. J., and R. Kleinsasser. 1992. Linguistics, language pedagogy, and teacher's technical cultures. In *Georgetown University Round Table on Languages and Linguistics 1991*. Washington, D.C.: Georgetown University Press.

Saxe, D. W. 1999. Curriculum standards and public policy. Curriculum Standards: National and Pennsylvania Perspectives. Pennsylvania Association for Supervision and Curriculum Development.

Scholefield, W. 1997. The teaching and learning of English in Japan since 1945: An overview. *Babel* 32 (1): 16–21, 37–38.

Schön, D. 1983. *The Reflective Practitioner*. New York: Basic Books.

Schrum, J. L., and E. W. Glisan. 2000. *Teacher's Handbook: Contextualized Language Instruction*. Boston: Heinle and Heinle.

Schubert, W. H. 1986. *Curriculum: Perspective, Paradigm, and Possibility.* New York: Macmillan.

Schwartz, A., P. C. Duo, and M. Djamou. 1999. Curriculum standards in the foreign languages. Curriculum Standards: National and Pennsylvania Perspectives. Pennsylvania Association for Supervision and Curriculum Development.

Scollon, R., and S. W. Scollon. 1995. *Intercultural Communication: A Discourse Approach.* Cambridge, Mass.: Blackwell.

Sercu, L. 1995. *Intercultural Competence: A New Challenge for Language Teachers and Trainers in Europe.* Vol. 1: *Secondary School.* Aalborg: Aalborg University Press.

Setz, W. (in progress). Classroom Diagnostics of Language Learning Autonomy. Ph. D. diss., University of Nijmegen.

Sharwood Smith, M. 1994. *Second Language Learning: Theoretical Foundations.* New York: Longman.

Shohamy, E. 2001. *The Power of Tests: A Critical Perspective on the Use of Language Tests.* New York: Longman.

Shohamy, E., S. Donitsa-Schmidt, and I. Ferman. 1996. Test impact revisited: Washback effect over time. *Language Testing* 13, 298–317.

Silverman, D. 1993. *Interpreting Qualitative Data: Methods for Analysing Talk, Text, and Interaction.* London: Sage.

Simons, P. R. J., and J. G. G. Zuylen. 1994. *Actief en Zelfstandig Leren in de Tweede Fase.* Tilburg: Mesoconsult.

Slavin, R. 1990. *Cooperative Learning: Theory, Research, and Practice.* Boston: Allyn & Bacon.

——. 1995. *Cooperative Learning: Theory, Research, and Practice.* 2nd ed. Boston: Allyn & Bacon.

Slavin, R., S. Sharan, S. Kagan, R. H. Lazarowitz, C. Webb, and R. Schmuck. 1985. *Learning to Cooperate, Cooperating to Learn.* New York: Plenum Press.

Smith, M. L., C. Edelsky, K. Draper, C. Rottenberg, and M. Cherland. 1990. The role of testing in elementary schools. CSE Technical Report 321. University of California, Los Angeles, Center for Research on Evaluation Standards and Student Testing.

Smylie, M. A. 1988. The enhancement function of staff development: Organizational and psychological antecedents to individual teacher change. *American Educational Research Journal* 25 (1): 1–30.

——. 1996. From bureaucratic control to building human capital: The importance of teacher learning in educational reform. *Educational Researcher* 25 (9): 9–11.

Solomon, J. 1997. Language teachers align curricula with standards: Preliminary results from a national survey. *ERIC/CLL News Bulletin* 21.

Spradley, J. P. 1979. *The Ethnographic Interview.* New York: Holt, Rinehart and Winston.

Stahl, R. J. 1995. *Cooperative Learning in Language Arts: A Handbook for Teachers.* Menlo Park, Calif.: Addison-Wesley.

Steele, R. 1996. Developing intercultural competence through foreign language instruction: Challenges and choices. In J. E. Alatis, C. A. Straehle, M. Ronkin, and B. Gallenberger, eds., *Georgetown University Round Table on Language and Linguistics 1996*. Washington, D.C.: Georgetown University Press.

Stern, H. H. 1989. Seeing the wood AND the trees: Some thoughts on language teaching analysis. In R. K. Johnson, ed., *The Second Language Curriculum*. Cambridge: Cambridge University Press.

Strauss, A., and J. Corbin. 1990. *Basics of Qualitative Research: Grounded Theory Procedures and Techniques*. London: Sage.

——. 1994. Grounded theory methodology. In N. K. Denzin and Y. S. Lincoln, eds., *Handbook of Qualitative Research*. London: Sage.

Stubbs, M. 1996. *Text and Corpus Analysis: Computer-Assisted Studies of Language and Culture*. Cambridge, Mass.: Blackwell.

Stuurgroep Tweede Fase. 1994. *Tweede Fase. Scharnier tussen basisvorming en hoger onderwijs*. The Hague: Stuurgroep Tweede Fase.

——. 1996. *Organisatie in het Studiehuis*. The Hague: Stuurgroep Tweede Fase.

Swender, E. 1999. *ACTFL Oral Proficiency Interview Tester Training Manual*. Yonkers, N.Y.: American Council on the Teaching of Foreign Languages.

Tedick, D., and C. Walker. 1994. Second language teacher education: Problems that plague us. *Modern Language Journal* 78 (3): 300–331.

Thompson, G. 1996. Some misconceptions about communicative language teaching. *ELT Journal* 50 (1): 9–15.

Thornbury, S. 1998. Comments on Marianne Celce-Murcia, Zoltan Dornyei, and Sarah Thurrell's "Direct approaches in L2 instruction: A turning point in communicative language teaching?" *TESOL Quarterly* 32, 109–115.

Toulmin, S. 1990. *Cosmopolis: The Hidden Agenda of Modernity*. New York: Free Press.

Tsui, A. B. M. 1995. *Introducing Classroom Interaction*. London: Penguin.

Tucker, M. S., and Codding, J. B. 1998. *Standards for Our Schools: How to Set Them, Measure Them, and Reach Them*. San Francisco: Jossey-Bass.

Tyler, R. W. 1949. *Basic Principles of Curriculum and Instruction*. Chicago: University of Chicago Press.

Van Ek, J., ed. 1975. *Systems Development in Adult Language Learning: The Threshold Level in a European Unit Credit System for Modern Language Learning by Adults*. Strasbourg: Council of Europe.

Van Els, T., T. Bongaerts, G. Extra, C. van Os, A. Janssen-van Dieten, and R. van Oirsouw, trans. 1984. *Applied Linguistics and the Learning and Teaching of Foreign Languages*. London: Edward Arnold.

Van Esch, K., E. Schalkwijk, A. Elsen, and W. Setz. 1999. Autonomous learning in foreign language teacher training. Paper presented at the AILA '99 Tokyo Twelfth World Congress of Applied Linguistics. August 3.

——. 1999. Autonomous learning in initial foreign language teacher training. In P. Faber, W. Gewehr, M. Jimenez Raya, and A. J. Peck, eds., *English Teacher Education in Europe: New Trends and Developments*. Frankfurt: Peter Lang Verlag.

Van Esch, K., E. Schalkwijk, and P. Sleegers. 1996. Zelfstandig Leren in de opleiding van leraren. *VELON Tijdschrift voor Lerarenopleiders* 17, 24–30.

Van Lier, L. 1988. *The Classroom and the Language Learner: Ethnography and Second Language Classroom Research*. London: Longman.

——. 1994. Forks and hope: Pursuing understanding in different ways. *Applied Linguistics* 15, 328–346.

——. 1996. *Interaction in the Language Curriculum*. London: Longman.

Van Patten, B., J. F. Lee, and T. Ballman. 1996. *¿Sabías que . . . ? Beginning Spanish*. New York: McGraw-Hill.

Vygotsky, L. S. 1978. *Mind in Society: The Development of Higher Psychological Processes*. Cambridge, Mass.: Harvard University Press.

——. 1986. *Thought and Language*. Cambridge, Mass.: MIT Press.

Wachob, P. 1995. Taiwan cram schools in the twenty-first century. In *Proceedings of the Fourth International Symposium on English Teaching*. Taipei, Taiwan: Crane.

Wada, M. 1999. English language education in Japan: A case study. Paper presented at the AILA '99 Tokyo Twelfth World Congress of Applied Linguistics. August 3.

Wada, M., ed. 1994. *The Course of Study for Senior High School: Foreign Languages (English)*. Tokyo: Kairyudo.

Wall, D. 1996. Introducing new tests into traditional systems: Insights from general education and from innovation theory. *Language Testing* 13, 334–354.

Wall, D., and J. C. Alderson. 1993. Examining washback: The Sri Lankan Impact Study. *Language Testing* 10, 41–69.

Wallace, M. J. 1991. *Training Foreign Language Teachers: A Reflective Approach*. Cambridge: Cambridge University Press.

Walz, J. 1989. Context and contextualized language practice in foreign language teaching. *Modern Language Journal* 73 (2): 160–168.

Wang, C. C. 1999a. English language teaching in Taiwan. Paper presented at the Annual Conference of the American Association for Applied Linguistics, Stamford, Conn., March.

——. 1999b. Communicative language teaching in EFL contexts: EFL learners' beliefs and attitudes toward classroom practices. Paper presented at the Annual Conference of the Second Language Research Forum, Minneapolis, September.

——. 2000. A sociolinguistic profile of English in Taiwan: Social context and learner needs. Ph.D. diss., Pennsylvania State University.

Wang, M. C. 1983. Development and consequences of student's sense of personal control. In J. M. Levine and M. C. Wang, eds., *Teacher and Student Perceptions*. Hillsdale, N.J.: Lawrence Erlbaum.

Wang, M. C., and S. T. Peverly. 1986. The self-instructive process in classroom learning contexts. *Contemporary Educational Psychology* 11, 370–404.

Wang, M. C., and B. Stiles. 1976. An investigation of children's concept of self-responsibility for their school learning. *American Educational Research Journal* 13, 159–179.

Warschauer, M., and R. Kern. 2000. *Network-Based Language Teaching: Concepts and Practice.* Cambridge: Cambridge University Press.

Wells, G. 1999. *Dialogic Inquiry: Toward a Sociocultural Practice and Theory of Education.* New York: Cambridge University Press.

Wenden, A., and J. Rubin. 1987. *Learner Strategies in Language Learning.* Englewood Cliffs, N.J.: Prentice-Hall International.

Wertsch, J. V. 1985. *Culture, Communication, and Cognition: Vygotskian Perspectives.* New York: Cambridge University Press.

——. 1991. *Voices of the Mind: A Sociocultural Approach to Mediated Action.* Cambridge: Cambridge University Press.

——. 1998. *Mind as Action.* New York: Oxford University Press.

Widdowson, H. 1990. *Aspects of Language Teaching.* Oxford: Oxford University Press.

Wiggins, G. 1999. Standards, not standardization: Evoking quality student work. *Educational Leadership* 48, 18–25.

Wolff, D. 1994. Der Konstruktivismus: Ein neues Paradigma in der Fremdsprachendidaktik. *Die Neueren Sprache* 93, 407–429.

Wong, B. Y. L. 1997. Clearing hurdles in teacher adoption and sustained use of research-based instruction. *Journal of Learning Disabilities* 30, 482–485.

Yun, M. 1998. Interview on National Public Radio, November 15, on *House of the Winds* (New York: Interlink Books).

Zeichner, K. M., and D. P. Liston. 1996. *Reflective Teaching: An Introduction.* Mahwah, N.J.: Lawrence Erlbaum.

Contributors

Liying Cheng, Queen's University, Canada
Adri Elsen, University of Nijmegen, Netherlands
Kiyoko Kusano Hubbell, Hosei University, Japan
Celeste Kinginger, Pennsylvania State University, United States
Diane Musumeci, University of Illinois at Urbana-Champaign, United States
Kazuyoshi Sato, Nagoya University of Foreign Studies, Japan
Sandra J. Savignon, Pennsylvania State University, United States
Eus Schalkwijk, University of Nijmegen, Netherlands
Ana Schwartz, Pennsylvania State University, United States
Wim Setz, University of Nijmegen, Netherlands
Minoru Wada, Meikai University, Japan
Chaochang Wang, Ming Chuan University, Taiwan
Kees van Esch, University of Nijmegen, Netherlands

Index

action research, 127

adopters, 120

American Council on the Teaching of Foreign Languages (ACTFL): National Foreign Language Standards (*see* National Standards for Foreign Language Learning, ACTFL); Oral Proficiency Guidelines, 20, 24, 118, 122, 203

aristocratic culture orientation, 167, 169

Army Specialized Training Program (ASTP), 21

assessment: alternatives, trend toward, 4, 91–92; for college entrance exams, Japan, 36, 47, 56–57, 64; computer-mediated, Illinois, 157–58, 160; and exam-oriented teaching, 36, 47, 56–57, 64, 144, 146, 176, 184–86, 210–11; in Japan, 36, 47, 56–57, 61–63, 64; and learner autonomy, 184–86; reform, accompanying curriculum innovation, 4, 128–29, 210–11; reform, apart from teacher beliefs or context, 108, 109–10; reform, as center-periphery

policy, 121, 123; state-mandated, United States, 121, 123; and strategic competence, 3; Taiwan, 132, 135–36, 141–42, 144, 145, 146, 149; top-down reform of, 91; and washback effect (*see* washback effect). *See also* conformity of teaching patterns

attitude. *See* learner attitudes/motivation

audiolingual methods, 5, 173

authentic materials, 97–98, 141

BALLI (Beliefs About Language Learning Inventory) scale, 6

Bartz, W. H., and M. K. Singer, 125

behaviorism, 168, 169, 170, 173

Berns, M., 5–6

Beyond the Classroom curriculum, 11, 15–16, 116

bottom-up innovation, 113, 121, 126, 129. *See also* center-periphery method; diffusion of innovation

bottom-up processing, 9

Breen, M., and C. Candlin, 115